THE WIRRAL

Alan Brack

Phillimore

First published 1980
Corrected reprint 1988

Published by
PHILLIMORE & CO. LTD.
Shopwyke Hall, Chichester, Sussex

ISBN 0 85033 679 1

Printed and bound in Great Britain by
REDWOOD BURN LTD.,
Trowbridge, Wiltshire

THE WIRRAL

CONTENTS

ILLUSTRATIONS

ACKNOWLEDGMENT

It goes without saying that a book of this nature cannot be written without a lot of help from a lot of people, both living and dead. As big fleas have little fleas upon their backs to bite 'em, every writer draws upon the works of past writers, and so on ad infinitum. He also relies heavily on the kindness of his friends who are ever ready to help by allowing their precious books to be borrowed, their memories to be searched and their brains to be picked. In particular I am grateful for the help of Ruth Lloyd, Wilf Briscoe, Ted McGenity, Roger Lancelyn Green and others who loaned material of one kind or another.

But, of course, one has to rely heavily on one's own experience and whilst most of this has been gained from over forty years' living in the area I must express my indebtedness to Leslie Radcliffe, the Editor of *Cheshire Life*, whose commissions over the years on behalf of that magazine have sent me into corners of the Wirral Peninsula where I might otherwise not have ventured and led me to meet interesting people I would otherwise not have met. Thanks are also due to that same magazine for so readily giving permission to use pictures from their library as illustrations, all of which were taken by their chief photographer, Cyril Lindley.

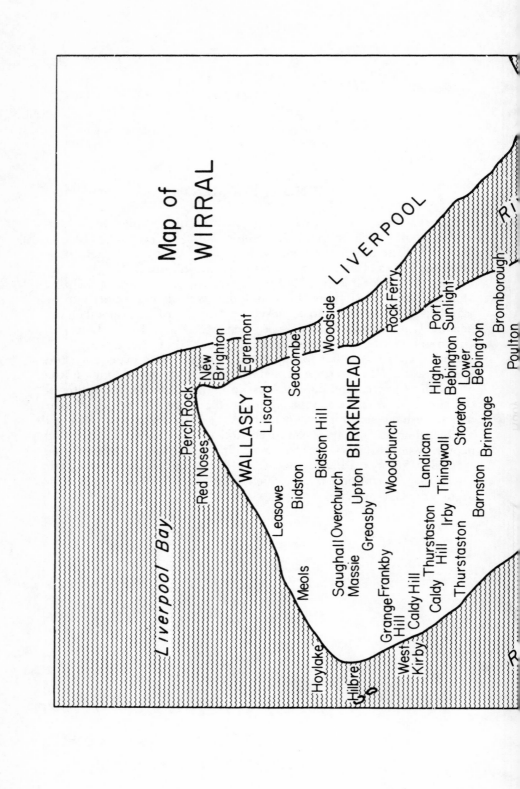

Map of
WIRRAL

Liverpool Bay

LIVERPOOL

RI

Perch Rock
Red Noses
New Brighton
Egremont
Seacombe
Woodside
Rock Ferry
Higher Bebington
Port Sunlight
Lower Bebington
Bromborough
Poulton

WALLASEY
Liscard
Bidston Hill
BIRKENHEAD
Storeton
Brimstage

Leasowe
Bidston
Saughall Overchurch
Upton
Woodchurch
Landican
Thingwall
Barnston
Meols
Massie
Greasby
Thurstaston
Irby
Thurstaston
Frankby
Caldy Hill
Caldy Hill
Thurstaston
Grange Hill
West Kirby
Hoylake
Hilbre

R

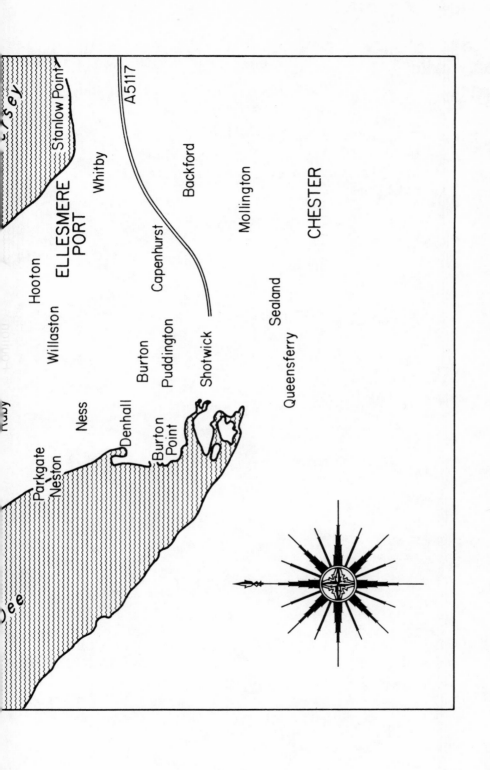

For EDITH

'A long square, or rather a rhomboide'

Before embarking on a profile of The Wirral Peninsula it behoves me first to draw an outline sketch of what I consider that area to be for nowhere is it officially defined.

Roughly speaking, it is that piece of land, about thirteen miles long and six to seven miles wide, which lies between the estuaries of the rivers Mersey and Dee with the northern edge bounded by the Irish Sea. That defines three sides of it; it is the base which is not clearly apparent.

In 1972 the Local Boundaries Commission, having studied the map and considered how they thought the area should be administered, eventually drew a wavering line from a point on the Dee just north of Parkgate across to the Mersey on the northern boundary of the town of Ellesmere Port. From its starting point it weaved its way up towards Gayton then, as though following a drunk trying to find his way home on a dark night, it veered unsteadily south to avoid Raby. When it approached Willaston it sheered away as though it had no right to enter and pressed on towards the M53 Mid-Wirral Motorway. There, as though failing to find a way through the traffic, it rebounded southwards; keeping Hooton on its right, until it finally lurched across the A41 Birkenhead–Chester road near the Hooton crossroads and so straight into the Mersey between Eastham and Ellesmere Port.

The land to the north of this line, said the Boundaries Commission, is Wirral; to the south is Ellesmere Port.

To be precise, they said that the area to the north of this line is the Wirral Metropolitan District of the new Metropolitan County of Merseyside. To the south is the District of Ellesmere Port (since renamed Ellesmere Port and Neston) in the County of Cheshire – and they left not a few people decidedly miffed.

For a start, they upset most people who had been left in Wirral but put into the County of Merseyside when, ever since counties were invented, they had been part of Cheshire and proud of it. This was especially so in the case of those living outside the towns of Birkenhead, Wallasey and Bebington. I know a man bearing an ancient Cheshire name whose career took him to other parts but who always vowed that, come retirement, he would lose no time in returning to his native heath. Which he did. When the day came he bought a house in West Kirby and was most upset to find that, despite the fact that he would be living decidedly on *Dee*side, not only did part of his rates go to the County of *Mersey*side but that, too, was his address. West Kirby (or Hoylake or Meols or Heswall), *Merseyside*, he protests, sounds as wrong as it is geographically inaccurate. Many other people feel the same and, despite Post Office warnings about probable delays, simply use 'Wirral' on their notepaper and pretend that Merseyside does not exist. There are even die-hards who will persist unto their dying day in using 'Cheshire', come what may.

In the same way, residents of Neston and Parkgate, and Burton, and Willaston and Hooton, objected to being ousted from official Wirral and becoming a part of Ellesmere Port. *They* had been part of Wirral almost since it became a peninsula and, damn it all, isn't the Wirral Stone – the very foundation-stone some say – still there in Willaston for all to see?

So the residents of these places also insisted on keeping 'Wirral' in their addresses and, what's more, so did the residents of Ellesmere Port, but for a different reason.

Ellesmere Port was unequivocally delighted that it had been left in Cheshire and out of Merseyside and carried on happily as before until the Post Office decreed that Ellesmere Port's correct postal address was 'Ellesmere Port, *Merseyside*'. No mention of Wirral, let alone Cheshire.

Not unnaturally, it brought a howl of protest and only after a lot of pressure did the Post Office yield slightly by allowing that Ellesmere Port District (including, of course, its suburbs and villages) could use the term 'South Wirral'. But it had to be followed by the postcode 'L (for Liverpool) 64'.

And cocking a final snook, all letters posted anywhere in Wirral, be it north or south, bear the Liverpool postmark.

Out of all this there is one person who had reason to feel more aggrieved than anyone else and that is Viscount Leverhulme. He awoke one morning to find his home, Thornton Manor, Thornton Hough, was now in the County of Merseyside – and he was the Lord Lieutenant of *Cheshire*! A special dispensation had to be obtained to permit his continuing in office.

(By an odd quirk of fate this has now been counter-balanced. The recently-appointed Lord Lieutenant of Merseyside, Wing-Commander Kenneth Stoddart, lives in Cheshire – in Willaston).

For the purposes of this book, therefore, I obviously cannot accept the boundaries of what is officially Wirral today but nevertheless I must draw the line somewhere. So, free and unfettered by any politico-economic restraints, I declare the southern boundary of my field of interest to be the A5117 trunk road, extended in the west to include the village of Shotwick. Its validity can be seen at a glance if you look at the road map. In fact, if ever Wirral became an independent state this road would certainly mark the southern border. Approaching from North Wales through Queensferry, past the steel works at Shotton, the first Customs post would undoubtedly be established at the traffic lights where you turn left to enter the Peninsula on the A550 to Birkenhead; the other would be at the roundabout just before the Stanlow oil refineries where the road meets the M56.

I know this does not match up exactly with the old Hundred of Wirral, but it is about a Ninety-Nine and I feel it makes little difference if my line of demarcation slices off a sliver of Cheshire which probably has more in common with Chester than Wirral.

As for the actual shape of the Wirral Peninsula I can do worse than quote the description by William Webb which he included in his book, *King's Vale Royal*, published in 1616:

'I have laboured to cast the Hundred of Wirral by the dimensions thereof into some resemblance, and though, geometrically considered, it comes nearest to the figure of a long square, or rather a rhomboide, yet because the lines are not straight lines, nor the opposite ends equal in their distance, we must take it, as it is, irregular; and the nearest resemblance that I can give it, is the sole of a lady's pantofle* for the furthest north-west end, compassed with the sea, falls somewhat round; then it narrows itself both ways, and between Bebington on the east, and Oldfield on the west side, falls narrow of the sole; then it widens itself either way to Stanney, on the one side, and Burton on the other, where it is broadest; then narrowing again till it points with the tip of the toe upon Chester liberties'.

In the 360 years since that was written the edges of the peninsula have been frayed somewhat by the combined ravages of the elements and the hand of Man, but the figure of 'a long square, or rather a rhomboide' is a fair representation.

And the name of the peninsula? Wirral? Or *The* Wirral? The pedants never use the definite article, saying it has no historical precedent, but the plain fact is that nine people out of ten today talk about going to or living on *the* Wirral leaving 'Peninsula' unsaid. It is a habit known to grammarians as ellipsis.

*A slipper

Moreover, who can say what is *correct*? The name has been spelled a dozen different ways over the centuries and how it was pronounced in the past is a matter of conjecture. It is all a matter of common usage at any given period and common usage today is undoubtedly THE WIRRAL.

ONE

A Place Apart

The early history of the Wirral is not at all well documented. It was noted in Domesday Book and as well as from William Webb it received passing mention from other itinerant chroniclers like John Leland, William Camden and Daniel Defoe, but it was not until the nineteenth century that anyone sat down and accorded it specific treatment. George Ormerod naturally included a section on Wirral in his famous *History of the County of Cheshire* published in 1819, but the first comprehensive study was that of William Williams Mortimer, whose *History of the Hundred of Wirral* was published thirty years later (and republished in facsimile in 1972). And Mortimer himself remarked on the scarcity of historic detail: 'At the present moment it would be more easy to obtain a History of Switzerland, or of China, than one of Wirral, while the majority of readers are perhaps more familiar with the Cantons of the one, or the Provinces of the other, than with the topography and records of the Hundred'.

The fact is that there is not that much history to tell – not of any substance anyway. The Romans, the Vikings, the Saxons, and the Normans were all in occupation at one time or another, but ask the average Wirral schoolboy or girl what they know about its early days and they are likely to tell you that the peninsula was once so covered in trees that a squirrel could hop from branch to branch all the way from Blacon Point to Hilbre (a popular myth); that the monks of Birkenhead Priory started the regular ferry service to Liverpool by rowing people across the Mersey; and that the place abounded with wreckers and smugglers. Oh, yes – and King William III came to Hoylake and embarked there for Ireland on his way to fight the Battle of the Boyne and that is why there is a road in Hoylake called King's Gap.

There is also a suggestion that the Battle of Brunanburh was fought on Wirral soil in AD 937. This was an important battle, involving an estimated 100,000 combatants, fought by Athelstan, King of the Mercians and West Saxons, a grandson of Alfred the Great, against a combined army of Welsh, Irish, Scots, and Danes. But no-one knows for certain where Brunanburh was and claims have been put forward for 39 other places ranging from Dumfriesshire in the north, to Devonshire in the south, and Humberside in the east. But a very reasonable case has been made that Brunanburh lay where Bromborough now stands.

I remember the late Mrs Anne Anderson of Bromborough, a much-respected local historian, expounding it to me a few years ago and she was in no doubt at all. The only account of the battle is given in the *Anglo-Saxon Chronicle*, the main literary relic of those days, but being in poetic form it suffers from the poet's usual imprecision. However, all the factors mentioned, together with the rough similarity in name (Bromborough was once Brunburgh and even now, Mrs Anderson insisted, should be properly pronounced *Brum*borough) fit in nicely with the Bromborough theory. The Viking Society, in fact, decided that this was the likely place: 'In no other locality (they said) does the context of geography, politics and place names accord so well with the few facts we possess concerning the contest'. Unfortunately the factors can also be made to fit a theory that the battleground was in north Lancashire near Burnley which also happens to be on the River Brun. And there the matter rests.

Indisputable however is the one-time importance of Parkgate and Hoylake on the Dee shore as embarkation places for sailing to Ireland. This lasted for centuries until the 'High Lake' (there are a variety of spellings) silted up. The pool provided an anchorage for ships awaiting favourable winds and so important was it that in the year of the Spanish Armada there was great concern that the Spanish might actually try to occupy Hilbre Island and so effect a blockade and sever the link with Ireland.

King William's famous visit to Hoylake was on 12 August 1689 when he embarked his troops to wage war in Ireland against the Roman Catholic James I and his French allies. His subsequent victory at the Battle of the Boyne came on 12 July in the following year and that day – Orangeman's Day – has been celebrated in Northern Ireland and by Protestant Irish everywhere ever since. But with scant regard for history the Orange Lodges of Merseyside always choose to spend that day at Southport.

William III, however, was not the first royal visitor to Wirral. In the twelfth century Henry II set sail from Shotwick Castle on his Irish expedition and in the thirteenth century Edward I also set out from there to oppose the Welsh. He was also twice a visitor to Birkenhead Priory.

But the most exciting and colourful blue-blooded visitor was James, Duke of Monmouth, the illegitimate son of Charles II and one of his mistresses, Lucy Walters. In pursuit of his campaign to thwart the accession of the Duke of York (later James II) he undertook several barnstorming tours through the western counties of England and Wales to gain support and popularity with a razzmatazz that no modern PR man could have managed better. For most of the journey he travelled by coach accompanied by a vast retinue of supporters and servants. When they neared a town the nobility and gentry in the party were sent on ahead to break the news that Monmouth was coming and arouse the populace to a state of excited anticipation. Then after an interval the Duke would arrive all alone on horseback with his servants following at a respectable distance and the excitement would rise to fever pitch. Thus he arrived in Chester in 1683, but unfortunately the excitement escalated into hooliganism during which the cathedral was damaged. After a couple of days he wisely moved on into the Wirral.

He came to Wirral to attend the races at Leasowe on what Mortimer claims was 'probably the oldest gentlemen's racecourse in the country' and where it is said the forerunner of the Derby was run before it was moved, first to Newmarket and then to Epsom. The Duke, with his full retinue in all their finery, was there for two days, spending the intervening night carousing (or possibly plotting) in Liverpool. On the first day he took part in the principal 'plate' for a stake of 60 guineas and – it almost goes without saying – he won. Next day he took part in two foot races over 20 roods (about 110 yards), one with boots on, the other with boots off. Naturally, he won those, too.

But three years later he was twice a loser. His ill-equipped army of peasants met the King's men at the Battle of Sedgemoor. He lost both the battle and, subsequently, his head.

It must be mentioned, too, that Handel is believed to have stayed at Parkgate while he was making his way to Dublin for the first performance of his *Messiah* and is said to have made last-minute alterations there after trying out parts of the oratorio with some of the Chester Cathedral choir. This is disputed by some historians who aver that he took one look at the heaving waters of the Dee and moved on to Holyhead, crossing by the short-sea route.

There are many others who were born in, lived in, or have had connections with Wirral who have achieved greatness, notoriety, or fame – like Emma Lyon who became Lady Hamilton, the mistress of Lord Nelson; 'Lottie' Dod from Bebington who was arguably Britain's greatest-ever sportswoman; F.E. Smith, the great lawyer and statesman who became the first Lord Birkenhead; J.L. Garvin, legendary editor of the *Observer*; and Arthur Christiansen, equally legendary an editor of the *Daily Express*; Wilfred Owen, the First World War poet; and Lord Selwyn Lloyd.

But from an historical point of view nothing of much significance happened between the departure of King William and the arrival of William Laird. The peninsula remained an area of scattered villages and hamlets whose occupants were engaged in farming or fishing (and even smuggling and wrecking) as late as 150 years ago and the biggest place was the market town of Neston.

And from all accounts not a few of the farmers were a little slip-shod in their husbandry. For the most part it was dairy country and Mortimer rebuked them for the state of their hedges: 'They are generally speaking exceedingly bad, and from the slovenly manner in which they are made up, they very imperfectly answer the purposes for which they were designed; many are allowed to run so wild that they cover two or three yards on each side of the ditch, and are so high as in a great measure to prevent the circulation of air in small fields; there are some farmers who scarcely think it necessary to cut a hedge, unless thorns are wanted to repair the gaps, or some other such occasion requires it, and then the work is performed most carelessly.'

A certain William Palin, who won a Royal Agricultural Society prize for a report on the state of farming in Cheshire, also found the Wirral farmers' methods to be less than efficient except on one farm where he witnessed the use of 'Alexandra's Draining Plough'.

'It was drawn by sixteen horses, yoked eight abreast, then six, then two; by the first operation soil to the depth of sixteen inches was thrown out, by the second soil to the depth of eight inches more was cast up, leaving the drain twenty-four inches deep and five inches wide. . . .'

Sixteen horse-power! It must have been a splendid sight.

In the eighteen-twenties steam-powered boats came into general use and the Mersey ferries were able to work to a regular time-table instead of being wholly dependent on wind and tide. The river crossing could now be accomplished in ten minutes whereas, hitherto, if the conditions were unfavourable, it could take half a day. This encouraged many a prosperous merchant and businessman to move house from over-crowded, ever-growing Liverpool 'over the water' to the peace and calm of the Wirral countryside.

These pioneer commuters – they were nothing less – came and built large villas in spacious grounds, first on the Mersey's edge at Tranmere and Rock Ferry and then in the Claughton and Oxton areas.

Not least of the attractions for the gentry was the hunting. In those days no man was a Gentleman unless he rode to hounds and the Wirral Peninsula abounded with foxes and other huntable creatures. Henry K. Aspinall in his delightful, meandering, anecdotal book, *Birkenhead and its Surroundings* (1902), says that the immediate cause of his father removing to the Cheshire side of the Mersey was the exciting news that

Sir Thomas Stanley of Hooton Hall had decided to establish a pack of fox-hounds.

The Hooton meet, in fact, attracted many notabilities and the exiled Prince Louis Napoleon was a regular visitor. But even in those days fox-hunting had its opponents.

'It was well-known', writes Aspinall, 'that the venerable Rector King of Woodchurch destroyed foxes near his rectory. One hunting morning, my father, my brother and I were riding on the Woodchurch road to a meet at Thingwall when we met the rector in his gig. He and my father pulled up at the same time. "Good morning, rector." "Good morning, Mr Aspinall." "I am really sorry for you, rector." "Why, Mr Aspinall?" "Because, rector, you will never go to heaven." "Why not, Mr Aspinall?" "Because only Christians go to heaven; and no Christian ever shot a fox in hunting country." '

How times change. Over the years the fox in Wirral – and indeed all creatures great and small – have steadily retreated before the house-builders, the road-makers and the rail-layers. But of late the fox, especially, has been staging a come-back, even into the town centres. Instead of red-faced, red-coated, horse-borne Gentlemen on his tail, however, he is now hunted by van-borne men in white coats and wellington boots armed with cyanide smoke canisters.

As Liverpool became more and more built up many people living there gazed across the Mersey at the well-nigh virgin land of Wirral and thought longingly of the joys of leading an after-business country life much as many today dream of cottages in North Wales or the Lake District. So temptingly near it was, and yet so far, and at the time Aspinall senior moved to Birkenhead the population was little more than a hundred. Then, in 1824, a Scots engineer named William Laird, who had successful business interests in Liverpool, also moved across to take up residence. But he saw the place in an altogether different light.

Laird saw the Woodside area as the ideal site for creating an exclusive Edinburgh New Town-style suburb of Liverpool, away from the hurly-burly of the town but within easy reach of it. But after he had bought the land for this enterprise he heard of land being sold cheaply on the edge of Wallasey Pool and, as his first venture in Wirral, he established there a boiler and iron works which later became a shipyard turning out iron ships – and, indeed, the first-ever iron ship.

This was the age of steam and more industries soon followed, all of them on the Mersey banks of the peninsula. Extra ferry terminals were opened and a natural consequence was that traffic – still horse-drawn at this stage – vastly increased.

A contractor named Thomas Brassey, later to become the world's most renowned railway-builder, built a new turnpike road from Tranmere to Bromborough. It was wholly macadamized and today would be termed a by-pass. It was a costly enterprise for the times, involving as it did the erection of a large bridge across Bromborough Pool, but it obviated the need for coaches to make the journey from Chester to Birkenhead through a number of little villages with narrow, unmade roads. The road was called, as it still is, the New Chester Road, and with subsequent extensions is the present A41.

One of the places by-passed was Eastham, which for centuries enjoyed great importance. The main mode of travel and conveyance of farm produce from Cheshire and North Wales to Liverpool had been by coach and cart to Eastham Ferry (or Carlett Ferry as it was then) thence by boat down the Mersey for the rest of the way. The opening of the new road meant that the journey could be made via Tranmere Ferry and a short sail across the river with a great saving of time.

The year 1840 saw the building of Wirral's first railway. Planned by George Stephenson, it ran from a station in Grange Road, Birkenhead, to Chester and, not surprisingly, John Aspinall, Gentleman, was totally opposed to the idea in the belief that it would ruin the fox-hunting. But when it was completed he not only found it made little difference but, to his huge delight, he was able to travel on the train and take his horse with him to join meets in deepest Cheshire.

The new road and rail service coupled with the reliably regular ferry services really marked the awakening of Wirral from its centuries-long pastoral slumber. Within the next 25 years or so it underwent a vast change. Birkenhead and Wallasey grew into sizeable towns and clusters of houses rose round the various ferry termini at Rock Ferry, New Ferry, Seacombe, Egremont and New Brighton. Industries were established along the Mersey shores. In 1854 Price's Patent Candle Company of London, looking for a site for a factory in an environment more healthy than their Battersea works, built a candle-making works on the south side of Bromborough Pool and on 60 acres of adjoining land laid out a village for their workers. (Its more famous near-neighbour, Port Sunlight Village, was not established until 1888.)

By this time Birkenhead was spreading like lava from a new volcano. Its first town hall had been opened in 1835, Claughton and Oxton were soon brought within the town's limits and in the year that happened 123 acres of marshy land between Claughton and the town centre were turned into Britain's first municipal park. In 1844 the first stone of Birkenhead's docks were laid and, in 1847, the first two docks and Birkenhead Park were all opened on the same day.

Though it was the steam-propelled ferry which opened up the Wirral Peninsula, it was the Mersey Railway which consolidated the development. It usually comes as a surprise to outsiders to learn that Merseyside has an underground railway system at all and an astonishing revelation that it dates back as far as 1886. In that year the Prince of Wales opened the first section under the Mersey from James Street Station, Liverpool, to Green Lane Station, Birkenhead, with an intervening station at Hamilton Square. It was a notable feat of engineering and the first underwater railway in the world.

It was the advent of this railway which really brought about the development of the 'top end' of the Wirral which faces on to Liverpool Bay and along the Dee shore as far as West Kirby. Some omnibus services had been established between Birkenhead and these parts by the mid-nineteenth century, but they hardly allowed for quick commuting to Liverpool. The residents (according to Mortimer) were 'principally boatmen or fishermen who have frequently evinced the greatest courage and alacrity in rescuing unfortunate mariners from the horrors of shipwreck'. But in 1866 the railway was extended to Hoylake and in 1878 to West Kirby and the whole character of the area began to change.

The shore from Meols to West Kirby became a popular place to visit in the summer and on the sheltered western slopes of Grange Hill large houses were built as residences for Liverpool merchants and men of means for whom the distance from their place of business was not of great concern.

Developments had also been taking place gradually on the Mersey banks to the south of Eastham at a spot called Netherpool, near Whitby. Here a new eight-mile-long canal from Chester entered the river so providing access to the sea for a canal which began at Ellesmere in Shropshire.

The engineer in charge was a William Jessop but after a few months he was joined by the engineer who had been in charge of cutting the original canal from Ellesmere, the daddy of all canal engineers, Thomas Telford. Under his direction a mooring basin was made and a toll house built. Trade developed slowly but surely and in 1843 Telford was recalled to build a much larger dock and bigger warehouses. Mortimer (writing in 1847) comments on how ' a few years since there were on this site only one public house, three small cottages, a mere shed as a substitute for a warehouse; and one set of locks. Now it has about two hundred houses, many of them of neat aspect and commodious interior, a Church, several schools, a splendid and most ample range of warehouses erected on arches by which branches of the canal are brought under them, and, above all, a magnificent floating dock, containing upwards of sixty thousand yards of water space'.

It was the beginning of Ellesmere Port.

The interior of the Peninsula for the most part remained delightfully rural right up to the First World War. Only in the nineteen-twenties did places like Upton and Heswall become in any way urbanized with insidious, uncontrolled development giving cause for alarm. On 22 May 1928 a public meeting was called at St Michael's Church Institute, Claughton, 'to organise action to protect Wirral from disfigurement or injury.' It led to the formation of The Wirral Society and over the fifty years since the society has steadfastly pursued that aim, with such stout allies as the (even older) Wirral Footpaths and Open Spaces Preservation Society and the The Wirral Green Belt Council, a sort of local 'parliament' of varied organisations all with an interest in protecting the environment.

The combined efforts of these and other kindred bodies could not, of course, stem the tide, only try to control its flow, and the late Sir Patrick Abercrombie, the famous architect and town-planner, was once moved to write: 'Is it too late to save the remnants of Wirral? Anyone who knew the Peninsula thirty years ago and returned today to find himself in Upton or on Thurstaston Hill might well say its beauty has gone beyond recall.' And that despairing cry was uttered more than forty years ago, in 1936! But when you know that Sir Patrick was the founding-father of the Council for the Protection of Rural England you can see why he felt so strongly.

However, despite the undeniable and inexorable march of the developers and industrialists through the Peninsula there was – and still is – much left to admire. There is still a substantial 'green belt'; the views from Thurstaston Hill and Caldy Hill are still spectacular. The view from Bidston Hill with two vast council housing estates at its feet may have deteriorated, but it still provides a marvellous panorama of the world-famous Liverpool waterfront and the two cathedrals. Burton and Caldy villages remain delightfully picturesque; Shotwick and Puddington have not been touched, and Port Sunlight and Thornton Hough are in good hands and well cared for. And I am sure the professor would have been overjoyed to see how a dozen miles of disused railway track alongside the edge of the Dee have been transformed into the imaginative Wirral Country Park.

No, all is not yet lost. There have been changes, enormous changes, but Wirral's popularity as a place in which to live is undiminished. It has a character of its own; it has an identity of its own. It remains a place apart.

TWO

100 to 100,000 in 100 years
Birkenhead

For many people living no more than a gallon of petrol away from Merseyside the town of Birkenhead is the place where you arrive if you drive through the 'old' Mersey Tunnel from Liverpool. It may also be a shipbuilding firm called Cammell Laird, a struggling football team named Tranmere Rovers and, for those of a certain age, the one-time Argyle Theatre.

Less than 200 years ago Birkenhead was a delightfully unspoiled headland called Birchen Head (headland of birches) which reached out into the Mersey estuary between the tidal inlets of Wallasey Pool and Tranmere Pool. But the industrialists and the entrepreneurs of the nineteenth century saw it only as low-priced undeveloped land, and though Hitler did his best to wipe out some of their unlovely work he only made things worse, while the post-war planners who were charged with putting it to rights have not yet produced a New Jerusalem.

For all that, the rise of Birkenhead from a straggling hamlet of a hundred to a metropolis of a hundred thousand in just a hundred years is a fascinating story.

But sometimes I wonder what might have been had such things as Planning Acts and such bodies as the Nature Conservancy Council and the Royal Society for the Protection of Birds been in existence when William Laird established his boiler works on the shore of Wallasey Pool. Wallasey Pool was a mile wide at its mouth and extended for two miles inland and was a sheltered water for boating, probably the scene of good fishing and, being muddy at low water, doubtless the haunt of wading birds. Laird would have been up against it. So if you lament at all the despoliation of the Mersey banks of Wirral then I suppose he is the man to blame.

On the other hand, he is also the man who gave us Hamilton Square, freely acknowledged to be one of Europe's finest enclosed spaces, and he established the shipbuilding firm which, though it has had more than its fair share of vicissitudes over the years, has produced many famous ships and provided work for generations of Birkonians. He is the man who laid the foundations of modern Birkenhead.

The foundation of ancient Birkenhead is ascribed to a Norman baron, Hamon de Mascy (the spelling of his name varies) in the twelfth century. Though he lived some 50 miles away in Dunham Massey near Altrincham in Cheshire, he possessed a large part of the Wirral Peninsula and decided to build a Benedictine priory on the Mersey headland. As priories go it was – as the ruined remnants still show – on the small side, housing only 16 monks, and his motives for establishing it can only be guessed at.

It has also been suggested that there were simple, practical reasons. There was a need for a ferry across the Mersey which would be more reliable than depending on the whims of the fishermen and also to provide somewhere at which pilgrims and travellers could obtain hospitality. These were things which the Benedictines could provide in keeping with their way of life. Their motto was *Laborare est orare* (To work is to pray) and far from spending their time in prayer and contemplation as did monks of other orders they made a special point of cultivating the land and looking after the needs of wayfarers.

The lands and rights of pasture which were given to the Priory constituted what is now thought of as Birkenhead with the exception of Oxton, Tranmere and Prenton, and extended to Higher Bebington, Saughall Massie and Bidston. They had granges (or granaries) in Grange Mount (between the present Alfred Road and Euston Grove) and the path which led to them is today's Grange Road.

The Prior was empowered to hold a court in the Manor of Claughton and enjoyed the rights to wreck and wreckage, fishing rights, keel-toll, and anchorage. When he rode out he was attended by his chamberlain and other monks and, to all purposes, was the over-lord – albeit a benevolent one – of Wirral with most of the privileges and dignities of a baron.

The Priory received two royal visits in its time. In 1275 and again in 1277, King Edward I stayed there in the course of his campaign against the intransigent Welsh. The second visit lasted five days, from 31 July to 5 August, and while he was in residence he received envoys from the King of Scotland. The latter sojourn is commemorated in a stained-glass window in Birkenhead Town Hall.

In the course of time the moral obligation of the monks to provide hospitality for all who knocked on their door put such a strain on the Priory's resources that they were forced to become more businesslike and King Edward II was petitioned for the right to build lodging houses for cross-river travellers and the right to sell food to them. In 1330

Edward II granted a further charter which confirmed this right and also granted a privilege which, as much as the Priory ruins themselves, has made the monks remembered in the annals of Birkenhead. It was the right of ferryage from Birkenhead to Liverpool *in perpetuity*.

That the ferry still operates by royal mandate is proudly indicated by gilded crowns on top of the ferry gangway posts.

The reign of the Benedictine priors over the Wirral lasted for years, but since no records have been found not a lot is known about their activities. What little *is* known has been derived from other sources, but it seems that during those four centuries life in the Wirral Peninsula was largely untroubled and changed little.

It was Henry VIII who shattered the calm with his dissolution of the monasteries in 1536. Birkenhead Priory was among the first to go and the property and rights were assumed by the king. The Prior was retired on a pension of £12 a year and the monks dispersed, but where they went is a matter of conjecture. Whether the buildings were deliberately wrecked at the time, as many others were, or whether they fell into decay with neglect, is not known either.

You might suppose that the Priory buildings themselves, as the very womb from which Birkenhead sprang, would have been cherished and that the beautiful Birchen Head would have been preserved as, say, Runnymede is preserved, and in the protective custody of the National Trust. Alas, no. The introduction of the steam ferries opened the gateway to a new world, not rich in gold so much as opportunity which could lead to gold, and the entrepreneurs who moved in saw the peninsula only in terms of virgin territory 'up for grabs'. Similarly, the people in possession, the Price family, were presumably not unhappy to sell land and seize the manna which fell so unexpectedly into their laps.

For all these early industrialists did for Birkenhead, with the notable exceptions of Hamilton Square and Birkenhead Park, they hardly improved the scenery. The headland of birches disappeared under bricks and mortar, Wallasey and Tranmere Pools were polluted with household and industrial effluent then artificially re-aligned and turned into docks and quays, and the sandy, rocky shore was gradually eroded. No consideration whatsoever was given to the Priory ruins and some of these developers even removed some of the Priory stonework for use elsewhere. And though the Chapter House was still in full use as Birkenhead's only place of worship and its graveyard as the area's only place of burial, the engulfing tide of industry contemptuously cut it off from the river with which it had been so closely linked for seven centuries and surrounded it on all sides with incongruous and unsightly neighbours.

Except for one very close neighbour. In 1819, as his part of a land deal, Francis Price, the Lord of the Manor, used some of his new-found wealth to build a church alongside the Chapter House which had become too small for the rapidly growing congregation. It was dedicated to St Mary and in due course became the Parish Church of Birkenhead.

Not until 1896 were the Priory ruins – the oldest priory remains in Britain – at last afforded some of the respect they deserved. An appeal was launched and sufficient funds were raised by private subscription to purchase the site from the Price family (save for the Chapter House which belonged to the Church authorities). They were handed over to Birkenhead Corporation and preservation work was put in hand.

The Chapter House, which became a place of worship following the Dissolution, is the only complete Norman structure on Merseyside. But if you want to see them for yourself and you are a stranger to Birkenhead you may have some difficulty in finding them – unless you are sharp enough to realise that the streets above the Mersey Tunnel exit, bearing names like Pilgrim, Friar, and Priory, must surely have some connection. Approach from Chester Street, look for a sign PRIORY INDUSTRIAL ESTATE and you are there. You will see the entrance at the end of a short road called St Marysgate.

Ownership of the ruins by municipal inheritance is now vested in the Borough of Wirral and they are in the care of the Department of Leisure Services. Lack of funds for their upkeep (insofar as you can keep up a ruin) caused their closure for a time but after much pressure the Department of the Environment eventually recognised the Priory as an 'ancient monument'. Since it is over 800 years old one cannot but wonder what the criterion is. However, one result of the tardy acknowledgement is that grants became available and the Williamson Art Gallery and Museum were able to supply a custodian. It is now open to the public during the week and in the restored undercroft there is an exhibition and relics relating to the Priory's history.

If you are unable to visit the Priory during the week you might like to attend a Sunday morning service in the beautiful Chapter House. Holy Communion is celebrated at 11am on the first and third Sundays and matins are held on the second and fourth. There is no evening service. Not only will you be swelling the regular congregation of a dozen or so, but you will be saying your prayers in the oldest place of worship on Merseyside.

Compared with the Priory, St Mary's Church died in its infancy, lasting only 150 years. As the original nineteenth-century streets and houses round about were demolished to make way for the Mersey Tunnel approaches, the trading estate and other projects, the congregation declined and the church declined with it. In 1970 it was declared unsafe and closed; in 1974 it was demolished. The spire and one wall still remain standing as a relic of Birkenhead's first parish church. The wall has been supported by two newly-built brick buttresses, one proudly endorsed E II R, the other 1978, a device which hitherto I thought was only used on newly-erected buildings and not on one which was ending its days.

The departure of the monks from Birkenhead seems to have had little effect on the area's way of life. The king granted most of the Priory estates and rights, including the ferry and its boats, to Ralph Worsley, of Worsley near Manchester, who had served him at court and had become Lord of the Manor of Claughton. From Worsley they passed into the hands of Thomas Powell of Denbigh, who had married one of Worsley's daughters, and he converted a wing of the Priory into a house which he called Birkenhead Hall. The Priory chapter house remained in use as the manor's chapel. In 1713 the estate was bought by John Cleveland, a Liverpool merchant who was also Liverpool's member of parliament and a former mayor. The street in Birkenhead which bears his name is the town's longest but his proprietary interest was one of the shortest for he died just three years later. He left two sons and a daughter, but both sons died without issue and history repeated itself in that the manor, lordship and estates again descended through the female line to the Price family.

This was the situation in 1815 when the most significant event ever witnessed on the River Mersey occurred. It far outweighed the launchings of the *Mauretania* or the *Ark Royal*; or the explosion of the gunpowder-ship, *Lottie Sleigh*; or the sailing of the emigrant ships; or even the arrival of the American troops during the last war. It was the unheralded arrival of the good ship *Elizabeth*. At 40 tons gross, with a length of only 59 feet and a draught of 4 feet, the *Elizabeth* was not exactly a queen of the seas and her voyage upstream to what was then the bathing resort of Runcorn was hardly in the same class as a trip up the Amazon. But she nevertheless rates a prominent place in the history of Merseyside. She was the first-ever vessel to enter the river powered by steam.

At this time Birkenhead was still no more than a straggle of houses with a population of around a hundred and enjoying a brief career as a health resort. The Woodside shore where, as the name suggests, the trees almost met the water, was a picturesque place with bathing machines and donkey rides, and rocks alive with crabs and periwinkles. Francis Price had developed part of the land between what is now Chester Street and the river with a few villas, while hotels had been built at both

Birkenhead Ferry and Monks Ferry approaches. But three-quarters of a mile of deep tidal water put these delights tantalisingly out of reach of most Liverpudlians.

The ferry service was, to say the least, erratic. Totally at the mercy of wind and tide, the crossing could take up to half a day if conditions were unfavourable. Even then, disembarkation on the other side could sometimes be a very wet, hazardous and undignified business through the shallows astride the back of some none-too-careful boatman.

The arrival of the *Elizabeth* puffing steadily and contemptuously through the water quickly showed that ferryboats powered by steam could provide a regular and safe crossing at any state of the tide and whatever the state of the weather. And just two years later the steam-paddle boat, *Etna*, began a regular service from Queen's Dock in Liverpool to Tranmere. Never was a vessel more appropriately named for the consequences were to be of volcanic proportions.

The next decade saw the beginning of the 'colonization' of Birkenhead and district. Henry Aspinall's father took up residence in 1824 and it was undoubtedly a most delightful place in which to live:

> 'My father took up his abode in a very pretty house near the river. . . .
> Fronting the house, a large grass field sloped down to the river side.
> Here the Hooton hounds met twice each season; and the hunt
> breakfasted at my father's house.
> I remember my mother used to go to Liverpool to do her shopping;
> and I recollect my being sent to the ferry to say my mother would be
> down in a few minutes, would they please detain the boat for her;
> which they did.'

William Laird arrived on the scene that same year but, of course, he did not come to follow the hounds. He had been in business in Liverpool since 1810 and saw Wirral as land ripe for development. His first thought was to build the exclusive residential suburb for Liverpool businessmen.

In the event, his boiler works came first. On the north side of Wallasey Pool he established the Birkenhead Iron Works and very soon afterwards he expanded this into a shipyard where he built the world's first iron ship. And the clanging of his riveters and the smoke from his furnaces must have shattered the agrarian calm of Wirral like a firework thrown at a vicarage garden party.

To build his elegant 'suburb' Laird called on James Gillespie Graham, an architect from Edinburgh. He produced a grid-iron street plan in the style of many an American city, with a large square and a central ornamental garden for the exclusive use of the residents as its

main feature. It was intended that all the houses should be stone-faced –
using the creamy-coloured Storeton stone – and, all in all, it was the
most ambitious town planning scheme of the nineteenth century.

Unfortunately, a fundamental mistake was made in laying out the
streets long before any houses could be built and ten years after they
were begun only Hamilton Square (named after Laird's mother-in-
law's family) had been completed.

The constant quoting of dates and statistics in a book which is not
intended to be an erudite historical work could become a bore, but in the
case of Birkenhead it seems necessary to do so simply to illustrate the
speed of its phenomenal growth. Thus, in 1810 the population was 105;
in 1821 it was 200. Ten years later it was more than ten times that figure
and by 1851 it had soared to nearly 25,000.

Obviously, some form of local government had become necessary
long before this point had been reached and in 1833, on the petition of
a group of residents (but not without considerable opposition), Royal
Assent was given to 'An Act for paving, lighting, watching, cleansing,
and otherwise improving the Township or Chapelry of Birkenhead, in
the County Palatine of Chester, and for regulating the Police thereof,
and for establishing a market'. To effect these measures the Act allowed
for the appointment of a Board of Improvement Commissioners and
empowered them to raise a loan of £8000 on the credit of their rates and
tolls.

In addition to a market hall, watch-houses and watch-boxes were to
be built and watchmen, night patrols and beadles were to be appointed
whose duties were to use their utmost endeavours not only to prevent
fires, but also 'to keep watch and ward within the Township, and to
prevent murders, burglaries, felonies, and other outrages, disorders and
breaches of the peace'.

All of which might suggest that early Birkenhead was a place of no law
and much disorder, but the fact is that the first police force established
under the Act consisted of just one constable and three nightwatchmen.

The success of the shipyards prompted ideas for further developing
Wallasey Pool and, in 1827, William Laird eagerly agreed to a plan put
to him by the most famous engineers of the day – Telford, Stephenson
and Nimmo – that the pool should be dredged, a wall built across its
mouth and a ship canal cut right across the flat land of northern Wirral
to the Dee estuary just south of Hoylake. This would not only create a
port to rival Liverpool, but it would have an entrance and exit outside
the jurisdiction of the Corporation of Liverpool, so avoiding their

notoriously heavy harbour dues. It would, in fact, have been within the limits of the Port of Chester. Parliamentary powers were sought to proceed with the plan but Liverpool Corporation were not to be caught napping and while plans were being drawn up they quietly spent £150,000 buying up most of the land on the south side of Wallasey Pool, so scuppering the scheme.

But twenty years later, having no use for the land, the Corporation sold it off in small lots and, in 1843, were astounded to learn that they had been hoist on their own petard. The land had been sold at auction and to push up the price the Corporation let it be known that purchasers could have the right to build docks on it if they chose. They had in mind small graving docks and small boat-building yards, but the purchasers (who included William Laird's eldest son, John, and William Jackson who were both to play such a prominent part in the rise of Birkenhead) formed a consortium and promoted a Parliamentary Bill for the building of 'a great floating harbour'. It was virtually the scheme of twenty years before minus the canal.

As for the new town, the Improvement Commissioners (who also included John Laird and William Jackson among their number) set to work with a will. A meeting room for their own use, a bridewell, and a market were erected in Hamilton Street on land donated by Francis Price; sewers were laid and roads were paved. And as nothing succeeds like success, the new town attracted new industries and new businesses, and workers came in their wake. So more shops and more houses were built, and more sewers had to be laid and more roads to be paved.

In 1840 William Jackson and his brother, John, built a gas works on the edge of Tranmere Pool and though the pungent smell of the gas sometimes overwhelmed the town this was accepted as part of the price of progress and a year later gas lights appeared in the main streets.

The year 1840 also saw George Stephenson's railway line to Chester opened, but 1843 must go down as one of Birkenhead's most momentous years. In that year alone the Woodside Hotel and several churches were built, the Jackson brothers opened a waterworks, the town's boundaries were enlarged to include Claughton and part of Oxton, and Thomas Brassey established his Canada Works at Wallasey Pool.

Thomas Brassey was one of the most remarkable of all the remarkable men who were active in early Birkenhead. Born at Bruerton in Cheshire, he was trained as a land agent and came to Birkenhead at the age of 21 to open a branch office for his Chester employer. He later became agent to Francis Price, but ultimately bought some lime-kilns and a brickworks and launched out on his own. One of his first big contracts was for the supply of bricks for the building of Liverpool's new Custom House (destroyed in an air raid in 1941) and he delivered these to the site by floating them across the Mersey on specially-made rafts.

At Storeton Quarry one day he met George Stephenson who advised him to try his hand at railway contracting and, though his first tender was unsuccessful because of his inexperience, his tender for building the Penkridge Viaduct and ten miles of track on the Grand Junction Railway between Liverpool and Birmingham was accepted.

This marked the beginning of his remarkable career. His Canada works were built (and so called) on his winning the contract to build the 540 mile-long Grand Trunk Railway of Canada from Quebec to Lake Huron. In the event, because of undreamed of difficulties with the Canadian winter, the feeding and housing of his English and Irish navvies, disease, frostbite, and a constant shortage of labour, he and his partners lost nearly £1 million. Nevertheless, the Canada Works, which built all the locomotives, carriages, wagons, rails and ironwork for the bridges – all of the highest quality – provided employment for 1200 men.

That same year the Improvement Commissioners, prompted by William Jackson (who fully deserved his subsequent knighthood for this piece of initiative alone) purchased some 226 acres of marshy ground on the Claughton side of the town to make Britain's first public park.

The park was laid out by the doyen of all landscape architects, Sir Joseph Paxton, and subsequently provided the inspiration for many other park developments, not least New York's Central Park. It was an imaginative enterprise. About a hundred acres of land round the perimeter were set aside for building houses and the sale of the building plots more than offset the cost of the construction of the park itself. Then Paxton, who was at first totally dismayed by the conditions of the site and only won over by William Jackson's persuasive tongue, showed equal resourcefulness by excavating two large lakes which completely drained the marshes. He then used the spoil from the lakes to create islands and hillocks which were planted with trees and flowering shrubs. These broke the flatness of the site and provided walkers with elevated views of the town. A winding carriage drive was laid out around the parkland and between this and the road were the building plots.

The plots of land were sold on condition that the houses built on them conformed to a minimum size and were of a style and quality of which the Commissioners approved – which, like Hamilton Square, meant they were houses for the well-to-do middle class. They were to be an informal mixture of villas and terraces but, true to the story of Birkenhead as a whole, the plan was never fully completed.

The park was divided into two parts, Upper Park and Lower Park, with Ashville Road running between, and nine lodges were built at the various gates. They were each in a different architectural style, and though some of them in recent years have suffered through neglect and vandalism, pressure brought by architects, councillors, and the 'Friends of Birkenhead Park' has rescued them in the nick of time.

At the main entrance, where Park Road East meets Conway Street and Park Road North, a pair of lodges is linked by a monumental triple arch of Storeton stone which, even in this sophisticated age, still provides a surprise for anyone who comes upon it for the first time. Inspired by the Arc de Triomphe in Paris, it is a majestic and exalting monument to the boldness and enterprising spirit of those years.

The year after construction of the park began, one thousand navvies set to work turning Wallasey Pool into a docks system which was called the Great Float. On Easter Monday morning, 1847, the first two docks were declared open and the afternoon of the same day saw the opening of Birkenhead Park. One dock was called 'Egerton' after Sir Philip Egerton MP who laid the foundation stone, and the other 'Morpeth' after Lord Morpeth who opened them. A few hours later the first ship arrived and the first cargo was discharged. It was no more than a load of guano from Patagonia, but as far as the crowd was concerned it was pure gold. Birkenhead had become a port.

The docks opening was followed by a huge banquet in a new warehouse on the quay and the opening of the park was followed by a programme of (so called) Rural Sports. Despite it being a day of wind and rain there were sack races, hurdle races and donkey races ('no carrots allowed'). There was a chase for a pig with its tail soaped; a blindfold wheelbarrow race; a greasy-pole climbing competition ('with Good Hats and Baragon Coats on top for the successful Competitors'); and a grinning match through horse-collars ('the ugliest one to have five shillings'), while 'Lads not exceeding eighteen years' were invited to see who could swallow fastest three basins of Hot Stirrah (a sort of porridge) 'no treacle allowed'. There were also two Foot Races (one confined to women) and, in keeping with the prevailing mood of the town, both races were 'Open to the World'.

By the time the population had reached five figures the original town market had proved too small, so a new building was erected in Market Street South. An acre and a quarter of enclosed and covered space, it was not only said to be the finest in the land ('Covent Garden not excepted') but with its cast-iron arcades and two interior fountains it was also considered to be 'one of the most graceful and perfect structures of its kind in Europe'. It grew to become renowned as a market with a character of its own and a reputation for a bargain, attracting people from all parts of Lancashire, Cheshire and North Wales. By comparison, the new market within the Grange shopping precinct is as lacking in character and atmosphere as the average bus depot.

And so it went on. A police station and extensive lairages were constructed, Woodside Ferry rights were acquired and large sums of money were spent on new ferryboats and landing-stages. The gas and water works were taken over and more new streets were laid out. It was all go.

The new Birkenhead Park became an attraction famed beyond the town, and as the railways spread and offered excursions people came from all over the north of England just to stroll about and take in the scene, to picnic, and to listen to the band. On bank holidays especially, they came in thousands from the cotton mills of Lancashire and the woollen mills of Yorkshire, and throughout the day the town's pavements rang with the clattering of clogs.

They also came to watch the cricket. Birkenhead Park Cricket Club was actually founded a year before the park was officially opened and the matches were a great attraction. In those days there were few rules, especially in the number of players taking part in a game, and in August 1847 no less than 77 players were involved in a single match!

Some 20 years later, the Park team, having soundly beaten all the principal local teams on both sides of the Mersey, fielded a team of 18 against 'An All-England XI' which contained some of the foremost cricketers of the day. It was a three-day match and aroused such excitement in the town that employees of some of the local firms were given a half-day's holiday to go and watch it. The match was drawn and the creditable performance of the local team was ascribed largely to the performance of Rylott, their professional bowler (bowling, being a chore, was considered more proper to professionals) who was carried shoulder high to the pavilion by an excited crowd when stumps were drawn.

The park was also a centre for horticultural shows, carnivals, sporting occasions, parades of one kind or another, temperance and evangelical meetings and, it is said, at the appropriate time of the year, the hour of closing was delayed so people could listen to the song of the nightingale.

The houses which remain on the Park's perimeter today have, for the most part, been sub-divided into two or more dwellings or made into flats and flatlets, or put to other uses like clubs and nurses' homes, but it needs little imagination to see what they were like in their hey-day.

A short terrace of elegant houses on Cannon Hill on the sweeping curve where Park Road South meets Park Road West merits special mention. With proper detachment, Edward Hubbard in the *Cheshire* volume of Sir Nikolaus Pevsner's *Buildings of England* merely says: 'Its symmetrical Italianate façade seen across the Lower Park forms an important feature of the landscape.' It was no place of his to mention that at the time he was writing the terrace had degenerated into a near-derelict slum with the front gardens completely laid waste. It was an eyesore which brought indignant petitions from residents round about. But eventually Cannon Hill was emptied of its uncaring occupants, beautifully restored, and turned into 36 modern flats by Merseyside Improved Housing Limited, a non-profit-making organisation which has rescued from decay many old Merseyside properties of architectural merit. The stonework is now as clean and as fresh as the day it was put into place, artificial stone pillars imitating the originals have been placed at the entrance and the gardens tidied up. Two adjoining villas are also being renovated as I write. It is a heart-warming sight.

Sir William Jackson himself built a magnificent Italianate house on rising ground facing Cannon Hill. Known as the Manor House (he was Lord of the Manor of Claughton), and sometimes as Claughton Hall, it is described in such glowing terms by Mortimer that one cannot but lament that it was ever demolished in favour of the 'semis' which now occupy its site on Manor Hill. Set in ten acres of grounds, it had 20 bedrooms and a richly-decorated interior of which the drawing-room 'presents a *coup d'oeil* rarely exhibited. The sides are divided by gold mouldings into panels in which are six exquisite paintings, upwards of eight feet high, of landscapes and figures – compositions of Italian scenery in the Watteau style'.

At the top of the staircase was a gallery with four marble columns, the floor of which was inlaid with a mosaic of oak, rosewood, satinwood, maple, sycamore and ebony; a mosaic which, says Mortimer 'has never been attempted before'. And should you think that warm-air central heating is something modern then note that 'every bedroom was ventilated by a stream of fresh air, previously warmed, entering over the door and passing through the ceiling behind the cornices'.

Elegant houses for elegant families were much in evidence in the town a century ago and many of them still remain, albeit their grandeur is faded. Villa estates, enclosed and protected by toll gates, were erected on sites which usually afforded the best views of the river scene. Clifton Park, Rock Park, and Egerton Park were all built then, though the delights of Clifton Park were ruined within a few years as residents found the smell from the gas works too much to stomach.

In Rock Park, Rock Ferry, Number 26 was the home of Nathaniel Hawthorne, the American writer and one-time US Consul in Liverpool. He moved in on 1 September 1853 and in his diary he wrote:

'Rock Park is covered with residence for professional people, merchants, and others of the upper middling classes. It is the quietest place imaginable there being a police station at the entrance and the officer on duty allows no ragged or ill-looking person to pass. There being a toll, it precludes all unnecessary passage of carriages; and never were there more noiseless streets than those that give access to these pretty residences. On either side there is a thick shrubbery, with glimpses through it of the ornamented portals, or into the trim gardens with smooth shaven lawns, of no great extent, but still affording reasonable breathing-space. They are really an improvement on anything, save what the very rich can enjoy, in America'.

From this house Hawthorne made many excursions into the Wirral and North Wales, all recorded in his *Journal*, and here he finished writing one of his best-known books, *Tanglewood Tales*, a collection of short stories for children from the Greek mythology.

Rock Park has slipped down the social scale since those days and many of the houses are showing their age, the 'upper middling classes' having long gone elsewhere. Yet it remains a pleasant and intriguing backwater despite the fact that a few years ago it was unforgivably vandalised in the name of progress.

In spite of protests from residents, conservationists, and the general public a by-pass to relieve congestion on the New Chester Road was cut right through the centre of Rock Park. Among the houses then demolished was Number 26.

Oxton Hill was another enclave of the comfortably off, but it was not built to a preconceived plan. This heather and gorse-covered mount offering extensive views of the Mersey shipping was quickly developed after the steam-ferry services were introduced and five horse-buses a day ran between Oxton Village and Woodside to cater for commuters to Liverpool. The area was favoured by the successful merchants and small manufacturers and while their houses were a little less grand than those in adjoining Claughton they were still elegant and spacious. Built piece-meal on plots of land leased from the owner, the Earl of Shrewsbury, their individual styles and sizes were dictated by the tastes and resources of their owners. The result was an irregularity of architectural design which gave individuality to the area, and though age has withered it to some extent, the pedigree is still apparent.

There are also rows and streets of smaller houses and cottages, singly and in groups, at haphazard angles and equally diverse in character, and a walk round the leafy roads is a fascinating experience. There are pleasant surprises, too, when you suddenly come across somewhere like South Grove, a lane which has never known macadam, or a narrow byway like Spring Villas where the approach to the houses precludes anything wider than the handlebars of a bike or a baby's pram.

Inevitably there has been new development, not always in keeping with the surroundings (though, to be fair, the architect in some cases has taken the trouble to be sympathetic) and the alarm has been raised that Oxton's charm could be destroyed if nothing is done to stop it. Happily, Oxton Village has now been declared a conservation area so that now not a tree can be felled nor a wall demolished without permission.

It is a part of Birkenhead that most outsiders do not know about. It is not a bad idea to keep it that way.

Although the new town had germinated well and seemed firmly rooted, the workers who had celebrated the opening of the two small docks in such fine style were not to know that the money to proceed further had run out. All construction work was stopped soon afterwards and this, coinciding with a decline in orders for new ships at Laird's, brought widespread unemployment. It was during this period of depression that Henry K. Aspinall, in his capacity as one of the Improvement Commissioners, coined a phrase which lives on yet, albeit perhaps with a different connotation:

'At this time, when Birkenhead was at its lowest ebb (he wrote in his reminiscences) and the public were continually calling the Com- missioners to account for what was considered extravagant street making, sewerage, and other necessary outlays for a new town, the writer in one of his speeches at a Commissioners' meeting denounced the all but slanderous denunciations in the press and indignantly referred to Birkenhead as "the city of the future". This phrase seems to have stuck'.

The depression saw thousands of workers, both skilled and unskilled, leave the town and grass grew on the empty streets. In 1850, however, means were somehow found to resume work on building docks to some extent, but this time structural failures through bad engineering and design came on top of further financial troubles.

In 1855, rubbing salt into the wounds, the entire docks system was taken over by their fierce rivals, Liverpool Corporation.

Three years later, however, Liverpool's dock interests were in turn vested in a new body, the Mersey Docks and Harbour Board, and in due course the work on the Birkenhead side was resumed, but in a somewhat desultory fashion compared with the vigour with which extensions and improvements of the docks on the Liverpool side of the river were pursued. Nevertheless, resumption of the work on the docks system slowly revived the town's fortunes. New industries moved in and the population rose again. Wallasey Pool had become unsuitable for Lairds' shipbuilding activities and the firm moved to Tranmere Pool, the site they occupy today. But in doing so they obliterated the last vestiges of the once-beautiful Birchen Head.

In 1860 a brash, fast-talking American arrived in the town with a proposition which he had unsuccessfully toted round most of the large cities of
Europe. This 'city of the future' he felt would be just the place where his
idea might be accepted.

Thirty-year-old George Francis Train, from Boston, Massachusetts,
was an advocate of horse-drawn street railways. A great success in many
cities and towns in the USA, they had not found favour on this side of the
Atlantic, but the broad streets of Birkenhead seemed well suited. And it
was in keeping with the enterprising and progressive spirit with which
the very air of Birkenhead was imbued that the Improvement Commissioners, urged on by the go-ahead John Laird, adopted his scheme.
The first route, one and a quarter miles long, ran from Woodside Ferry
along Argyle Street and Conway Street to Birkenhead Park entrance.
And by today's standards, with all the rigmarole of planning applications, advertisement, committee considerations and, frequently, a
public inquiry, the whole enterprise proceeded with extraordinary
speed. From the moment of receiving permission to proceed, forming a
company, recruiting labour, obtaining materials, laying the track, and
building the four cars, took just six weeks.

As with the opening of the first docks and Birkenhead Park, the
inauguration of the tram service – the first in Britain – was followed by a
splendid banquet. A temporary banqueting-hall was erected in the yard
of Mr Main, the coachbuilder, and (according to a contemporary
account) 'Mr Train, who is a most fitting representative of "Young
America" and who does not approve of doing anything in the old jogtrot
fashion, determined to make a series of innovations in connection with
the details of a *déjeuner* to celebrate the opening of the line'.

He began with a novel four-fold invitation card which he sent out to
all the important people he could think of (1200 in all), including all the
crowned heads of Europe, the Pope, and Garibaldi. None of them came
(and the only royal regrets came from Queen Victoria; the rest did not
reply), but some 350 men of substance did sit down to what was without
doubt a lively occasion. It could hardly have been otherwise when you
consider that no less than nine official toasts were drunk (all of them
'with immense enthusiasm') ranging from 'The Queen' to 'The
Corporations of the Kingdom' and that just as many, or more,
spontaneous extra toasts were drunk in between.

The toast list bore this injunction:

'Instead of the old-fashioned lumbering omnibus style of after-dinner
speaking let us introduce the elements of enjoyment and good nature
. . . the regular toasts are few (*sic*) in order to make room for the many

volunteers. Good speakers and good singers are present. Five-minute speeches will allow for all who wish to speak. Don't leave the table if you can help, and when the ranks get thin, close up'.

A brass band struck up appropriate music as the occasion demanded – like 'I'm a Yankie Doodle-Dandy' for Train himself – and altogether it must surely go down as one of the most sustained lunches in history. It began at two o'clock in the afternoon and lasted until eight o'clock in the evening.

The invitation card also listed all the advantages (over the horse-*bus*) of –

THE FIRST CIS-ATLANTIC RAILWAY
SAVING OF TIME – NO JOLTING – LESS CONFUSION – LESS NOISE – FEWER ACCIDENTS – NO MUD – LESS DUST – MORE REGULARITY – MORE ATTENTION – MORE COMFORT – BETTER LIGHT – BETTER VENTILATION – GREATER FACILITY OF INGRESS AND EGRESS – IN SHORT, SUPERIORITY IN EVERY RESPECT OVER THE OLD OMNIBUS. LADIES WELCOME IT – CHILDREN ENJOY IT – IT IS THE RICH MAN'S COMFORT – THE WORKING MAN'S LUXURY.

Not without some justification, Train added at the bottom of the card the words:

VENI, VIDI, VICI.

The cars were 'light green outside, fine-line vermillion inside and beautifully ornamented' and travelled at about 7 miles an hour. The horses' collars were trimmed with bells in the Parisian style and no less than 4360 passengers were carried on the opening day. Every yard of the way throughout the entire day the trams passed through dense crowds cheering as lustily as though they were greeting Queen Victoria herself.

The excitement of this year had hardly died down when Birkenhead was made a Parliamentary Borough. At the first election the man they chose to represent Birkenhead at Westminster was (who else but?) John Laird, who had stood as a Tory. As the son of the town's founder, the largest employer of labour, and very highly respected in his own right, his election might have seemed a foregone conclusion, but he had a formidable Liberal opponent. This was Thomas Brassey's eldest son, also named Thomas (later Lord Brassey), who was a large employer and very popular, and Laird won only by a narrow majority. To mark his election as MP he provided funds to build the General Hospital. (Later, he paid for the building of the adjoining School of Art which bears his name.)

The years which followed saw the successive erection of buildings and the establishment of those institutions and amenities which an ever-growing community demanded, among them Flaybrick Hill Cemetery in a disused quarry between Tollemache Road and Boundary Road. Now one would hardly expect that a simple proposal to turn a quarry into a much-needed burial ground would have excited feelings of any intensity, let alone violence. But when the plan was announced there was an immediate outcry from the Roman Catholic community because no special provision had been made for them. They demanded that part of the cemetery be set aside for their exclusive use and a Roman Catholic chapel provided.

Over the years there had been frequent outbreaks of violence between the 'Orange' and 'Green' elements among the Irish labourers who had settled in the town and this particular issue caused riots which only abated when the Catholic demands were hastily met.

An even worse situation has gone down in local history as the Garibaldi Riots. In this same year, 1862, Garibaldi made his first unsuccessful attempt to overthrow the papal rule of Rome and, not unnaturally, he was denounced vehemently from every Roman Catholic pulpit. So when the Birkenhead Parliamentary Debating Society proposed to discuss the Italian patriot's exploits at one of their meetings a mob set out to stop them. Fights broke out, windows were broken, and shops were wrecked and looted. Extra police and a company of soldiers had been drafted into the town in anticipation of the disturbances, but General Sir Edward Cust of Leasowe Castle, the then chairman of the magistrates, decided that the town's own police force augmented by some special constables would be able to cope without any outside help. Events proved him wrong and, as a result, the town's police force was strengthened and a military man was appointed head constable.

A few years later, however, there was an unbelievable alliance of all religious factions in the town against a common adversary – the Government. It was a situation akin to the more recent Tameside saga when that borough refused to accept the Labour Government's edict to introduce comprehensive education. And, like Tameside, it was a dispute which was watched with interest throughout the country.

In the case of Birkenhead it was a refusal by the Town Council to implement the Education Act of 1870 and set up a School Board (and, consequently, so-called Board Schools) to provide free 'elementary' education under state control for all children between the ages of five and thirteen not otherwise receiving any.

Education in Birkenhead was firmly in the hands of the churches, who argued that a state education would not only be a Godless education, but – the most telling point – a burden on the rates. Even when it was shown that of the 4200 children on the rolls of the church schools only two-thirds attended regularly and that some 3000 others were in receipt of no education at all it made no difference. Successive polls taken over the years on motions to establish a school board were roundly defeated one after the other. This prolonged defiance of the Government's wishes was obviously a matter of some local pride, for Philip Sulley in his *History of Wirral* published in 1889 wrote: 'Schools are attached to all the churches and the town *enjoys the distinction* of having successfully resisted the introduction of the School Board'. In fact, they 'enjoyed' this distinction for no less than 23 years until 25 May 1893 when the Town Clerk received a directive from the Education Department in London that a School Board was to be set up without further ado.

In 1877 Birkenhead became a County Borough but neither John Laird nor Sir William Jackson lived to see this day.

Laird died in his seventieth year on 29 October 1874 following a riding accident. His family intended the funeral to be a private family affair, but the people of Birkenhead were not to be denied a demonstration of the great esteem in which he was held.

A newspaper report at the time described the scene:

'At the time of the funeral all the shops and public houses in the town were closed, flags were seen floating at half-mast from many buildings and the shipping. The great Laird's works at Monk's Ferry were silent, and thousands of people congregated in the neighbourhood of the residence of the late member, along the short route to St Mary's Church, and in the churchyard. A very pleasing and almost imploring expression of respect to Mr Laird was made by the employees of Laird Brothers, to the number of 1300 they marched past Mr Laird's residence four abreast. Proceeding along Bridge Street and Church Street, they arranged themselves on each side of the street, from the north-end of the works to the churchyard. . . .

Upon the solemn cortege starting, the Birkenhead Commissioners, immediately joined the procession; they were followed by representatives of various public bodies on both sides of the Mersey, and by about 300 gentlemen, after whom came 28 private carriages.

The blinds of the houses along the route were drawn down, and as the procession passed, the marks of respect shown by the crowd were universal'.

His coffin was placed alongside that of his father in the grey granite vault in the old Priory grounds within a rivet's throw of the great shipyard which, more than anything else, had made known the name of Birkenhead.

Sir William Jackson died fifteen months later in London. His body was brought up to Birkenhead for burial in the family vault at Flaybrick

Hill cemetery and the townsfolk similarly turned out in force to accord him a funeral which reflected the admiration in which he had been held.

Proposals to seek borough status had been made on several occasions, even as early as the eighteen-forties, but nothing positive had been done. When the idea was again put forward in 1875 the support was such by this time that a committee of influential ratepayers was formed to report on it. They considered the proposition for six months and then produced a report which drew no conclusions nor made any recommendations. This so incensed a number of important citizens that they called a meeting, formed their own committee of 300 and successfully petitioned the Queen for an Order in Council granting a Charter of Incorporation to the town. So, in 1877, just 53 years after William Laird had crossed the Mersey from Liverpool to establish his residential suburb, Birkenhead became a borough with a council and, fittingly, the first elected Mayor was his grandson, John Laird, Junior.

The population was now approaching the 80,000 mark and increasing steadily. There was great overcrowding in the town. The houses which were built up to and immediately after the First World War did much to relieve the congestion, but they were far removed from the dream city of William Laird and James Gillespie Graham. Dreary rows of small terraced houses along the ruler-straight streets, with not a tree nor a blade of grass to brighten the scene, gave the town centre an overall drab appearance, despite the presence of Hamilton Square and Birkenhead Park.

There was some demolition and rebuilding during the nineteen-twenties, and the first council houses were then erected, but during the air raids of the last war over 2000 dwellings were destroyed and more than 26,000 seriously damaged (and 464 people were killed, 288 of them on a single horrendous night in March 1941).

When the war ended Birkenhead was unbowed, maybe, but badly battered and house-building received priority, with vast council estates being built on the rural periphery. The largest of them is at Woodchurch, which until then was a quiet hamlet behind the Arrowe Park Hotel. It consisted of a few cottages, a little village green and an interesting old church with a Norman tower. Some restoration work was done in 1934, but the work of the previous centuries was not obliterated. What has been obliterated is the hamlet itself, engulfed by the new estate.

Yet, opposite Woodchurch, across the few remaining fields in this part of the town, can be seen a small cluster of houses and a farm which constitute Landican. So far it has miraculously escaped the developers, be they private or local authority.

The post-war years also brought a traffic problem. As commuting habits changed and more people travelled to work by car, the peak-hour congestion on the roads leading to the Mersey Tunnel became so bad that something had to be done. In due course it brought forth the Tunnel Approaches Scheme, a plan to separate the Tunnel traffic from the town traffic. The scheme involved the demolition of much old property, the erection of sweeping flyover roads and the construction of a huge marshalling area where the queueing cars could be accommodated in serried lines without holding up other traffic. The work took many years and is a success. But it completely changed the face of Birkenhead and whether the flyovers enhance the town's appearance or not is a matter of personal opinion.

In the meantime the second road tunnel from Wallasey to Liverpool was opened. The queues of cars vanished and the marshalling area has not been needed.

All this was followed by the boldest of all the schemes – the Grange Precinct and Market. Conceived in the nineteen-fifties and planned to be built for £4½ million, its aim was to make Birkenhead the shopping centre for the whole of Wirral and beyond. With more than 100 shops of varying size, from the big departmental store to the little sweetshop, a new market with 250 stalls, three pubs and a bank, it was a daring enterprise for a local authority to undertake.

But its construction was dogged by long strikes, bankruptcies of sub-contractors, council wrangles and financial crises, and since the scheme involved the demolition of some 47 acres of houses and shops at the same time as the wide-scale clearances needed for the flyovers, the town centre lay disembowelled for nearly 20 years.

It was 1969 before building of the Precinct got underway and 1975 before the first shop was opened. In the meantime the original cost had quadrupled to £18 million.

Nevertheless, the scheme was architecturally pleasing and has proved such a great success that plans are afoot for extending it further. It has been like a heart transplant, giving the town a new life and many of those motorists who used to come out of the Tunnel and pass straight through now have good cause to stop and look around.

THREE

A place for people
Wallasey

To a degree, the story of Wallasey runs parallel with that of Birkenhead. It, too, owes its growth and emergence as a town of importance to the introduction of the steam ferries and, later, the arrival of the Mersey Railway. But instead of industry it attracted people. It became predominantly a dormitory town for the businessman and the white-collar worker; even as late as 20 years ago a Liverpool University professor observed that 'Wallasey is the embodiment of middle-class suburbia, a single-class town occupied by the office population of the "city" precinct of Liverpool facing it across the Mersey'.

It speaks volumes that whereas Birkenhead's first council dwellings had been built under the Housing of the Working Classes Act of 1890, Wallasey Council did not have enough council houses to deem it necessary to set up a special housing department until 1945. On the other hand, a municipal golf course and a municipal swimming baths were built as early as 1908–9.

Since the end of the last war large council estates have been built at Leasowe, Moreton, and in part of Saughall Massie so that Wallasey today is far from being all pin-stripes and bowler hats; donkey jackets and jeans are equally prevalent. What's more, at the time when Wallasey was absorbed into the new Wirral District the council was actually in Labour hands, albeit their majority was one.

It is interesting to note, too, that even during its high-Tory years Wallasey nevertheless spawned three notable trades union figures – Lord Citrine and Sir Thomas Yates, both former chairmen of the TUC, and Fred Jarvis who is the present secretary of the National Union of Teachers.

The erstwhile borough of Wallasey was made up of a string of one-time villages which stretched across the top right-hand corner of 'the long square' with a coastline bordering on the Mersey and Liverpool Bay. It was, in fact, almost an island on the north side of Wallasey Pool. Had the plans of Telford, Stephenson, and Nimmo to cut a ship canal through to the Dee Estuary been realised it would have been completely cut off except for linking bridges.

Until the advent of the second Mersey road tunnel and the M53 motorway, entry to the town was via one of three routes across the Birkenhead docks system, unless one took the very long way round through Leasowe.

For the first-time visitor such access is not without novelty. The choice lies between the Four Bridges, a chain of swing bridges over those docks nearest the river; Duke Street Bridge, an impressive mammoth lift bridge over the middle of the Great Float and Poulton Bridge further inland. This is another swing bridge which takes the road from the north end of Birkenhead to Poulton over the entrance to Bidston Dock.

This latter bridge is often called the Ha'penny or Penny Bridge for during the lifetime of the very first swing bridge – a wooden one – a toll was imposed. In 1896 the toll was doubled to a penny, but today it is free. (For many years this bridge bore a prominent notice declaring 'Speed Limit 4 mph' which puzzled motorists by its apparent absurdity. It was, however, for the benefit of the goods trains which also used the bridge.)

Now whilst these routes can provide a closequarters view of cargo vessels which might fascinate strangers, they are not without their hazards which can infuriate the locals. Ships moving into and out of the docks do so at high tide and naturally have the right of way, so when the bridges open to allow passage through them there is often a frustrating hold-up for anything up to half an hour. A few years ago the Mersey Docks and Harbour Board erected illuminated signs advising the expected delay and motorists can now work out whether to wait in the queue or whether there is time to race round to one of the other bridges before the same ship arrives there. Hitherto one had to make a lightning-quick mental estimate based on one's knowledge of the speed of the ship, one's place in the queue and the time taken to lower the bridge. Such calculations could go wildly astray, however, as a second ship cast off and followed in the wake of the first; or if the ship passing through was in fact the second and the first had reached the other bridge.

Mortal man has never uttered a more anguished cry than: 'The bridge is up!'

That Wallasey was once regarded as an island is implied by its name. The Saxons called it 'Wallas-eig' – the island of the Welshman – and in Domesday Book it is called 'Walea', and it is thought to have provided a refuge for the early inhabitants of the Wirral Peninsula against invaders.

The people were not Welsh in today's accepted sense and you won't find any bi-lingual road signs about. The name was bestowed on the area by the Norsemen about the 9th or 10th century AD who had, in turn, occupied the Wirral after some two hundred years' occupation by the Anglo-Saxons. That these 'Welshmen' were left unmolested in this little corner is understandable. Apart from being protected by the waters of Wallasey Pool, the land to the west as far the mouth of the Dee was either marsh or sandhills which flooded easily and was very inhospitable.

So, being surrounded by water on three sides – a peninsula within a peninsula – 'native' Wallaseyans down the years naturally came to depend very much on fishing for a living (and in the eighteenth century even became well-known for their kippers). But they had a very profitable sideline in smuggling and wrecking. A Royal Commission which enquired into the establishment of a police force in England picked out this part of the world, along with Cornwall, as being the worst in the kingdom for wreckers: 'They will rob those who have escaped the perils of the sea and come safe on shore and will mutilate dead bodies for the sale of rings and personal ornaments'.

In 1863, a nonagenarian, James Stonehouse, in his absorbing *Recollections of old Liverpool*, wrote that in his young days and in the middle of the seventeenth century:

'Wirral was a desperate region. The inhabitants were nearly all wreckers and smugglers – they ostensibly carried on the trade and calling of fishermen, farm-labourers, and small farmers; but they were deeply saturated with the sin of covetousness, and many a fierce fire has been lighted on to the Wirral shore on stormy nights to lure the good ship on the Burbo or Hoyle Banks, there to beat, strain, and throb, until her timbers parted, and her planks were floating in confusion on the stormy waves. Fine times, then, for the Cheshire men. On stormy days and nights, crowds might have been seen hurrying to the shore with carts, barrows, horses, asses, and oxen even, which were made to draw timber, bales, boxes, or anything that the raging waters might have cast up. Many a half-drowned sailor has had a knock on the sconce whilst trying to obtain a footing that has sent him reeling back into the seething water, and many a house has been suddenly replenished with eatables and drinkables, and furniture and garniture, where previously bare walls and wretched accommodation only were visible'.

As for smuggling, Stonehouse wrote:

'Fine times the runners used to have in my young days. Scarcely a house in north Wirral that could not provide a guest with a good stiff glass of brandy or Hollands. The fishermen used to pretend to cast their nets to take fish that then abounded on our coasts, but their fishing was of a far different sort. Formby, on this side, was a great place for smugglers, but the smuggling they did was nothing compared to their Cheshire compatriots. I don't think they wrecked as the Cheshire people did – these latter were very fiends'.

Smuggling, if not wrecking, persisted well into the nineteenth century and the spoils were removed to several well-proved hideouts. They might have been hidden in the caves which ran a considerable way inland in the rocks at New Brighton. Since the building of the promenade they have been almost hidden from view, but the outcrop of sandstone rocks known as Red Noses and Yellow Noses because of their colours can just be seen today by the Portland Court block of flats. Alternatively, the contraband might have been loaded on to donkeys and taken across the dangerous marshes of Bidston Moss to the village of Bidston and sometimes even as far as the old windmill at Saughall Massie. In either case, temporary storage might first have been found in the cellars of a notorious tavern on the shore at Egremont.

Stonehouse again:

'It was known as "Mother Redcap's" from the fact of the owner always wearing a red hood or cap. She was a great favourite with the sailor-men and had their entire confidence. She had hiding-places for any number and the men used, on returning from their voyages, to deposit with her their pay and prize-money until they wanted it'.

It is said that as their 'banker' she often had thousands of pounds in her custody, yet when she died suddenly after a very short illness, and soon after a successful privateer had returned to port, little or nothing was found.

Mother Redcap's real name was Poll Jones and by one of those odd quirks of circumstance her daughter married a Customs Officer!

The house itself was erected about 1595 and it seems to have been purpose-built or at least purposely adapted for its nefarious role. Its red sandstone walls were three feet thick and, as if that were not substantial enough, were further 'fortified' with stout planks from the plentiful supply of wrecked ships. It had a five-inch thick, studded oak door and the windows were fitted with strong shutters. It also had a novel anti-burglar device. Immediately inside the threshold was a trap door leading to a nine-foot deep cellar which was used for storing some of the spoils. The front door was secured on the inside with several sliding bars and any successful attempt at forcing the front door would automatically draw back the bolt of the trap door. One step inside and the intruder would take an involuntary drop into the cellar.

The house was amply provided with emergency exits and hiding places, both for men and money, and at the rear was a dried-up well and a large cave with a passage leading somewhere to safety – but not, as is generally now accepted, to the Red Noses at New Brighton as some past writers would have us believe.

Though originally only accessible from the shore, when the Mersey Docks and Harbour Board built the river wall Mother Redcap's became high and dry on Egremont Promenade. When Egremont was urbanised in the late nineteenth century the old inn found itself an incongruity in an unreal setting across the bottom of Caithness and Lincoln Drives off Seabank Road.

In 1862 the inn came into the possession of Mrs Maddocks who promptly cancelled the licence and, it is presumed, simply used it as a house or café. In 1888 it was bought by a Mr J. Kitchingham, a Wallasey-born solicitor with a practice in Warrington. He made extensive alterations, turning it into a handsome residence. When the promenade was built he donated that portion of land in front of his property to the Council on condition that it should never be used for vehicular traffic. And when he said never, he meant never. When the authorities on just one special occasion allowed some carriages to pass over it he was so outraged that instead of bequeathing the house to Wallasey, as he said he would, he left it to the people of Warrington for use as a convalescent home. Even though the offending carriages were carrying royalty on an official visit! In the event it was found to be unsuitable for such a purpose and was sold. Over the succeeding years it had a chequered life as a café and several kinds of clubs. Finally, some enterprise failed and it became empty, to become totally vandalised and destroyed by fire. Now all that remains is the empty site, the cellars and caves buried deep beneath bulldozed earth. There are vague plans to build on the site and, who knows, perhaps today's mechanical excavators might unearth the fortune which many people feel may still be hidden there. Wallasey has few buildings of any antiquity or, for that matter, little of anything to show of times gone by and it is a great pity that no-one took the initiative to save Mother Redcap's. What it may have lacked in architectural merit was surely off-set by its history and curiosity value.

Another building which would seem to point to a lack of historical awareness on someone's part is Wallasey's oldest house. I wonder how many present-day Wallaseyans know where it is? Thousands pass it every day in their cars and on buses, but they can be forgiven if they scarcely glance at the time-worn cottage at the corner of Limekiln Lane and the busy Poulton Bridge Road. When it was built by William Bird in 1697 it would be facing towards the mouth of Wallasey Pool. Today it is menacingly hemmed in by the Brobdingnagian tanks of the United Molasses Company, as though forced into a corner with only a tiny garden with a fig tree and an overgrown privet hedge to shield it. One more tank would have obliterated it. It is a sad little scene but, as we know from what happened in Birkenhead, when the need arises industry is no respecter of history. The wonder is, I suppose, that the house has survived all these years.

The clandestine activities of Wallasey folk gradually faded as the area became more populated. In 1830 James Atherton, a retired builder from Everton, bought 170 acres of sandhills above the Red and Yellow Noses with the aim of creating an exclusive seaside resort fine enough to rival those on the south coast – another Brighton, in fact; and he called it *New* Brighton. Every house to be built would be detached, in ample grounds, and have a panoramic view of the Mersey and its shipping. In a prospectus inviting investment in the scheme he stated that:

> 'As a Bathing Place it has peculiar advantages, not only from its being the nearest point to the open Sea, but it also possesses the most beautiful Beach, The Sands are hard and clean, free from Mud, Gravel or Quicksands, they are many miles in extent and cannot be equalled for the purpose of Exercise, whether in Carriages, on foot, or on Horseback.
>
> New Brighton also possesses a more interesting Sea View than any other Watering Place can boast, being constantly enlivened by the passing of Vessels to and from the rich and flourishing Port of Liverpool, in many instances approaching so near as to admit of persons on the shore conversing with those on board'.

He was not exaggerating. On occasions when the wind and tide was right after a long calm or stormy weather, an armada of up to 300 ships might be seen sailing past on their way to the open sea.

He went on to suggest that his plan (which included hotels, a church, a market place, shops, reading room, billiard room and Post Office) would make New Brighton 'a most agreeable and desirable place of resort to the Nobility and Gentry of all the neighbouring counties'. Alas, it did not work out that way. Some fine houses were built (and some of them still exist, especially in Wellington Road), but what was good for the bosses, it seems, was also good for the workers. Within a few years terraces of cheap boarding houses were built and New Brighton slipped sadly down the social scale. Fifty years later it had achieved a notoriety as (to quote Sulley) 'the favourite resort of Liverpool and Lancashire trippers and roughs'.

Atherton did not live to see this happen. He died in 1838 with only part of his scheme realised, but Atherton Street perpetuates his name.

The district of Egremont also grew out of a housing scheme similar to but less grand than Atherton's. The developer was John Askew, a man of many parts – a former slave-ship owner and captain, Liverpool's harbourmaster, a land speculator, and originator of the Egremont Ferry, though in the latter role he was found sadly wanting.

Always a man with an eye to the main chance, he was one of the consortium in the projected scheme for the ship canal through to the Dee (and, like his partners, made a handsome profit when they re-sold the land they had bought to Liverpool Corporation). He built up a large house for himself on a site which straddled the boundaries of Liscard and Seacombe and called it 'Egremont' after the town in Cumbria where he was born. And since the development was neither wholly in Liscard nor Seacombe either the area assumed the name of his house.

Thus, the Wallasey we know today grew piecemeal and it was some time before the various pieces were joined together.

Wallasey Village and Liscard were the two main districts and the first 'incomers' settled, not unnaturally, round the ferry points at Seacombe and Egremont. Soon there was a need for some form of local government to unite and control the area and in 1845 a Bill was enacted 'for Paving, Lighting, Watching, Cleansing and otherwise improving the parish of Wallasey, and for establishing a Police, and also a Market within the said Parish, and for other purposes'.

The 21 Commissioners duly appointed, however, did not by any means take advantage of all the powers which the Act gave them. Six years later the police force numbered only three (one chief, two men), there was no public lighting, no public supply of water, and the roads were still dirty and unmade. Worse still, they had been totally neglectful in the matter of sanitation and this invoked a petition to the Board of Health from 'the inhabitant householders' complaining about the inefficient state of the sewerage and drainage:

'We have to observe that all the drains and sewers from the houses and water closets of the village of Seacombe deposit their filthy contents upon the shore, the stench from which is not only highly offensive to the senses but extremely prejudicial to health'.

The shore referred to was that on the edge of Wallasey Pool which James Stonehouse had found so delightful a place to visit and fish when he was a boy. It was also polluted with effluent from the various works which had been established there and the twice-daily tide was relied upon to flush it away. When work began on the docks system and an embankment was built across the mouth of the Pool the cleansing action of the tide was lost.

The petition brought an official inquiry and (could you see this happening today?) all the Commissioners were sacked. The Commissioners were replaced by a Local Board of Health which, despite its seemingly restrictive title, administered the area for the next 40 years, and did it well. They not only improved the sewerage and water supply, but built roads, lit the streets, and even built that first stretch – from Seacombe to Egremont – of Wallasey's promenade.

All these improvements, plus the establishment of some horse-bus and, later, horse-tram routes, attracted more and more people. At the first national census of 1801 the population of the parish of Wallasey was 663; fifty years later it was 8339 and by the end of the century – after the opening of the Mersey Railway – it had soared to 53,000. By 1951 that had almost doubled to 101,369 and Wallasey was the third largest town in Cheshire.

Wallasey is unusual in that it does not have an obvious centre from which the various districts radiate. Like Birkenhead, the eventual County Borough of Wallasey was an amalgam of one-time villages but, unlike Birkenhead, they were strung out in a line along the edge of the Mersey and tended to keep their separate identities longer.

Liscard, in the middle of the chain, came to be recognised as the accepted centre. The police headquarters, the magistrates' courts, the central fire station, the main post office, the central hospital, and Central Park are all there. But the Parish Church is in Wallasey Village and the Town Hall is a ten-minute bus ride away in dingy Brighton Street in Seacombe. The strange decision to site the administrative centre here was arrived at – after years of discussion and several changes of mind by the Council – on the curious argument that the 'centre' could easily change from Liscard to, say, Wallasey Village but the main inlets and outlets will always be Egremont and Seacombe. So they chose a site mid-way between the two.

That particular council will scarcely go down in history for its foresight. Egremont Ferry closed down in 1941 (after the landing-stage was wrecked for a second time by a ship colliding with it) and now the future of Seacombe Ferry is in the balance. They seemed not to take into account that further development could only be to the north and the west of the borough so making the Town Hall ridiculously 'off-centre'.

The foundation stone was laid by King George V in 1914, but when it was completed it was pressed into use as a military hospital and not opened for municipal purposes until November 1920. Without doubt it is one of the finest municipal buildings in this part of the country ('strikingly monumental in so unmonumental a town', says Edward Hubbard), but its outward magnificence can only be appreciated to the full from the vantage-point of a ship in mid-Mersey. The building faces the river and it must be unique in that its main entrance is 'round the back'.

One of the attractive features of Wallasey is its three and a half mile-long promenade from Seacombe to Harrison Drive. (Indeed, it is one of the attractions of the Wirral Peninsula that, if you have a mind to, you can still walk along the edge of two of its three sides, all the way from Seacombe to Parkgate).

Since Liverpool's decline as a passenger port and the move of the main cargo business to the north docks at Bootle, however, there is no longer much to see on this walk in the way of shipping other than the occasional unglamorous oil tanker and the smaller vessels destined for Garston, Runcorn, Ellesmere Port and the Manchester Ship Canal. If you are there at the right time, the arrival or departure of the Irish and Isle of Man boats make a brave sight and even the criss-crossing of the Wallasey and Birkenhead ferries cause most people to stop and gaze, even though between the two of them it is something which happens every ten minutes or a quarter of an hour for most of the day. You are also in a good position to obtain a fine view of Liverpool itself. Making the walk doubly pleasurable is the fact that it is traffic-free for half of the way; you will notice the quiet immediately. The motor-car is only catered for on the mile and a quarter stretch between New Brighton and Harrison Drive.

The first hundred yards brings you to Guinea Gap Baths, those early (and one of the country's first) municipal swimming baths where, it has been claimed, more national and world records have been broken than anywhere in the land – so many, in fact, that its measurements have more than once been checked to make sure it was of standard length.

Immediately beyond Guinea Gap is the Town Hall and about three quarters of a mile further on is Mariners Park. This estate of bunga-lows, flats, a few houses and a small infirmary is a retirement village for seafarers and widows of seafarers, known locally as 'The Mariners' Homes'. There is a parkland setting with roads and buildings named after individuals or shipping companies which donated the money for building. These men of the sea enjoy an elevated view of the River Mersey and the Liverpool docks they know so well.

Until recently two large redbrick buildings dominated the site – Gibson House and Cliff House. The former accommodated seamen's widows; the latter, with its 135-feet high clock tower, was for 95 years until it closed in 1977, The Liverpool Home for Aged Mariners. It was closed because the cost of modernisation to bring it up to present-day standards was prohibitive and with the advent of the welfare state and the reduction in the merchant fleet the number of 'aged mariners' needing such accommodation had dwindled.

Built by a Mr William Cliff, a Liverpool merchant, in memory of his daughter, Rosa Webster, its purpose was to save ageing seamen from the workhouse. In later years it became a home for retired bachelor and widower shipmasters and officers. I paid them a visit a few years ago and found all the atmosphere of a gentlemen's club, with the lounge full of hide chairs and the chairs full of men ready to reminisce without the formality of the drop of a hat, or just dozing and dreaming of voyages gone by. The sound of a siren from a ship leaving dock brought a quick eye to the powerful telescope mounted in the big bay window and a commentary on who she was, whither she was probably bound and what she was carrying and even speculation on who might be at the helm.

The building has been demolished. What a pity the clock tower could not have been left standing.

Beyond the Mariners' Homes is Vale Park and, if it is a fine Saturday in summer, amateur painters will be displaying their work for sale on the railings.

A couple of hundred yards on again and you are in New Brighton – Merseyside's own seaside resort which, over the last thirty years, has been in sad decline. The reasons why are too complex to spell out here but, in essence, it has been as much a victim of the changing times as any redundant factory worker.

Immediately ahead lies the empty site where stood the Tivoli Theatre (where Lily Langtry starred on the opening night), and almost opposite on the right was the now demolished New Brighton Pier. On the raised ground to the left where an estate of houses has been built was the site of New Brighton Tower.

New Brighton Tower was in a splendid situation. On a natural, expansive, tiered mound it was a replica of Blackpool's tower, only bigger. It was erected in 1897–1900 at a cost of £120,000 and with a height of 621 feet (compared with Blackpool's 500 feet) it was the highest structure in Britain at the time. It was a pointer to the ambitions of those developers who followed James Atherton and sought to turn his superior residential suburb and health resort into a holiday centre, not just to rival Blackpool but to excel it. Set high on a vast red-brick 'base' which housed a theatre and a large ballroom, it had but a short life. During the First World War its maintenance was neglected to the point where there was doubt about its saftey. The cost of renovation proved beyond the resources of the owners and it was demolished between the years 1919–21. The surrounding area was laid out as a fairground, football pitch and cycle track and continued in use until a few years ago.

The theatre in its day staged every conceivable type of entertainment, from musical comedy to all-in wrestling and, right from the outset, an attraction which seems alien in such a setting but one of which I am sure James Atherton would have approved as in keeping with the type of resort he visualised. A resident musical director was appointed, an orchestra was formed, and New Brighton Tower became widely known for its symphony concerts. The musical director was a young man of twenty-nine who was later to achieve fame as one of Britain's best-known conductors and composers. He was Granville Bantock, who came to New Brighton following a distinguished career at the Royal College of Music. In his three years at the Tower he organised and conducted a remarkable series of concerts and his limited orchestral resources (initially, anyway) did not preclude his attempting large-scale works. He was also a champion of British classical music and (when the orchestra had been augmented to 60 players) among the composers who came to the Tower and conducted their compositions were Sir Hubert Parry, Sir Charles Stanford, Sir Frederic Cowen and Sir Edward Elgar – though only Stanford had been knighted at the time. Bantock himself was knighted in 1930.

Granville Bantock's concerts might well have been taken for granted in a staid watering-place or a culture-conscious spa but in view of the social level to which New Brighton had sunk by that time they were a remarkable achievement.

Just beyond the Tower the 'Ham and Egg Parade' had become notorious. Officially known as Aquarium Parade, this was a narrow promenade with collection of cheap and tawdry eating-houses whose owners touted for business on the doorstep, each trying to out-shout the other. The sands were disfigured with hucksters' stalls and tatty sideshows, and drunkenness and brawling were prevalent. The rest of Wallasey was ashamed of it. The council eventually took steps to clean up the place and in 1905 managed to purchase the Aquarium Parade. It was immediately pulled down and gardens were laid out on the site. A sea wall was built along part of the shore and on the land thus reclaimed the fine Marine Promenade was built.

In a few years New Brighton had recovered its respectability and by the time the First World War broke out it had become well established as a popular holiday resort and the playground of Merseyside. During the years of its existence the old Local Board of Health had pursued a policy of acquiring the front of their parish as it became available and building sea walls to counter tidal erosion. A bonus arising from this initiative was a public right of way and the subsequent promenade.

In 1927, the then council, keeping up the good work, obtained Parliamentary sanction to extend the promenade for a further mile or so all the way from New Brighton to Harrison Drive. But ambition seized their minds and instead of a simple sea wall topped with a conventional iron-railed walk along the water's edge they decided that this was the opportunity to make New Brighton into one of the finest resorts in the British Isles. The plan called for a massive concrete wall to be built out on the shore and on the reclaimed land in between they would build a vast promenade lined with smart hotels and superior guest houses. There would be an open-air swimming pool, the largest and finest in Europe, a boating lake, a car and coach park and approach roads and 46 acres of gardens. Such a noble scheme demanded a noble name. It would be called King's Parade.

The work which started in 1931 in a controversial atmosphere, was opposed by those who thought the money would be better spent joining with Liverpool and Birkenhead in the building of the Mersey Tunnel in return for obtaining an entrance and an exit within the Wallasey boundary. The promenade and the approach roads, and the swimming pool and boating lake were completed by the time war broke out in 1939, when all work came to a stop.

Forty years later the hotels and the guest houses have still not been built and where there was once a beautiful sandy shore there is now a wind-swept highway bounded by a fortress-thick wall just high and wide enough to deny promenaders a view of the sea. Originally seats were set into the wall every couple of yards for the whole length, but contrary to the accepted idea of a sea-front seat these all faced inwards. Time, weather and vandals have caused their total disappearance.

Nevertheless, it is a very ill wind which blows no good and King's Parade is a utopia for motorists. Here they can come and park for hours on end – without charge. And come they do. From all over Lancashire, Cheshire and the Midlands, when the weather is fine they make for New Brighton, park their cars, release their children and dogs to play on the grassy acres where the hotels should have been built, devour their sandwiches, and return home.

At other times King's Parade provides a welcome amenity for the locals. The extra-wide carriageway, the approach roads and the roundabouts together form what must be Britain's finest hazard-free training ground for learner-motorists. On most Saturday and Sunday mornings a car without an L-plate is conspicuous.

New Brighton itself does not benefit by one penny from any of this activity and since the end of the last war its fortunes have gone steadily downhill. In its hey-day it depended heavily on the ferry service from Liverpool. A trip on the boat to New Brighton was to the Northerner what a trip down the Thames to Margate was to the Cockney. But the writing was on the wall even before that when, in 1936, traffic had declined so much that the ferry service was restricted to the summer months. Yet, even as late as 1965, it was still carrying a million passengers in the period between Easter and the end of September, albeit at a heavy loss.

Then came the motor-car boom and people began to travel further afield for their holidays. This was followed by the relatively cheap airborne package holidays abroad and the decline was accelerated. In 1969 the Tower ballroom and theatre were destroyed in a tremendous fire and at the end of the 1972 season the pier was closed. In 1973 the number of passengers carried on the ferry had dwindled to below the 200,000 mark and the service was discontinued entirely. Soon afterwards the ferry pier and bridge were removed, but although there was an attempt to revive the attraction of the main pier it proved unsuccessful and that, too, was demolished in 1978. But enough remains to demand that something positive should be done. Apart from Britain's longest promenade, there is still Europe's largest open-air swimming pool, and Britain's largest indoor amusement arcade, and Merseyside's only bowling-alley, and the Floral Pavilion Theatre. And all those empty acres.

One much publicised grandiose plan for the building of a 40-acre Disneyland-style theme park, with water park, indoor arena seating 10,000 people, a theatre, casino and several top-class hotels occupied the council's mind and public debate for over three years. Hopes were high, only to be dashed when it transpired that the entrepreneur involved had much more imagination than hard cash.

Whatever the outcome, there are two New Brighton edifices which were built just before Atherton came on the scene and look as though they will endure for all time – Fort Perch Rock and Perch Rock Lighthouse.

Fort Perch Rock (or Perch Rock Battery), standing four-square on a sandstone outcrop which is frequently surrounded by water at high tide, looks as though it might have been plucked straight out of the desert. A real Beau Geste-like fort, it was built to protect the seaward approach to the Mersey and originally boasted 18 guns with the main fire-power aimed towards the Rock Channel which all ships then used. There was accommodation for 100 men and officers. The proposal to build such a fort was first mooted during the Napoleonic Wars, but so protracted was the argument between the Corporation of Liverpool and the Government as to who should pay for it that by the time it was completed and ready for action the Battle of Waterloo had been over for 11 years and Napoleon had been dead for six.

The fort was designed by a Captain John Kitson, Royal Engineers. Work began on 31 March 1826 and was completed on 30 April 1829. That seems a commendable performance when one remembers that this is the most exposed corner of the Wirral Peninsula and some time must surely have been lost through bad weather and high tides. But what really impresses me is the precision of Captain Kitson's costings. His estimated cost was £27,065 0s. 8d. The actual cost was £26,965 0s. 8d.

In the 150 or so years since the fort was built its guns have fired just three shots in earnest – two in the First World War and one in the Second. (There was regular gunnery practice, of course, and the New Brighton fishermen would wait until it was over then retrieve the cannon balls and sell them back to the fort). The two occasions were immediately after the declaration of war, as though the officers in charge could hardly wait to 'have a go'. The excuse for opening fire was the same in each case. A small sailing vessel had dared to approach the Mersey in defiance of the new emergency regulations. The skippers in both cases (one a Norwegian) pleaded ignorance and an understandable inability to 'pull up' without adequate notice.

In 1914 the first shot was intended to pass across the bows of the intruding vessel but the elevation was too high and it soared overhead to land on the Lancashire coast in the sandhills of Hightown. There an indignant resident retrieved the shot, put it into a bucket, and took it to the Headquarters of the Mersey Defences where he lodged a strong protest. For the second shot the elevation was lowered but that one, unfortunately, struck the bow of a liner lying at anchor.

During the last war, to confuse the enemy spy-planes, the Battery was camouflaged as a tea-garden, with the roof painted to look like a lawn crossed with paths and a large white sign proclaiming TEAS.

The fort was occupied by the military until 1954. Then in the absence of any practical use for the building, the War Department put it up for auction and it was sold for £4000, reopening to the public as an amusement arcade and café. The venture was not a success and after a period of closure it was bought in 1976 by Mr Norman Kingham, the well-known Merseyside architect, who lives in one of James Atherton's villas in Wellington Road and thus looks out upon the fort from his windows. He is busy restoring the interior to something like its original appearance, but it is a formidable and expensive task. Over the years since it was built the interior has been subjected to many alterations as changes in armament were made and thousands of tons of sand, rubble and concrete in-filling must be removed.

Plans for the future depend on what is revealed when the old courtyard and parade ground have been excavated (and when I was there last there was not a little excitement because their excavations had unearthed the original latrines).

The building is already being put to practical use. The Aircraft Wreck Recovery Group have established a fascinating museum of bits and pieces of crashed war-time aircraft, both British and enemy, which have been dug out of hillsides and brought up from lake bottoms, and some of the rooms will be used for exhibitions and meetings. There is a café and licensed bar and residential facilities have been provided for bird-watchers.

For many years, as an aid to shipping entering the River Mersey a pole, known as a perch marker, was located off New Brighton. It was so frequently destroyed by shipping colliding with it that in 1812 a Royal Navy surveyor, Lieutenant Evans, suggested that it should be replaced by a permanent and more substantial light. No action was taken until the marker was wrecked yet again in 1821 when a Mersey pilot boat collided with it during a storm. Even so, it took another six years of discussion and argument before work was started on a proper lighthouse. Work began in 1827 but was protracted because it could only proceed in the summer months at low tide and it was 1830 before it was completed.

Like the fort, Perch Rock Lighthouse was built to last and it is a marvellous example of the stonemason's art. Made out of Anglesey granite, each stone was expertly hand-shaped and dove-tailed into the next. Apart from the fact that the lighthouse looks solid and durable their expertise cannot be really appreciated because the whole structure was finally coated with a layer of *puzzolana*, a cement made from the volcanic dust of Vesuvius which becomes increasingly harder as it ages.

The lighthouse, like the fort, cost £27,000, is 90 feet high and its light could be seen for 15 miles. It shone for the last time on 1 October 1973 and it, too, is now in the ownership of Norman Kingham. He has restored the interior and, as in the Fort, has provided domestic and sleeping accommodation for bird-watchers or anyone who wants to get away from it all. 'It's marvellous to get up at dawn', he said, 'and look *down* at the birds.' He also added that it is a perfect place for a honeymoon! When Norman Kingham laid on electricity to the lighthouse he sought permission to light up the lantern once again and so revive a few Merseyside memories. But permission was not forthcoming. The M.D. & H. Company felt the restoration of the light, even much-reduced in power, might cause some confusion.

Harrison Drive, the road leading from Wallasey Village to the end of King's Parade, has given its name to a popular stretch of shore which has so far escaped depredation. It is the place where the locals go when they want to go down to the beach.

The shore at this point borders on Wallasey Golf Club's course and the club, which was formed in 1891, has its place in the history of the game in the shape of a former club captain, Dr Frank Stableford, who devised the particular type of competitive golf which bears his name.

Harrison Drive also marks the beginning of The Embankment, another man-made structure which all north-west Wirral hopes will have the durability of the fort and the lighthouse. With the King's

Parade sea wall, it holds in check the mighty winter poundings of the sea and prevents the waters of Liverpool Bay from sweeping in and inundating all the low-lying land right back to the foot of Bidston Hill. The dangers of losing this part to the sea were voiced as far back as the eighteenth century as winter gales and high tides constantly gnawed away at the shoreline. Barriers of a sort were erected from time to time but seldom lasted long and no substantial measures were taken until a man of some eminence, General Sir Edward Cust, took it upon himself to write a long letter to the mayor of Liverpool outlining the dangers and urging immediate action.

Sir Edward had good reason for sounding the alarm, for, in the event of the sea breaking through, he stood every chance of being the first to be engulfed for he lived almost on the shore in Leasowe Castle. To be fair, he did declare his interest. He also pointed out that not only would scores of small landowners be affected but that Liverpool Corporation land and property in Wirral would also be put at risk if a calamity were to happen. His arguments were heeded and a year later an Act of Parliament had been obtained and work started on building the embankment.

For many years the maintenance was the responsibility of the Wallasey Embankment Commissioners and a special Embankment Rate was levied on all householders living below the 25-foot tide level. This was an area of some 6000 acres and included parts of Birkenhead. In the nineteen-sixties, after lengthy negotiations the embankment became the responsibility of Wallasey Corporation. It passed in turn to the new Wirral District Council and its maintenance is now borne by the general rate.

People living above the 25-foot tide level may feel this is something of an injustice, but the fact is that without adequate protection from the ravages of the sea an area of more than five square miles could be in jeopardy.

The original embankment, which had needed regular repair over the years, was in such bad state that in 1973 the Council embarked on an intensive ten-year reconstruction programme at a cost of £1 million a year. Now there is a vast, sloping concrete revetment, impressive to look at but hardly a thing of beauty. But what it lacks in aesthetic appeal it makes up for in the invigorating elevated footpath it provides.

Harold Edgar Young, writing in his *Perambulation of the Hundred of Wirral* in 1909, did not have the advantage of this grandstand view, but there is no doubt about the esteem in which he held the walk:

'I have heard the sea complaining on many shores, and know what it is like to see the Indian Ocean coming tossing in, and to lose myself within the tangle of the China Seas, or to watch from a great headland the long roll of the Pacific Ocean. But in its way there is nothing more enjoyable than on a fine breezy day to set off from New Brighton, along the shore of the Mersey Estuary, and walk to the Estuary of the Dee'.

Between the Embankment and the first half-mile of the ruler-straight Leasowe Road lie Wallasey's famed market gardens – or what is left of them. At one time they covered a large area stretching inland to Bidston Moss, but they have gradually been reduced by development until now just a short stretch remains between Greenleas Road and Leasowe Golf Course. Before any sort of barrier was built the area flooded regularly at very high tide, and when the tides receded they left behind a deposit of sand which helped to lighten the clay. In the course of several generations families like the Websters, the Joynsons, and the Deans, brought the soil to a remarkable state of fertility and husbandry to a fine art. A notice proclaiming 'Wallasey New Potatoes' painted on the window of a greengrocer's shop in May is still the promise of an epicurean treat.

Beyond the gardens, in the shadow of the Embankment, are the long, low-lying links of Leasowe Golf Club which pass through what was once the back garden of Leasowe Castle. It is the oldest club in Wallasey and their first captain was John Ball, one of the most outstanding golfers of his day.

Leasowe Castle itself is something of a mystery. Architecturally it is a hotch-potch and it can really only be justified being called a castle because it has served as an Englishman's home. The mystery is why it ever came to be built. It was erected in 1593 by Ferdinando, the fifth Earl of Derby, and originally was no more than a squat octagonal tower surrounded by a moat standing all alone in the middle of (what was then) the vast expanse of the north Wirral 'leasowe'. It is conjectured that it was once just a private stand for watching the racing on the course which, at a later date, attracted the Duke of Monmouth. It has been fairly well established, however, that the race-course was a couple of miles away on land which has now been washed away. The other theory is that it was built for watching hawking. If so, Ferdinando must have thought that hawking as a sport was here to stay; the walls are three feet thick.

Within the next 40 or 50 years four square gabled turrets were added and it became a residence, changing hands several times, but by the end of the seventeenth century it became unoccupied and acquired the name of Mockbeggar Hall, a term in common use in those days for any large property which was derelict. The building was eventually restored and reoccupied, again changing hands several times, until in 1802 it was bought by Lewis Boode, a West Indian planter. It was in the Bill of Sale on this occasion that the name 'Leasowe Castle' was first used. In 1818 Lewis Boode's wife, Margaret, a daughter of the Rector of Liverpool, carried out some alterations and made additions to the building. But, sad to relate, in 1826 she was killed in a fall from her pony trap in Breck Road. Her daughter erected a memorial tablet on the wall at the spot where she died. The tablet can still be seen but it was moved from its original position some years ago to allow for road improvements.

The daughter, Mary Anne Boode, became 'bedchamber woman' to Queen Victoria's mother, the Duchess of Kent, and in 1821 she married Colonel the Honourable Edward Cust, Member of Parliament for Grantham. Their respective duties obviously entailed spending most of their time in London and they had little use for Leasowe Castle. Cust had the idea of promoting Leasowe as a holiday resort with the Castle as its nucleus. In 1828 he issued a prospectus proposing the building of holiday homes 'with a view of the sea and so arranged as to afford shelter against the violence of the winds. They will communicate with each other by a covered way opening to the South on to a Pleasure Ground, and the plan contemplates the addition of shops together with a Chapel for the Established Church and a Building that may include a Reading Room, Baths and Billiards.'

The prospectus also extolled the excellent sea-bathing, the fine private beach free from quick-sand, the excellent horse-riding to be had on the leasowe itself, and its easy access 'being not more remote from Chester than from Hoylake and Hoose Hotels, whilst owing to recent improvements in the communications, it is as accessible as the former and infinitely more so than the latter'.

For all that it did not succeed. The Castle served as a hotel for some years but eventually the Custs (by now General the Hon. Sir Edward and Lady Cust) made it their 'country' home and both played a very active part in Wirral affairs. While they lived in the Castle further alterations and additions were made. The library was lined with bog oak taken from the submerged forest at nearby Meols, while the dining-room was adorned with the fireplace, chimney piece, and panels of Henry VIII's notorious Star Chamber court.

The Cust family remained in possession until 1895 when the then baronet, Sir Charles Cust, put the property up for sale by auction. It was bought by a company which turned it into the Leasowe Castle Hotel. This venture lasted until 1908 when it changed hands yet again and became a convalescent home for railwaymen. During the First World War, however, it was used for housing German prisoners.

Leasowe Castle remained a convalescent home for nearly seventy years. As with the Mariners' Homes at Egremont, a culmination of changing times, fewer railwaymen, and the facilities of the welfare state rendered it obsolete and it closed in 1970. After its closure it was offered to the then Conservative-controlled Wallasey Council for the knock-down price of £30,000 with all fixtures, fittings and furniture, but they could see no use for it and declined to buy. The Labour councillors argued hotly that it should be acquired for public use and were incensed when, ultimately, it was bought privately for the same sum and planning permission was given for its conversion into luxury flats. Before conversion could begin, however, a local election saw the Socialists returned to power by one seat. The planning permission was withdrawn and a compulsory purchase order was issued. The thwarted owners promptly sold all the contents by auction and the Council were left to buy the empty shell, not at the bargain price previously offered but at the current market value – and that had risen to £113,000.

For some years the building lay empty, being used only as a tempo-rary depository for papers and records from Wirral boroughs. Inevi-tably, thieves stripped lead from the roof and in some of the rooms fungi as large as dinner plates were growing. Mockbeggar Hall loomed again. But happily in 1981 it was acquired by Kenneth Harding who has restored and refurbished it – and, in a sense, put the clock back. In 1982 it reopened, as it had been in 1895, as the Leasowe Castle Hotel.

A few hundred yards beyond Leasowe Castle stands another building, historic and listed, but also empty and looking for a future. This is Leasowe Lighthouse and it has been empty since 1908 when it was deemed no longer necessary and the keeper moved out into a cottage nearby. She – yes, it was a woman – was Mrs Mary Elizabeth Williams, and not only was she the first woman lighthouse keeper, she was the only one of her day. Her husband also worked for the Mersey Docks and Harbour Board who owned the lighthouse and they had 13 children, the youngest of whom, Dolly, is living in Hoylake. She told me something of life in the lighthouse which, with such a large family, was not surprisingly somewhat cramped, and how her mother carried three gallons of oil up 132 steps each day to replenish the lamps. She also told me of a particular problem which faced the removal men when finally the time came to move out. How to bring the piano down the spiral staircase from the top floor? In the end they took out the 'innards' and sawed the rosewood case in two. At ground level a cabinet-maker dowelled the two parts together again and it was re-assembled. But how did it get up there in the first place? Dolly explained it was taken up before the iron spiral staircase was installed. The original staircase was made of wood, but following a disastrous fire in a lighthouse elsewhere it was replaced and the piano was trapped.

The white-painted, brick-built lighthouse dates from 1824, despite the presence of a 1763 datestone above the door. This came from its predecessor which was located nearer the water's edge and abandoned (and later demolished) as the sea encroached. Several local writers over the years have claimed that the earlier lighthouse was the first in England but this is not so. The Romans had a *pharos* at Dover, the remains of which can still be seen, and coastal lights of one sort or another if not actual lighthouses were in use in the Middle Ages. Conventional tower lighthouses first came into use at places on the south coast nearly a hundred years before the Leasowe light.

FOUR

Bebba, Brun and Scirard

Bebington and Bromborough

The Municipal Borough of Bebington came into being on 20 August 1937 when, by Royal Charter, 'a new body politic and corporate' was created. It covered an area half as big again as Birkenhead, its population eventually rose to 53,000 and it had its own Member of Parliament. But, as with all the others, it disappeared into the maw of the new Wirral Borough in April 1974 and its municipal history must therefore rank among the shortest anywhere.

The 37 years it lasted were not really long enough for it to establish its identity as a town and, in essence, Bebington was an exact but later counterpart of Wallasey – an administrative linking of distinct and separate communities.

The district from which the borough took its name is of ancient origin. It consisted of two villages, Higher Bebington (or, sometimes, Bebington Superior) and Lower Bebington (or, sometimes, Nether Bebington) – or even Little Bebington and Great Bebington according to the period in history – and although not mentioned in the Domesday Book they were both certainly in being at the time. The name, in fact, is generally considered to be of Anglo-Saxon origin and, since 'ton' means farm or stedding, there must have been a tribe called Bebing, probably led by Bebba – or so the theory goes.

Great Bebington (Lower Bebington, that is) was in the possession of the Lancelyn family by the end of the eleventh century, but Sulley conjectured that at the time of the Conquest it was vested in one Osborne Fitz Tezzon. Little Bebington (or Higher Bebington as we know it) on the other hand was owned by Robert de Bebington who got it from John, Lord of Worleston, 'to be held by the render of a red rose on St John's Day'.

St John's Day, however, is 27 December and though it would not be too difficult today, where in the world of Wirral would one find a red rose on that day in the eleventh century? Was it, for some reason, a devious condition making payment nigh impossible? The likely explanation, is that the St John mentioned is St John the Baptist. *His* day is

24 June which is not only Midsummer's Day but also an official Red
Letter Day. A token payment of a rose on that day would seem
reasonable.

For hundreds of years the two Bebingtons remained little more than
rural hamlets and only at the beginning of the nineteenth century did
they come to notice when stage-coach traffic between Chester and
Birkenhead increased. The coaches used the Old Chester Road
through the lower village and at their peak as many as 30 a day passed
through. Then, as elsewhere, the steam-ferry brought newcomers who
discovered its rural delights and it became yet another desirable, over-
the-water commuter base.

As the population increased first Higher Bebington, then Lower
Bebington, became Urban Districts, and neighbouring Bromborough,
which was also growing apace, achieved the same status ten years later.
In 1921, all three were merged into the one authority known as 'The
Bebington and Bromborough Urban District '. In 1933 the boundaries
were further extended to take in another ten villages and with the larger
area it was decided that their title should be shorter, presumably to save
time, printing ink and paint. But what should it be?

There developed a straight fight for their honour between Bebington
and Bromborough. Bebington had the advantage of being a UDC
before Bromborough, but the latter argued that their village was just as
important, equally venerable, and certainly more historic. As I outlined
in my first chapter, there was the possibility that the important Battle of
Brunanburh had been fought there; they could point to Bromborough
Cross where a weekly market had been held as far back as the year 1278
under a charter granted by King Edward I when he stayed the night
there on his way to Birkenhead; and, in its time, it had been the most
important market town in Wirral. They could point to St Patrick's Well
in Brotherton Park, which is said to have been found and blessed by the
good man himself when passing through about the year AD 432. They
could also reasonably claim that it was the better-known of the two
places, what with Bromborough Pool, Bromborough Dock, and Bromborough Telephone Exchange.

When it came to the vote, the Bromborough councillors were
narrowly defeated and so the Urban District of Bebington came into
being.

With such a spread of responsibility it is understandable that it was not
very long before full municipal status was sought. But the individual
villages which constituted the new district continued to lead their own

separate lives (and, for that matter, still do). Thirty-seven years was not long enough to achieve a proper blending.

Higher Bebington lies on the eastern slopes of Storeton Hill and is undistinguished except as being a pleasant place in which to live. In Village Road there are still a few cottages which once housed quarrymen from Storeton Quarry which lay alongside the road running from Prenton to Clatterbridge.

The rock strata of Wirral generally are red or yellow sandstone but at this point some geological convulsion millions of years ago brought towards the surface a much harder whiter stone. This was quarried extensively for building for 1700 years and to see examples of it today look at Birkenhead Town Hall and the houses in Hamilton Square, or the nave and tower of St Andrew's Church, Bebington.

The quarries ceased working in 1907 and were later filled with stone from the Mersey Tunnel workings and elsewhere, but they will be remembered in the history books not for their stone so much as the discovery 150 years ago of a thin stratum of softer rock about 60 feet below the surface which contained a number of foot-prints and tracks of prehistoric animals. Several species were represented, but the clearest and most exciting were those of the Cheirotherium. My journey through the dictionary in pursuit of a precise definition turned out to be ponderously in keeping with the nature of the beast:

Cheirotherium, a Triassic labyrinthodont with hand-like footprints . . . *labyrinthodont*, an extinct stegocephalian amphibian of Carboniferous, Permian and esp. Triassic times, so called from the mazy pattern of a section of the teeth . . . *stegocephalia*, an extinct order of tailed amphibians.'

Experts have deduced that it was a large beast with a small hand which walked slowly on its hind legs dragging a long tail, not unlike a large non-hopping kangaroo, but with short legs and hand-like feet.

The discovery caused a sensation in international scientific circles and some of the footprints carefully excavated found their way into museums all over the world. Happily, two examples can still be seen locally – in the porch of Victoria Hall and in the porch of Christ Church, King's Road, Bebington.

Of the two Bebingtons, Lower Bebington has always been the more important in that it lay on the way to somewhere. As well as being on the Birkenhead to Chester road, the Birkenhead to Chester railway line eventually ran through it. The parish church was there and, in due course, it was there that the UDC and the Municipal Borough had their offices. It naturally followed that the new town hall and civic centre should be built there, too.

Much that was in any way historic, however, has been swept away, including a house which stood next to the Rose and Crown belonging to an eccentric stonemason named Thomas Francis. It was demolished only a few years ago to make way for road improvements. Francis was born in 1762 and was in business as a stonemason and contractor. He must have done fairly well for the house was no two-up and two-down cottage but a commodious detached villa with a large garden. What made it memorable were the embellishments which he added. There was a figure of Britannia above his door and in the porch below there was a sculpted tableau which was seen by Nathaniel Hawthorne and described in his *English Note-Books* a few years after Francis's death:

> 'We peeped through the gate and saw a piazza beneath which seemed to stand the figure of a man. He appeared advanced in years, and was dressed in a blue coat and buff breeches, with a straw hat on his head. Behold, too, a dog, sitting chained. Also close beside the gateway another man, seated. All were images, and the dwelling with the inscriptions and the queer statuary was probably the whim of some half-crazy person.'

Francis also chiselled conundrums on the walls of his garden, both inside and out (three of them have been preserved and are set in the wall just inside the gateway of the nearby Mayer Park). When Napoleon threatened to invade England he promptly built a stone 'Martello Tower' on which he mounted wooden guns pointing in the direction of Birkenhead. It is said, too, that he had been known to invite friends to dinner and when they were seated at a table laid with all the promise of a great repast he would, with great flourish, whip off the covers of the large tureens to reveal a main course of a single, roast, trussed sparrow. Another of his idiosyncrasies was to spend his birthday lying in a coffin (and making his poor wife do likewise) and as they both grew older and their bodies heavier, the coffins were suitably altered. The object behind this behaviour is not known, but Francis seemed to give much thought to his ultimate fate. With the reluctant permission of the rector, he dug a grave for himself in St Andrew's Churchyard, lined it with stone and (weather permitting, presumably) spent his Saturday evenings slumped in it at reflective ease smoking his pipe.

When he died in 1850 he had reached the ripe old age of 87.

No account of Bebington would be complete without reference to the amazing Mr Mayer – silversmith, goldsmith and jeweller; antiquarian, horticulturist and philanthropist, and much more besides.

Joseph Mayer was born in Newcastle-under-Lyme, but set himself up in business in Liverpool. He prospered to such a degree that he became a wealthy man. He lived for most of his adult life in Rock Ferry, but in 1864, at the age of 61, he moved to Bebington and lived there until his death 20 years later. From the moment he set foot in Bebington he made it his business to brighten and enrich the lives of the inhabitants. He took part in all the activities, served on numerous committees, and distributed largesse in all directions.

As a young man he was an avid collector of antiques and *objets d'art* and as he grew rich he was able to indulge his great interest, travelling all over Europe collecting items which took his fancy. He was a man of discernment and in this way he built up a magnificent collection of antiquities, historical relics, ivory and pottery. Most of these treasures he shared with the public in a museum which he established in Colquitt Street near his business premises in Liverpool. Among his acquisitions was a remarkable collection of archaeological specimens which once belonged to an eighteenth-century clergyman, the Reverend Bryan Faussett, of Kent. These included many Anglo-Saxon relics, including a masterpiece known as the Kingston Brooch. After his death his grandson offered the brooch to the British Museum, but they declined it on the grounds that they were not interested in British history! Thus snubbed, and understandably not a little aggrieved, the grandson sought to sell it elsewhere and found a ready buyer in Joseph Mayer; but after meeting him he not only sold him the brooch but the entire collection.

In 1867 Mayer presented the whole of his museum (valued even then at £80,000 – and at present-day prices, what? £2 million, £3 million?) to Liverpool Corporation and it was put on display in Liverpool's new museum. In 1941 some of the collection was lost when the museum was bombed and burned out during an air-raid, but among the items salvaged was the Kingston Brooch. It is now back on show today in, appropriately, the Treasures Gallery of the ground floor of the rebuilt museum.

Mayer also built up one of the world's greatest collections of mediaeval ivories and they, too, can be seen beautifully displayed in the Museum's Humanities Gallery.

The year before this munificent gift to Liverpool, Mayer had established at his own expense Bebington's first public library, finding accommodation for it in the house which had belonged to the eccentric stonemason almost adjoining his own house. It was an immediate success and soon he was looking round for larger premises. Most opportunely, a farmhouse with a barn attached, together with some five acres of land, just on the other side of his house became vacant and he straightway bought it. He had it altered and adapted, added a tower in which he installed a clock for the benefit of the public, and it became the Mayer Library. With subsequent alterations it continued to serve the people of Bebington right up to 1971. It is now used as council offices.

The five acres of land were turned into a public park, known today as Mayer Park.

Later in the same year a baker's shop and an outbuilding adjoining the library became empty and Mayer promptly bought them, too, had them suitably adapted and opened a public art gallery. The next year he had the whole lot demolished and a new building erected to serve as a public museum. It almost goes without saying that he provided all the exhibits.

After his death the museum became the town's meeting place, re-named Mayer Hall, and when the Urban District was formed the upper floor housed the council chamber.

So extensive were Mayer's benefactions it was as though he regularly sat down and wracked his brain to see what else he could do for the public good, and there is no doubt that the dissemination of his fortune on these various enterprises gave him great satisfaction. Nor was his philanthropy confined to Liverpool and Bebington; he did not forget the town of his birth. In Newcastle-under-Lyme he established another splendid library in the High School and, among other things, improved the mayoral chain.

Apparently feeling that the Mayor was inadequately adorned in relation to the size of the town he asked leave to take the chain away to his Liverpool workshop where, with his skill as a goldsmith, he remodelled it. When the Mayor got it back it was not only aesthetically more pleasing but bigger and heavier and altogether more valuable.

Mayer was not solely a 'Lord' Bountiful; he played a full part in public affairs. He was active in the cultural life of Liverpool and was one of the founders, and for several years president, of the esteemed Historic Society of Lancashire and Cheshire. He also served on numerous committees in Bebington itself and was an early chairman of the Bebington Local Board (the precursor of the UDC) and was largely responsible for the introduction of gas and water into the town.

In 1860, when the Volunteer Movement was sweeping the country, Joseph Mayer raised two companies which formed the Volunteer Borough Guard of Liverpool and was their commanding officer. Five years later, he raised and fitted out, at his own expense, the Bebington Corps of Volunteers and became their Commandant, a position which he held for ten years.

Another of his great interests was horticulture, which he was in a position to pursue in the grand manner. His biggest achievement was bringing the *Victoria regia* water-lily into flower for the first time in

Europe in the open. This had only previously been accomplished in heated glasshouses at Kew and Chatsworth House. The native habitat of this gigantic plant is the River Amazon. Its leaves are three to five feet in diameter and substantial enough to support a young boy, while its flowers are 18 inches across. Mayer grew it in an artificial pool in the grounds of his house, creating suitable conditions by erecting a small boiler nearby and heating the water with a four-inch pipe. The plant's flowering caused a sensation in horticultural circles where such a thing had been thought impossible outside tropical climes, and hundreds of people came to see it for themselves.

The house he lived in, standing back from the road between Mayer Hall and the Rose and Crown, he called Pennant House after Thomas Pennant, the naturalist, whom he greatly admired. Today it is in use as council offices and the gardens form part of Mayer Park.

Joseph Mayer died in January 1886 at the age of 83 and was buried in St Andrew's churchyard. And Bebington mourned that day as deeply as Birkenhead had mourned John Laird and Sir William Jackson a decade earlier.

Although Lower Bebington remained little more than a hamlet until the last half of the last century it was nevertheless able to boast in St Andrew's Parish Church one which has often been described as the finest in Wirral and can certainly lay claim to being one of the oldest. It is known that a church first stood on the site in Saxon times. It was built of Storeton stone (at a time when most churches were built of wood) and this 'white' church caused the area to be known for a time as 'Whitchurch'. But the church has been much altered and extended at roughly 200-year intervals so that it is neither wholly Saxon, Norman, Mediaeval, Gothic nor Victorian but a mixture of the lot.

The Borough of Bebington in its short life prided itself on being progressive and in the nineteen-sixties embarked on a ten-year plan of major works known as the Lower Bebington Scheme. It did not provide for anything revolutionary, including as it did such items as improved street lighting, new roads, more council houses, better drains and the like – the bread-and-butter requirements of a modern municipality. But it included completion of their civic centre. This had been in official minds since the Borough was constituted, but first the war and then the economic restraints which followed held it back. Permission to proceed in stages was eventually given and the splendid town hall, library, civic hall, council offices and police station which have been built, together with the 'Mayer' complex opposite, make an attractive town centre.

This was to be the heart which would pump life into Bebington and give it the civic identity it lacked, but, of course, the local government reorganisation nipped that ambition in the bud.

But Bebington also needed to establish its identity beyond the civic bounds. Taking up Bromborough's arguments before the merger of the three Urban District Councils, who outside Merseyside had ever heard of the place? It was a Parliamentary constituency, it is true, but councillors who attended party conferences as 'the delegate from Bebington' frequently had to explain exactly where it was. And it did not help their image-building that the borough had to depend on Birkenhead for its bus services and, prior to nationalisation, for its gas and electricity, too. Nor did Bebington even have a telephone exchange with its name on (subscribers were on Rock Ferry or Mountwood), nor a main post office, and it was unfortunate that the town's excellent grammar school was called The *Wirral* Grammar School. Had the name of Bebington been used things might have been different.

The choir of Wirral Grammar School for Girls, under its well-known conductor, Doris Parkinson, was the best girls' choir in Britain in the nineteen-sixties. They won six Llangollen International Eisteddfod trophies, numerous prizes at various other festivals, including the BBC 'Let the People Sing' competition, and broadcast on a hundred occasions.

The Wirral Grammar School for Boys, situated next door, can claim an illustrious old boy in Harold (now Lord) Wilson. He was their first sixth former and won a State Scholarship from there to Oxford.

It was put to me a few years ago by one of the town's aldermen that what was needed to bring the name of Bebington to the nation's notice was a professional football team, and, he added, it did not have to be a good team, either.

The origin of Bromborough's name is obscure, but one of several theories suggests that it is Saxon and derives from *Brunburgh*, the town or stronghold of one Brun, a dark-haired man. In that case he could well have been a contemporary of Bebba. On the other hand, it has been suggested that the 'Brom' derives from 'brunnr', the old Norse word for springs or wells of which the district once had plenty.

Whatever its derivation, it has never lacked an identity, but many people who have only a nodding acquaintance with the place today might think of it as Stork Margarine, or Kelvinator Refrigerators, or Girling Brakes, or the power station. All of which would firmly stamp it in the mind as being an industrial centre.

By a most fortunate circumstance, however, the busy A41 New Chester Road which Brassey built slices the area in two. Thus, the industrial part on the banks of the Mersey is nicely segregated, more or less, from the residential part.

But as it has grown so has its past been erased and older residents recall how this old hall or that old house, and that old farm and this old cottage, have all been pulled down for redevelopment within fairly recent memory.

One thing which is still standing, however, is Bromborough Cross, though it is not entirely the original article. The charter which Edward I granted for the holding of a Monday market was given to the monks of the Abbey of St Werburgh (now Chester Cathedral) and its location beneath the cross was in the pious hope that it would promote honest dealing. It was also the place where farm labourers made themselves available for hire, indicating their wish for employment by dangling a straw from their lips.

The steps of the cross are the genuine thirteenth-century originals to which a new shaft and cross were restored in 1874. But the present cross is only a few years old, a gift of The Bromborough Society as a replacement when, incredibly, the first was stolen. Now why would anyone want to steal such an object? And, moreover, how did they do it? It could hardly have been a snatch-and-run impulse theft. I imagine it would have required a tallish ladder, proper tackle and transport. Did no-one see them at it?

In the years immediately before and immediately after the First World War almost all vestiges of ancient Bromborough disappeared in what was almost an orgy of demolition. All that remains of any antiquity, apart from the steps of the cross, is Pear Tree Cottage (which carries a datestone 1699), Stanhope House, and The Big Stone.

The Big Stone lies on the edge of the pavement near the Church School and seldom rates a glance from passers-by. Yet it is undoubtedly the oldest thing in Bromborough, being a granite boulder which was carried down from the Lake District by a glacier during the Ice Age. It is not unique (there are, for example, half a dozen similar, and much bigger, boulders in Mayer Park), but the remarkable thing is that it is still there and not buried under the tarmac.

Pedants may argue that I have not included Tellet's Farm in my list which, as can be seen from the datestone, was built in 1685. But the building has been disembowelled and now houses shops at ground level, while the rest of the building has been cement-rendered and pebble-dashed, cloaking any semblance of antiquity.

That Stanhope House still survives is due to the efforts of The Bromborough Society (formed in 1932 in dismay at the demolition of the beautiful Bromborough Hall), the Wirral Society, and the generosity of a Liverpool businessman.

This three-storey sandstone house was built by Joseph Spanne and was once known as Spanne's Tenement and dates from 1693. It was presented to the Borough of Bebington in 1939 by a local builder who had acquired the property for demolition (so keeping up the tradition!) and development. Happily, after protests by the Bromborough Society (motto: *Hold fast that which is good*) he saw the error of his ways.

The council decided that Stanhope House would serve admirably as a much-needed branch library and immediately gutted the ground floor for this purpose, leaving the two upper floors empty and neglected. By the nineteen-sixties the building was in such a sorry state of disrepair that something had to be done. Naturally, only one solution crossed their minds. Pull it down! But before they could do so they had to find another home for the library. So what did they do? They erected a 'temporary' wooden building in the front garden. The house was abandoned and deteriorated rapidly, and once again it was left to the Bromborough Society to do something about it. With the backing of the Wirral Society they brought its plight to the attention of Mr Raymond Richards (who had rescued and restored his own very beautiful home, Gawsworth Hall, near Macclesfield) and he generously offered to foot the bill for its complete restoration.

Eventually, a new library was built alongside a new community centre in Allport Lane and Stanhope House is now occupied again and looking as good as, or possibly even better than, it did at the dawn of the eighteenth century.

On the edge of Bromborough is Spital and/or Poulton Lancelyn. To some people it is two places, to others it is one and the same. The junction at the Three Stags Hotel is generally known as Spital Cross Roads and a short distance away is the railway station called Spital. The name derives from a house of ho-SPITAL-ity founded by William Lancelyn in 1170. It was the year of the murder of Thomas Becket, the Archbishop of Canterbury, and the house was dedicated to his memory.

The name Poulton Lancelyn is properly the seat of one of Britain's oldest families and of the Lord of the Manor of Lower Bebington and Poulton. The Lancelyn family has lived on this spot continuously for nine hundred years – ever since, and probably before, William came and conquered. Or, to put it another way, more than a century before the monks built Birkenhead Priory. The present head of the family is Roger Lancelyn Green and in his seventeenth-century home, Poulton Hall, he showed me an old iron chest. It was made in the twelfth century and holds the family papers. Among them was a light oak case containing a parchment roll 20 feet long and about the width of a roll of wallpaper which he rolled out along the landing as though putting down a carpet. It was a sight which would have turned the head of any genealogist – a family tree going back to the year dot. Highly illuminated with coats of arms, it was compiled in 1654 and has been kept up to date. It goes back for 33 generations, from Roger and his wife, June, and their three children, to the first of the line, Scirard (pronounced 'Shirrard'), *floruit* 1093.

The rest of the ancient parchments in the box provide documentary evidence of the tree's roots and its many branches. At the time of the Conquest the Norman barons, knights, and esquires were granted large tracts of land and, in a few cases, the original Saxon owners who had sworn fealty to William were allowed to keep what they had and even given more. It is probable that Scirard was one of these. His immediate descendant on the family tree is shown as Richard de Launcelyn and their exact relationship is not known. Possibly he was a son or grandson who changed his name for some reason, or a son-in-law who was a Norman knight married to a daughter of Scirard. But there is no doubt about the descent from there on.

At the time of the Domesday survey in 1080 Poulton was held by Osborne Fitz Tezzon. One of his descendants, Hugh de Boidele, in the reign of Richard I (1189–1199) gave Richard's elder son, Richard Lancelyn, a charter confirming the ownership of Poulton to himself and his descendants for ever:

'Hugh de Boidele to all, both present and future to whose knowledge the present page shall come, greeting. Know ye that I have granted, and by this charter have confirmed, unto Robert Lancelin, for his homage and service, all the land and tenements which Richard Lancelin, father of the aforesaid Robert, held of my ancestors; to wit, Pulton and Bebington, Apilton and Hull, with all their appurtenances, to him and his heirs. To have and to hold, of me and my heirs, in fee and inheritance, as his hereditary right, freely, fully, and peacefully, in wood, in plain, in meadows, in pastures, in waters, in ways, in paths, in mills, in fisheries, and in donations to churches, for ever'.

It goes on to ask that in return the Lancelyns should furnish him with the services of two knights and two armed men for 40 days each year and four men every third year for six days 'to make my outworks at Dodleston'.

The Lancelyn male line died out in the sixteenth century and the property descended to Elizabeth Lancelyn who married Randle Greene of Green's Norton, Northamptonshire, and so the Lancelyn Green succession was established.

Poulton Hall, hidden behind tall, majestic trees on the road to Dibbinsdale was built in 1653, but over the years it has seen many alterations and additions, like Tellet's Farm, rough-cast rendering cloaks its age.

A short distance away is the site of the ancient castle of the Lancelyns and faint traces of the earthworks can still be seen when the grass is mown short. Some of the old stones have been built into a garden wall and others have been used to pave the old stack-yard and barn. In front of the house is an open lawn backed by a copse of tall trees and rhododendrons which has from time to time in recent years been used most successfully as an open-air theatre. *Midsummer Night's Dream* was presented there in 1960, Milton's *Masque of Comus* in 1965, and 1965 saw Euripides' *Rhesus*. In 1970 Granada Television spent six weeks in the house and grounds making the very successful film version of Alan Garner's book, *The Owl Service*.

But the most spectacular open-air production was undoubtedly *Alice Through the Looking-Glass* in 1972, the centenary year of its publication. There was a cast of 120, including many distinguished people associated with drama, art, and education in Cheshire, the Wirral Grammar School girls' choir and dancers from the renowned Hammond School of Dance in Chester. The costumes were based on the original illustrations of Sir John Tenniel and designed by Jane Kingshill of Sadler's Wells, while the music was specially written by that most prolific of modern composers, Stephen Oliver.

The dramatisation was by Roger Lancelyn Green himself, an author of more than 60 books, among which is *The Story of Lewis Carroll*. He has also edited the Lewis Carroll diaries and a collection of Lewis Carroll's letters and is a long-serving member of The Lewis Carroll Society. With such credentials the production could hardly have been staged anywhere else – though 'staged' is perhaps not quite the right word.

The producer was Roger's wife, June – very well-known in her own right in Wirral and Cheshire amateur dramatic circles – and it was, in more senses than one, a revolutionary event in Britain's theatrical history. The many scenes were enacted in natural sets provided by Poulton Hall's lawns, trees and shrubs, and by the house itself. The audience – for the first time in this country – was accommodated on a *revolving* auditorium, an 8 Scout-powered roundabout which moved them from one scene to the next in much the same way as a television camera pans its way round a studio. This novel apparatus, seating 200, was designed by the Lancelyn Greens' elder son, Scirard (a name met with earlier, you will remember).

As might be expected, every room in Poulton Hall has its quota of Lancelyn Green memorabilia accumulated down the centuries, except for one small room on the top floor which has been set aside to the memory of one not to be found anywhere on the family tree; none other than Mr Sherlock Holmes. This is a remarkable reconstruction of

221B Baker Street, London, where Holmes lived with Doctor Watson, faithfully furnished and equipped by the Lancelyn Greens' younger son, Richard, when he was only 13.

Both Richard and his father are members of the Sherlock Holmes Society of London and the inspiration to recreate this room came from the television series of the nineteen-sixties. To anyone who has ever read a Sherlock Holmes story or seen one re-enacted on the stage or screen this room is immediately recognisable. Never described in detail in any one story, it is nevertheless frequently alluded to so that assiduous research through the 50 or 60 stories can piece together a fairly complete picture.

Life at the 'real' 221B apartment centred round the fireplace, and the plush-girded mantlepiece within easy reach of Holmes' armchair was a convenient dumping place for all the minutiae of his life. It was his habit to transfix his unpaid bills and unanswered correspondence to the mantelshelf with a knife. Within his arm's reach was his rack of pipes, and hanging on the surround his famous Persian slipper in which he kept his tobacco. Alongside his chair, the coal-scuttle which contained his stock of cigars. All this has been meticulously reconstructed; the papers, the knife, the scuttle, and the genuine Persian slipper are all there.

Scattered along the mantelshelf's length, among the pieces of loose tobacco ('plugs and dottles left from his smokes of the day before') and pill boxes marked 'Poison', is a plethora of items which in their turn have each proved vital to the solving of a case: a hand-written note reconstructed by Holmes from the merest fragment found clutched in the fist of a murder victim, a red leech preserved in spirit, some spent cartridges, a pocket watch, a (genuine period) telegram envelope, and an assortment of calling cards left by the many who sought the detective's assistance; and, of course, his large magnifying glass.

Do you remember the story of *The Speckled Band* where the murder 'weapon' was a poisonous snake, distinctively marked, which had been trained to slither into the victim's bedroom through the bell-rope inlet? Holmes thwarted this fiendish plot, of course, and it was the villain who got bitten – and there in a jar is the body of the snake preserved for posterity! There, too, in the hearth is the poker bent by that arch-scoundrel, Dr Grimesby Roylott, to show his strength after bursting into the room to threaten Holmes.

In the corner of the room is what Holmes used to call his 'table of smells' where he conducted 'weird and often malodorous scientific experiments'. On it, along with all the paraphernalia of chemistry, is Holmes' handsome brass microscope.

Close by, leaning against the wall, is a violin-case and, inside, THE violin. Dr Watson relates how Holmes told 'with great exultation how he purchased his own Stradivarius, which was worth at least five hundred guineas, at a Jew broker's in Tottenham Court Road for fifty-five shillings'. The observant Holmes had spotted the small label which Antonio Stradivarius used to place right inside the instrument. This violin of Richard Lancelyn Green's also bears a label with the famous name inside and he only paid fifty shillings for it. True, the name is prefixed by the words 'Copie de' but the moment when young Richard made his find in a junk shop was hardly less exciting.

And so it goes on. To try and itemise the entire contents of this room would tax the talents of a man from Sotheby's, but in this remarkable re-creation of '221B Baker Street' – which I am sure would have delighted Conan Doyle himself – Richard Green has built up an absorbing museum of Victoriana.

In the last ten years the name, Poulton Lancelyn, in many people's minds has come to mean the new housing estate bounded by Spital Road and Poulton Hall Road. It now has about 1400 houses and a population of about 5000 and, at a glance, is much the same as any other better-class estate built in recent years. Bijou houses with steeply raked roofs, dominant garages, open-plan front gardens, tiny back ones, and plenty of white-painted, ranch-type fencing. But amid all this newness stands, quite incongruously now, a venerable and dignified mansion which has not only survived but has acquired a completely new identity.

Attractively sited among tall, age-old trees, Poulton Hey was built about the middle of the last century as a dower house for a member of the Lancelyn Green family and high up in the outside chimney breast is the Greens' coat of arms with its familiar three stags. After it was last occupied by a Lancelyn Green it was divided and for many years served as two separate dwellings. When it eventually became unoccupied it remained empty for some time under threat from a possible motorway route and suffered heavily from those three afflictions to which old buildings are prone – dry rot, wet rot, and woodworm. Its demolition seemed inevitable.

About this time, however, the Rector and Church Council of Bebington Parish Church were seeking a site for a 'daughter' church on the estate and Roger Lancelyn Green generously offered Poulton Hey to them. The church could be built on the site and part of the land sold towards its cost. It seemed an admirable idea, but to everyone's surprise the subsequent planning application brought not the expected approval but a preservation order. The house was deemed to be of historical interest, possibly because in this area of new development it was a tenuous reminder of an era gone by.

It was a case of 'back to the drawing board' and the solution found was not only novel but probably unique. If we can't knock the house down and build a church, they said, then we'll restore the house and build a church inside. Which is what they did.

The ground floor became the 'church'. A velvet-curtained 'reredos' was hung against one wall, a dais with a simple communion table, a lectern, and communion rails, was installed, wall-to-wall carpeting laid, and a small organ brought in. In September 1977, Poulton Hey, thus resurrected, became Holy Trinity Church.

It is an excellent arrangement in that the upper floor is virtually their parish hall and thus all church activities can take place under one roof.

Apart from restoration and repainting the outside appearance of the old house has not changed much. Its modern role is not obvious except that on the gable-end facing approaching visitors is a stone cross betokening its ecclesiastical role. The curious thing is that the cross is not new; it was put there when the house was built well over a hundred years ago. Was its present use pre-ordained?

Since the above account was written the huge success of the church-in-a-house has brought about the building of a new Holy Trinity Church in the grounds with the house being used as parish rooms.

FIVE

Sheer industry

Ellesmere Port

By far the best way to approach Ellesmere Port is by parachute, dropping straight down into the town centre between the Civic Hall and the Central Library. Arriving more conventionally from any other direction could prove a disappointment. For Ellesmere Port is a modern boom town, which means, in essence, it is just a vast industrial complex with accommodation for the workers. True, there are parks and recreation areas which alleviate the workaday scene and thousands of trees have been bravely planted to off-set an otherwise featureless terrain, but I am sure that even the Mayor himself would agree that, visually, it is not the stuff of which greetings cards and calendars are made. But the town centre is impressive, with a most comprehensive shopping precinct and, what is balm to the eyes of any visitor these days, enormous free car parks alongside.

It all suggests the 'new town' concept and that is really what it is. A lot of it dates from only yesterday and, going back in time, only from the nineteen-fifties when the town expanded like an inflating balloon.

Though Ellesmere Port is in the County of Cheshire its native tongue is predominantly 'Scouse'. This has much to do with a deal which Liverpool did with the old Ellesmere Port Urban District Council in 1959 whereby, over the years since, some 20,000 Liverpudlians have been 'overspilled' into the town to relieve the city's unemployment and housing shortage. Provided they had found themselves a job in 'the Port' they were allotted council housing. There are many houses still looking new, new shops, new schools, new roads, and new factories, so that the abiding impression on leaving the town is of brand-newness.

Discounting the several villages and places like Willaston and Neston which go to make up the actual *Borough*, not much is left of any great age. Ellesmere Port itself is a name which had not crossed anyone's lips before 1796 and it was some years after that before it was in everyday use. Earlier it had been known as Whitby and the change was brought about by the cutting of a canal.

In 1793 an Act of Parliament authorised the construction of an eight-mile-long canal through the Wirral from Chester into the River Mersey to provide a deep-sea outlet for the Ellesmere Canal system in Shropshire, so enabling manufacturers in the Midlands and the Potteries to transport their wares directly to ships for export or conveyance round the coast.

The canal entered the Mersey through a series of locks in the tiny hamlet of Netherpool, but since the principal place at the time was nearby Whitby the area became known as Whitby Locks. However, it was often referred to as the 'Ellesmere Canal port' and that, in time, became shortened to 'Ellesmere Port'.

The canal was designed by the great Thomas Telford who, at the time of his appointment as engineer of the project, was actually superintendent of the Shropshire roads. The son of a Scottish shepherd, he was a stonemason by trade and I suppose it was reasoned that the construction of a waterway embodied much of the same principles as the construction of a roadway. He went on to become one of our greatest engineers and architects, responsible for the construction of over 1000 miles of road (including that from London to Holyhead), 1200 bridges (including the Menai Suspension and the Pontycysllte aqueduct), churches, docks and harbours, and many other canals (including the 61-mile-long Caledonian Canal, which took 21 years). He also wrote poetry and was a great friend of the Scottish poet, Thomas Campbell, and the Poet Laureate, Robert Southey, with whom he made a long but rather rough tour of Scotland.

The original intention was that the canal should be wide enough to accommodate the size of the barges used on the Mersey and the Severn. Had this been carried through Ellesmere Port might possibly never have materialised; the barges would merely have passed through a lock into the rivers and presumably little more than a lock-keeper's hut at either end would have been needed. In the event, it was decided to build a narrower canal which would only accept narrowboats, so facilities had to be built for the transhipment of goods between the sea-going vessels and the barges. Telford achieved this by the construction of a tidal basin which connected the canal to the Mersey with a series of locks.

The work was completed by 1801, but it took another 20 years or so for the trade to reach significant proportions. Then, with the gradual completion of a canal network with all towpaths leading to Ellesmere Port and a link with Liverpool, the original cargo-handling facilities became inadequate. Thomas Telford was called in again and was asked to lay out a comprehensive dock estate which would provide wharves, docks, and warehouses whereby cargoes from sea-going vessels of up to 500 tons could be transferred to and from the inland waterways craft or into warehouses for movement later.

For basic things like pig iron, clay, coal and flints, spacious wharves and sheds were provided, but the main feature of his plan was a large general warehouse cleverly linked at different levels with both the basin and the canal where cargoes could be handled under cover. He achieved this with a building supported on a series of swooping arches of such proportion and grace that in later years engineers and architects greatly admired it and artists painted it. The locals called the area 'Little Venice'.

Telford died in 1834 before the estate was finished and the work of completion was entrusted to William Cubitt. The work of construction of the dock estate was slow and it was not until 1843 that the plan was fully realised. Soon afterwards the Ellesmere and Chester Canal Company merged with a number of other canal and railway concerns and the group became known as the Shropshire Union Railway and Canal Company – and the canal as 'The Shroppie'.

From the outset the canal was not merely a cargo-carrying facility. The *Chester Courant* in its editorial of 12 June 1795 looked foward to its advantages for passengers with eager anticipation:

'The communication that will now be established between Chester and Liverpool is such as to promise the most substantial advantages to both places, to facilitate which no expense has been spared in the construction of the canal passage boat which in point of elegance, convenience and swiftness (added to the experience and civility of the captains) cannot but obtain an extensive share of the public's patronage, not only from the mercantile and trading part, but also from the people of leisure and fashion, as the passage will now be no more than a cheap and pleasant trip'.

With a horse-drawn boat along the canal section and transfer to a sailing-boat for the trip down the Mersey it was not exactly speedy: if conditions were unfavourable, the journey took a whole day or even longer.

The fares were: 'Along the canal in the best apartments 1/6 and 2/6; From the canal to Liverpool 1/-. By canal in other apartments 1/-; From the canal to Liverpool 6d.'

In the first month of operation there were more than 1700 passengers.

The advent of steam propulsion speeded up the journey and as early as 1823 the Ellesmere Canal Packet was advertised as leaving Tower Wharf, Chester, for Ellesmere Port every day to connect with a steam packet for Liverpool:

'The adoption of the STEAM BOAT, which is of the most approved construction, in preference to the sailing packet, gives a decided superiority to this mode of conveyance, and ensures the passage in three hours – frequently in less time.'

1   Caldy Village

2   Burton Manor

3   *Top* Bishop Wilson's Cottage, Burton
4   Birkenhead's 'Arc de Triomphe' – the main entrance to Birkenhead
    Park

5 *Top* Looking across Hamilton Square to Birkenhead Town Hall
6 Stanhope House, Bromborough, dating from 1693

7 *Top* West Kirby Sailing Club – home of champions
8 The Parade, Parkgate

9   The fishermen's church of St. Thomas, Parkgate; in its time it has served
three denominations

10   Did Shakespeare live here? – seventeenth-century Bidston Hall

11 *Top* Church Farm, Bidston
12 A night view of part of Shell U.K. Oil's Stanlow Refinery

13   *Top* Seventeenth-century Irby Hall
14   Irby Farm (1612), defiantly surviving in the village centre

15 Ashtree Farm, Willaston, dating from 1697

16   The windmill, Willaston – Wirral's largest

17 Now a cemetery chapel – Frankby Hall
18 The Wheatsheaf Inn, Raby – a free house since 1611

19 *Top* 17th-century cottage, Shotwick
20 Shotwick Hall – now a farm. Built by Joseph Hockenhull in 1662

21   Church Lane and the parish church of St Mary, Eastham

22   *Top* The Lady Lever Art Gallery and the War Memorial, Port Sunlight
23   Tudor-style houses in Port Sunlight village

24   The windmill, Bidston Hill

The large influx of labourers excavating the canal basin brought a big increase in local population, and as various industries were attracted by the facilities afforded by the canal terminus, Ellesmere Port rapidly took on the semblance of a real town. Houses were built for the workers, both by the canal company and other employers – notably the Wolverhampton Corrugated Iron Company – and ecclesiastically it was recognised as a separate parish in 1842. Its growth was further consolidated when the railway came in 1863, but it was still far from being wholly industrialised and for some years continued to be a place of holiday excursion for people from Liverpool and Lancashire. Then a great army of navvies arrived and started digging a ship canal from Eastham to Manchester.

The Manchester Ship Canal is one of the greatest engineering achievements of the Victorian era and its construction brought to an end years of bickering between Liverpool and Manchester. The exorbitant Liverpool dock dues amounted to what was virtually a Mersey toll bar and this had long caused resentment. The grim determination of the merchants of Manchester to put an end to such a stranglehold culminated in the courageous decision to turn that city into a seaport by building this 36 mile-long canal. The planned route cut right across Ellesmere Port's outlet to the Mersey: vessels to and from there were forced to use part of the ship canal and its entrance into the river at Eastham. The Ship Canal Company's attitude towards 'the Shroppie' was somewhat cavalier, but in time Ellesmere Port's position near the entrance came to attract new enterprises as others had been attracted by the earlier canal terminus and, as a consequence, the latter lost its supremacy as the town's chief industry.

In the years immediately following the First World War inland waterways generally lost custom in the face of competition from the railways and the growing use of road transport. Many canals, in fact, were owned by the railways and the Shropshire Union was one. It was owned by the London North Western Railway Company, who in 1921 announced that their canal operations would cease. Over the next year the whole Shropshire Union fleet of barges, the biggest in the country, was sold off.

The canal system remained open for other users and though they grew less and less each year the last war brought a resurgence and it was 1958 before the dock estate was finally declared redundant and closed down. In the years which followed it became derelict and the haunt of vandals and scrap metal thieves. The waters of the dock basin were rubbish-strewn, buildings crumbled, lock gates began to rot, and machinery rusted away. But Telford's graceful arched warehouse remained as a monument to a way of life that was past. Until one afternoon in June 1970. Somehow the warehouse caught fire and thousands of Ellesmere

Port residents watched in horror as the huge building was engulfed by the flames and slowly fell apart to tumble into the water below.

It is a British characteristic that whenever an aspect of the past dies someone with no professional interest whatsoever comes along to pick up some of the pieces to preserve as a reminder, just as happened, for example, with steam trains, early motorcars and trams. But there is invariably a time-lag, so that the task of rescue is never less than formidable. It has happened at Ellesmere Port where the Northwest Museum of Inland Navigation is now trying to re-create some of the one-time scene.

The Boat Museum, as it is more popularly known, was set up in December 1970 by a small group of enthusiasts who had individually shown an active interest in preserving canal boats. In 1974 Ellesmere Port council offered them the use of the derelict Shropshire Union buildings and the dilapidated dock estate as a base for their activities. The entire site was later declared a conservation area and parties of school children and youth organisations have cleared some of the debris, while members have spent many long hours of their spare time repairing and renovating an ever-growing number of boats of all sizes and functions ('the largest assemblage of historic canal craft afloat in Europe', they claim) and restoring what is left of the buildings and machinery. Their aim is to preserve the working craft in working condition and their ambitious plans are of necessity long-term.

The Museum opened to the public in 1976 and great strides have been made. It can never be complete, of course, without the splendour of Telford's warehouse but the boats and the static exhibits do give a good idea of what the canal basin was like in its hey-day. The Museum is easy to find and open throughout the year. It is situated adjacent to Junction 9 of the M53 and is well signposted. Buses from Chester and Birkenhead pass close by.

The opening of the Manchester Ship Canal in 1894 not only made Manchester an inland port but also put Ellesmere Port itself into the deep-sea business. A quay was built along the side of the canal and it became the first port of call. The quay (now long enough to be referred to as 'the docks') has been modernised in recent years and container-handling and roll-on/roll-off facilities have been installed. Electric cranes and diesel locomotives, and fork-lift trucks and straddle carriers rapidly deal with cargoes for or coming from ports in Europe and Scandinavia, the United States and Russia.

A mile away, along the canal towards Eastham is Manesty Wharf, originally built by Bowater's Paper Company to handle wood pulp for their paper mills. Following their departure in 1982 it is now used for the importation of forest products of all kinds. And a mile away upstream is Stanlow.

Stanlow is only just inside the boundary of 'my' Wirral and, quite honestly, I would rather it were elsewhere. That is being selfish for I am as dependant on its products as the next man and, unlovely as it is, this monster oil refinery occupies a site which was otherwise useless. Ormerod described it as 'a cheerless marsh' and 'a gloomy morass', while Mortimer considered it to be 'one of the most miserable townships in the county' and Sulley as 'the poorest and most desolate in Wirral.'

Stanlaw (as it was once known) was an area completely open to the elements and subjected to frequent flooding, but near the spot where the River Gowy flowed into the Mersey there was a rocky outcrop. On this spot in 1178 John de Lacey, 6th Baron of Halton and Constable of Chester, established a monastery of the Cistercian Order as a prelude to his pilgrimage to the Holy Land. It was a journey from which he was never to return, dying there in 1190. It has been suggested that he deliberately chose this site *because of* its bleakness for it would present a challenge to the Cistercian monks who lived on the principle of hard work and little in the way of creature comforts. Whatever the reason they were obviously not as fortunate as their Benedictine brothers who joined Hamon de Mascy's priory about the same time on the beautiful Birchen Head.

The abbey nevertheless flourished and through several bequests of land (as far afield as Blackburn in Lancashire) it became very rich, which seems a little ironic for an Order based on austerity. Riches or no, it came to pass that their faith was put to the test. In 1279 the abbey was struck by a great storm and the Mersey overflowed, causing tremendous damage. Seven years later, before they had fully recovered from this disaster, another storm wrecked the tower of the abbey church and two years after that a fire destroyed almost all the buildings.

To add to these misfortunes the site was often under three feet of water at spring tides. In the end they were forced to make urgent representations to the Pope for permission to move out. Permission was eventually granted for a move to Whalley Abbey in north Lancashire, but it was not until 1296 that this was achieved.

But Stanlaw was not finished. It remained in being as a cell of Whalley with just a dozen monks and lasted for another 300 years until the Dissolution.

What happened to the abbey at that time is not known, but a farm came to be established on the site and the farmhouse was probably built out of old masonry from the ruins. When the Ship Canal was cut it was isolated from the mainland.

The connection of Stanlow with oil goes back to the nineteen-twenties when Shell-Mex (as it was then), seeking a base for its activities, decided that somewhere on the Ship Canal near to good road and rail connections would be most suitable. They built a quay and bought Ince Hall, a manor house once noted for its beautiful gardens, where they established a refinery to make bitumen. A second oil dock, for Lobitos, followed in 1933, but it was not until 1949 on the eve of the great motorcar, road transport and oil heating boom that expansion began in earnest.

Now Stanlow is a great steel, sci-fi city, an ugly, overpowering city, an awesome sight and every time I pass in its shadow along that three-mile straight between the roundabouts at Elton and Little Stanney I feel small and insignificant.

It is one of the largest and most comprehensive refineries in the world. It covers 2,000 acres, has 30 miles of internal roads, 15 miles of rail sidings and 1200 miles of pipeline. It takes in 30,000 tons of crude oil every single day and turns out hundreds of oil-based products, from petrol to detergents . . . enough petrol to take 200,000 family cars from Wirral to London and back; enough aviation fuel for 32 Concorde flights from London to Washington; fuel enough to satisfy 17 power stations; 200,000 gallons of lubricating oil; 3 million gallons of gas and diesel oils; sufficient bitumen to surface $1\frac{1}{4}$ miles of a six-lane highway; wax to make the equivalent of 4 million five-inch candles – and much, much more. Every day of the year.

At the opposite end of the Borough there has been an equally impressive development where Vauxhall Motors arrived on the scene in 1958. And like Stanlow, the ground which now accommodates this giant factory has had an historic past. Before Vauxhall's it was Hooton Park Aerodrome and before that a race-course; but it was also the site of Hooton Hall, for more than five centuries the seat of one of Britain's distinguished families. The Stanley family came into possession of the Manor of Hooton through marriage when Sir William Stanley married Margery, the daughter of Sir William Hooton, and down the years, through various alliances of heirs and successors with heiresses of leading Cheshire and Lancashire families, their influence grew.

One of the early marriages brought them the bailiwick of the Forest of Wirral as betokened by the famous Wirral Horn. The 650-year-old horn still exists and is in the possession of the Earl of Cromer, former governor of the Bank of England, who now lives in Jersey – and how he comes to have it is a somewhat convoluted tale. The post of Master Forester of Wirral was granted by the fourth Earl of Chester to Alan Sylvester in 1120 together with the manors of Hooton, Storeton and Puddington.

This does not mean that the peninsula was one dense forest but rather a largely uncultivated place of rough pasture and frequent woodland over which strict forest laws operated relating to the taking of game. Alan Sylvester was succeeded by his son, Ralph, but he left no children and the forestership and the manors were granted to Alexander de Storeton who had married Alan Sylvester's daughter, Anabella. Alexander de Storeton, however, left only daughters, so the bailiwick and properties passed to Sir Thomas Bamville who had married the eldest daughter, Agnes.

Their son and heir, Sir Philip Bamville, in his turn, left only daughters and once again everything passed to the lucky man who had married his eldest. But was she, Jane Bamville, actually married at the time of her father's death? That was the question, for Sir William Stanley had claimed that he and Jane had actually eloped two years before on Sunday, 27 September 1282 and had been married at Astbury Church near Congleton. There William had declared: 'Jane, I plight thee my troth to take and hold thee as my lawful wife until my life's end.' And Jane replied: 'I, Jane, take thee, William, as my lawful husband.' And as this declaration of true love had been spoken in front of two credible witnesses the marriage was recognised.

The couple had taken this step to thwart Jane's father's plans to marry her off to his step-son and the opportunity to steal away with the man she loved came while the rest of the family were enjoying a banquet.

Thus, in such romantic fashion, did the forestership of Wirral come into the Stanley family.

The Stanley family's propensity over these five centuries to call most of their first-born sons William means that without a family-tree at one's elbow it is easy to become confused about which one did what – and between them they did much. In 1402 the then Sir William raised a force of lancers and archers to support Sir Henry Percy (the famous 'Hotspur'), son of the Earl of Northumberland, in the revolt against Henry IV. It culminated in the Battle of Shrewsbury and the death of 'Hotspur'. Fortunately, the King later pardoned Stanley for the part he played or the family line might possibly have come to an end there and then.

This particular Sir William's brother, Sir John, Knight of the Garter, was made Lord-Lieutenant of Ireland and married Isabella, the daughter of Sir Thomas Latham, so uniting a famous Cheshire family with a famous Lancashire one, and from this union sprang the Earls of Derby.

Yet another William Stanley fought at the Battle of Agincourt in 1415 and when his son – yes, William again – died 15 years later he was described as being in possession of manor and lands in no less than 22 places in Cheshire.

But among these many Williams was one whose conduct sadly lapsed from the high standards expected of such an illustrious line. He was the black sheep of the family if ever there was one. This one lived at the beginning of the seventeenth century. A fervent Roman Catholic, he became a distinguished soldier in the service of the King of Spain. The year 1578, however, found him in Ireland playing a prominent part in the English campaign against Munster. He particularly distinguished himself in successfully repelling after eight hours of desperate fighting an attack by 400 foot and 30 horse-borne troops, 'not having in his company six score persons to the uttermost'.

From Ireland he went to the Netherlands with the Earl of Leicester's expedition against the Spaniards and at the Battle of Zutphen saw his friend, the poet and soldier, Sir Philip Sidney, killed. Following the battle the Earl of Leicester made Stanley governor of the town of Deventer with a garrison of 1400 Irish soldiers. But within a few weeks, for some reason never explained, he committed an act of gross treason. He handed his garrison over to the Spaniards and worse, persuaded most of his troops to enter the service of the King of Spain.

He remained as Governor of Deventer, kept his rank, and even went so far as to aid King Philip's war against England by advising him on the best places for the Armada to attack. (Did he mention Hilbre and the Dee, I wonder?). He ultimately became Governor of Mecklin (today known as Malines) in what is now Belgium and died there.

His father, Sir Roland Stanley, outlived him – in fact, he lived to be 96 – and, ashamed of his son's treachery, he tried to make amends by contributing to the Armada defence fund. Possibly because of this, when he died his son's son, aged 7, was allowed to succeed to the title and the estates.

In 1715 Sir William Massey of Puddington died and left his estates to his godson, Thomas Stanley, who, not unreasonably in the circumstances, promptly took Massey as an additional name. In 1863 the last of the line to live in Hooton Hall died. He was Sir William Thomas Massey Stanley, but he died in Paris. He was the Stanley who established the pack of fox-hounds which so excited John Aspinall and he led such a profligate life of hunting, race-going, gambling and party-giving that he so ran into debt that he was forced to sell Hooton Hall and his estates.

Louis Napoleon III who had been a frequent guest at Hooton Hall during his years of exile in England repaid Stanley's hospitality by befriending him in his last years.

The heir to the baronetcy was his brother, Sir Rowland Stanley, who eventually came to benefit under the will of his great uncle on his mother's side, Henry Errington, and with a family precedent to follow he acknowledged the bequest by changing his name to Sir Rowland Errington. Sir Rowland's second daughter, Ethel, married Evelyn

Baring, the prominent statesman member of the banking family of Baring. In his capacity as British agent and consul-general for Egypt for over 20 years he was the virtual ruler of that country. For his services he was successively created a baron, a viscount and, finally, Earl of Cromer.

And among the possessions which his wife brought with her on marriage was the Wirral Horn.

There have been two Hooton Halls. The first, a large timber building, was erected in 1488 by licence from Henry VII and lasted for nearly 300 years until the Sir William Stanley of the day had it demolished and replaced by a mansion built of Storeton stone in 1778. When this building had to be sold the buyer was a wealthy Liverpool banker, Richard Naylor, who enlarged and Victorianised it, turning it into a very stately home indeed with a massive façade, colonnade and tower, together with a large banqueting hall and marble pillared picture gallery. Sadly, less than 50 years later, the Hall became unoccupied for several years and was eventually demolished, though for a long time some of the pillars remained starkly standing like the ruins of a Greek temple.

On the New Chester Road near the Hooton cross-roads you can still see the very fine lodges which give at least a hint of the opulent style of the Hall itself.

After some years as a race-course, the thousand-acre estate of Hooton Hall became an aerodrome and during the First World War was used by the Royal Flying Corps. Between the wars great efforts were made to establish it as a major airport, but (so to speak) it never got off the ground. When the Second World War broke out in 1939 it became an RAF base. The end of the war left behind it a great enthusiasm for flying and many wartime squadrons became auxiliary groups. Hooton housed three – 633 Air Observation Post Squadron, 610 (County of Chester), and 611 (West Lancs) Auxiliary Squadrons – and for more than 15 years the skies of Wirral were alive with the noise of Meteor jets. Battle of Britain Day in September every year was celebrated in style and drew vast crowds.

The aerodrome also housed the firm of Martin Hearn Limited which, at its peak, employed 5000 people repairing and servicing RAF aircraft and building gliders. Then, in 1956, a drastic Government economy drive brought about the disbanding of these squadrons of spare-time fliers and Hooton's aeronautical days were over.

For a few years part of the site was used for the annual Cheshire Show then Vauxhall Motors arrived and at a cost of £66 million built one of the largest and most modern motor vehicle factories in the world.

Production began five years later and with a workforce of 10,000 the firm is now Ellesmere Port's biggest employer.

Over the last 25 years industries of all descriptions have been setting up shop in Ellesmere Port ever since it was realised how conveniently it is situated and the population has grown correspondingly. It has not quite matched the speed of Birkenhead's early growth, but 150 years ago the population of Whitby was just over 800. Just after the turn of the century, when the Urban District of Ellesmere Port and Whitby was established, the figure had reached 4000. Today it is nearly 80,000 and still increasing.

SIX

The Urbanized Districts

Neston, Hoylake and Heswall

Outside the four erstwhile municipal boroughs in the Peninsula are three former urban districts – based on Neston, Hoylake and Heswall, though the last for some reason was called *Wirral* UDC.

Neston is by far the oldest of the three places, being an important place when Heswall was but a tiny farming hamlet and Hoylake non-existent. Indeed, until the rapid rise of Birkenhead it was the largest and most important town in Wirral. Furthest removed from Liverpool, Neston did not attract commuters in quantity until the post-war motorcar boom when it was found to be a most convenient place for people who worked in Ellesmere Port, Bromborough and Chester. By the nineteen-sixties its population had reached 12,000 and Cheshire County Council had faced up to its new popularity with a development plan which visualised an optimum population of 25,000.

In the Middle Ages it had enjoyed a period as the port for the packet service to Ireland, a role which it had taken over from Burton when the silting of the Dee had prevented vessels reaching there, just as Burton in its turn had taken over from Shotwick, which had taken over from Chester.

The building of a new quay (called thereafter The New Quay) was commenced in the first half of the sixteenth century at Little Neston, but work on it was slow and six years later it was still unfinished when funds ran out. Sporadic attempts were made to complete it, but all were hampered by lack of money. But the promoters – mainly Chester merchants – were nothing if not persistent and petitioned the king for help. As a result, by royal command in 1557 and again in 1560 special collections towards the cost were made in churches throughout the kingdom. I wonder how many people who dropped their pennies and groats onto the collecting plates even knew where Neston was? But funds were never sufficient for the work to be completed. Nevertheless while the depth of water was there Neston remained the main port for the Irish traffic.

The waters of Liverpool Bay and the Irish Sea can be wild and since the average size of the vessels was less than 100 tons the 120-mile crossing to Dublin had its hazards. Depending on the weather, it could take anything from 15 hours to two days or more. The alternative route was via Holyhead, which cut the sea passage to 60 miles but entailed an extra 100 miles journey by road. And in those days the roads were no less rough than the sea and the journey by stage-coach added an extra couple of days to the trip.

Inevitably, storms brought disasters. In 1775 two ships went down with all aboard and in 1806 the packet, *King George*, got no further than the Hoyle Bank off Hoylake when it sank, with only four people surviving out of a total of 117.

Within 50 years of being built silting made the New Quay unusable by anything other than small fishing boats. In 1608 a decree was issued for its demolition but nearly two hundred years were to elapse before the Chester merchants got round to selling the stone to Sir Richard Mostyn. It is said that some of it was used in building the sea wall along The Parade.

In the meantime the New Quay has become generally known as the Old Quay following the establishment of Connah's Quay further upstream where the unsuccessful attempt was made to revive Chester's fortunes as a port by canalising the stretch of river where the estuary narrowed.

For many years the larger vessels had to anchor in the open river waters of the Dee. Not only were there many complaints about lack of shelter from the elements but the disembarkation of passengers and the unloading of cargo into small rowing boats was not without its hazards. The cargo was taken upstream to Chester in the smaller vessels and the passengers proceeded by coach.

Throughout this period Neston continued to prosper. It had risen to a place of importance by virtue of the fact that travellers bound for Ireland frequently had to spend many days, even weeks, waiting for fair weather before sea-crossing could be attempted. Thus a big hotel and inn-keeping trade developed.

When William Webb was perambulating round the 'long square' he refers to 'the well-known town, parish church, and port of Great Neston; and the usual place where our passengers into Ireland do so often lie waiting the leisure of the winds, which make many people better acquainted with this place than they desire to be.'

Neston continued to be Wirral's most important town for many years. Even as late as the first national census of 1801, when Birkenhead's population was the much-quoted 110, Neston could boast of having 1486. It was, in fact, another 30 years after that before Birkenhead had grown big enough to supersede it.

Waiting travellers could also find accommodation in Parkgate itself which could boast almost as many inns as Neston. This area, however, was not always known by this name and the deep-water anchorage itself seemed not to have any particular identity. In 1610, however, there is a reference to it being at 'the parke gate'. This probably refers to Neston Park, an area between what is now Buggen Lane and The Square, which was enclosed for hunting purposes about the year 1250. When the shipping and its attendant trades and businesses became established round this new landing place it was natural that it should be spoken of as 'Parkgate'.

The port of Parkgate, as the principal terminal for the mail-packets, flourished throughout the eighteenth century and brought many important people to the place. John Wesley passed through on several occasions in one direction or another, employing his waiting time by preaching; Dean Swift was a frequent visitor on his way to London and back; and every Wirral schoolchild learns early on that George Frederick Handel also came there on his way to Dublin's New Music Hall for the first performance of his *Messiah*. Handel did not, in the event, set sail from Parkgate. The weather was unfavourable and he went on to Chester and stayed in the Golden Falcon Inn, using the time to make last-minute revisions to his score. He arranged with the Chester Cathedral organist for a number of choristers to meet him at the inn to try out the revised parts but their inability to cope with the music at first sight threw Handel into a tremendous rage. He eventually crossed to Dublin from Holyhead but he did return via Parkgate.

The glorious years of Parkgate's life as a port began to dwindle towards the end of the century as the silt built up. By 1791, unless it were a very high tide, ships had to anchor away from the quay and passengers and goods were ferried on small boats and even, like the passengers on the early Mersey ferries, carried on the backs of fishermen. By 1810, the Parkgate–Dublin service had virtually come to an end.

The silting-up was not wholly to blame for Parkgate's demise as a port. By this time the Port of Liverpool was well established and the Dee estuary was doomed as a shipping lane anyway.

The shipping decline was by no means disastrous for Parkgate for it had also developed a flourishing holiday trade and, indeed, for a time it was the most fashionable resort in the North of England. Sea-dipping had become the vogue and the waters of the Dee were not only considered to be especially salubrious but the prevailing north-west winds were regarded as particularly well-laden with health-giving ozone.

For the entertainment of the visitors there were the many inns and hotels of both Parkgate and Neston, a theatre in a narrow 'weint' called Drury Lane between the Union Hotel (now called The Ship) and the exclusive George Hotel (now incorporated in Mostyn House School), and the Assembly Rooms where concerts and dances were held. The theatre has long gone but the Assembly Rooms, with the distinctive cast-iron balcony, are now in residential use and called Balcony House.

Opposite Balcony House the sea-wall of The Parade does a side-step round a concrete base with some seats on it. This is known locally as The Donkey Stand because donkeys once stood there for hire, but it is really the site of a tall, narrow building which housed sea-baths for invalids. It was there before the wall was built so the wall had to go round it.

Among the distinguished visitors to Parkgate were Mrs Fitzherbert, who subsequently married the Prince of Wales, later George IV (but who was never Queen because she was a Roman Catholic) and Mrs Emma Hart (née Emy Lyon of nearby Ness, later Lady Hamilton), who was seeking a cure for a skin rash for which the mud of the Parkgate was supposed to be particularly efficacious.

The era as a watering-place ended in the early years of the nineteenth century and Parkgate was left to the fishermen. It became as famous for its shrimps as Whitstable for its oysters.

The life of the fishermen was hard; they had to contend with the Dee in its angriest moods just as did the sailors of old. I remember the late Councillor Billy Howe, Parkgate-born and bred, telling me the story of the Great Storm of 1919 and the havoc it caused. The wind never blew and the sea never raged more than it did that night and most of Parkgate's fishermen were caught out in the estuary. Their boats were 32-foot long 'nobbies' which in those days were moored to the sea-wall. Every man had a nick-name. There was, for example, Spurna and Tush, and Bad-Luck (the most successful), Why-Why and Six-Foot (the smallest), Geddy, and one called Slen. When the storm arose the sky blacked-out and the boats made for the shore guided only by the light from the acetylene car-lamps of the only car in Parkgate, belonging to Mr A.G. Grenfell of Mostyn House School. After struggling for hours they all eventually reached land but one, Slen, slipped when climbing out of his boat onto the sea-wall. His leather boots filled with water, dragging him down, and he was drowned. The date was 17 December 1919 – the very day on which a local soothsayer had prophesied the world would end and there were many who rated it a near-miss.

In due course the silt, and the marsh into which it developed, was such that after the nineteen-thirties the water only reached the sea-wall at very high tide. Today it is a coarse green and brown matted carpet stretching almost as far as the eye can see towards Wales and the water only covers it to lap the sea-wall when the highest Spring tides are swollen by the force of a strong wind. It is such a novelty now that people come specially to see it.

For all that Parkgate is no longer a 'seaside' resort and the marsh no thing of beauty, The Parade still attracts visitors simply because there is nowhere quite like it. From the Parkgate Road end the Boathouse Restaurant (now happily restored after an ignoble period as a club and a disco) is a line of buildings in a sequence of shapes and sizes which immediately draw the eye. Inevitably, there are some incongruous intrusions, especially the large garage, which detract from the overall scene, but along the three-quarters of a mile front there is still much remaining of Parkgate's hey-day. The black and white Boathouse itself is only about 50 years old and stands on the site of an old coaching inn called The Pengwern Arms, but many Wirral folk remember it with great affection as The Boathouse Tea Rooms when the owners were the Misses Wallace-Smith.

Apart from the Assembly Rooms which I have already mentioned, several old fishermen's cottages still exist and the odd-shaped house which constricts the roadway for a few yards is the former Watch Tower used by the coastguards.

The coastguards' cottages themselves are in Coastguard Lane off the little Mostyn Square, most of which is taken up by the village school (now a house – and notice the splendid patterned slate roof) and the church. The church, of local sandstone, could hardly be more functional – nothing more than four walls and a roof – but is interesting in that it has served three denominations. It was built in 1843 as a Congregational Church. Later the Presbyterians took it over and today it belongs to the Church of England.

Some of the other old cottages and buildings have been cement-rendered and pebble-dashed or, like the Ship Inn, modernised out of all recognition, but one adaptation which has undoubtedly enhanced the scene is the Mostyn House School which occupies what was once the Mostyn Arms Hotel and the George Hotel. This preparatory school for boys (and now girls) was founded over a century ago by the Reverend A.S. Grenfell whose son, Wifred, born at the school in 1865, was to achieve lasting fame as 'Grenfell of Labrador'. A doctor, he devoted his life to the eskimos and fisher-folk of Labrador where he established hospitals, orphanages and schools. His rescue from a drifting ice-floe in Northern Newfoundland and the story of how he stayed alive by killing and skinning three of his beloved dogs and wrapping himself in their pelts is one of the great survival stories of all time. In the school chapel there is a brass plate to 'Three brave dogs, Moody, Watch, and Spy, whose lives were sacrificed to save mine.'

This terrifying episode did not deter him from his medical and missionary work and he became a world-renowned figure. Knighted in 1929, he died in America in 1940. His ashes were interred at St Anthony, a settlement which he had founded on the coast of Newfoundland.

The school is still in the hands of the Grenfell family today (the present headmaster, Julian Grenfell, is a great-great nephew of the founder) and one of the unexpected delights of Parkgate, if one happens to be there at the right time, is to hear the school's carillon. It was erected as a memorial to the old boys who fell in the First World War and, incredible as it might seem, when the idea of such a memorial was mooted it brought a petition of protest from the residents fearful of the disturbance it would cause! It contains 37 bells and is played by one of a team of boys six times a day to signal such things as morning prayers, lunch and bedtime, and for accompanying hymns. The visitor can best be sure of hearing it at 4.30pm on Wednesdays and Saturdays during school terms when practices are held.

Shrimps were a Parkgate speciality, but the good old-fashioned ice-cream made and sold at Nicholls' shop for many years by the Thomas family (two brothers and their wives) still attracts customers from all over Cheshire and Merseyside. I have seen people even in winter patiently queueing outside the shop in pouring rain and in the teeth of razor-edged winds.

In Boathouse Lane and Parkgate Road, the approach roads to The Parade, the Parkgate Society has erected signs proudly proclaiming one's arrival in the Parkgate Conservation Area, thus implying that a proper respect is called for. The signs do not denote the actual parish boundaries. The Ordnance Survey map actually refers to Neston-cum-Parkgate, which is entirely appropriate because there is no obvious dividing line between the two. What seems inappropriate is the modern municipal link of the two with Ellesmere Port. It was the price they had to pay for not being included in the new County of Merseyside and being allowed to remain in Cheshire. On the face of it, it seems an odd arrangement. The two places are not only separated by eight miles, one on the Mersey and the other on the Dee, but one is a bustling industrial complex, the other a country town. Just how long Neston will remain a country town, however, is something which is worrying some people. It has now been awarded the dubious honour of becoming the centre of the new industrial revolution with the establishment of a factory for making the magical micro-processor, the so-called 'silicon chip'.

Up to a few years ago modern Hoylake (with which I include Meols, West Kirby and Caldy as there are no obvious boundaries between them) received a very fair share of space in the national press. If it were not the local-born MP for Wirral, the Right Honourable J. Selwyn Lloyd, CBE, TD, QC hitting the headlines as Foreign Secretary, or Chancellor of the Exchequer, or Lord Privy Seal, or Speaker of the House of Commons, or being subsequently ennobled, it was local-born Glenda Jackson, CBE, one-time counter assistant in the Market Street Boots,winning awards for her brilliant acting. Or it was the Royal Liverpool Golf Club playing host to the Open Golf Championship, or the open tennis tournament which attracted Wimbledon winners, or members of the West Kirby Sailing Club winning a British, a European, or a World championship. It could also have been the Duke of Edinburgh being secretly landed on internationally-famed Hilbre Island for a clandestine bird-watching holiday. In fact, if Hoylake had been a *real* seaside-resort depending on visitors for a livelihood it would not have needed a public relations officer to extol its virtues.

But as Hoylake did not want to attract the holiday-maker – not in large numbers anyway – such publicity was accepted like the wind from Liverpool Bay, as something which arrives unasked for and passes over.

But nothing and nowhere ever remains unchanged for very long and the area does not get into the news as much as it used to do. Glenda Jackson is still winning accolades almost as a matter of course and the West Kirby Sailing Club still produces champions with astonishing regularity. But Lord Selwyn-Lloyd has passed on, the open tennis tournament has folded and the Royal Liverpool Golf Club is no longer on the rota for the Open Championship.

Going back to the beginning, the Saxons, the Vikings, the Norsemen and (since some of their coins have been found) probably the Romans all had settlements here but after their various departures it only attracted a few fisherfolk. For the most part it was a rather dreary wasteland of scrub and sand-dunes popular only with the rabbits. But there was the 'High Lake'. This deep anchorage, sheltered by an extensive sandbank named Hoyle Bank, for centuries provided a safe roadstead for ships too large to sail up the Dee. It was also used by ships bound for Liverpool seeking shelter from a storm or for lightening cargo to allow safe passage over the sandbanks into the Mersey estuary.

The lake was also much used for the embarkation of troops for Ireland, especially in the sixteenth and seventeenth centuries. While arrangements were being made, and until the weather was right for sailing, the troops encamped on the 'leasowes' between Leasowe and Meols.

In the spring of 1689 a 10,000-strong army which had been mustered at Neston during the previous week sailed from the High Lake in an armada of 90 ships under the Duke of Schomberg to confront the forces of James II who had landed there from France. In June 1690, King

William III, accompanied by the Prince of Denmark 'and several other persons of quality', arrived en route to take personal charge of the fighting and lead the army at the victorious Battle of the Boyne the following year. The King spent the night of 10 June at Gayton Hall, the home of William Glegg, and before leaving next morning bestowed a knighthood on his guest. Seldom can the provision of dinner, bed and breakfast have been so generously rewarded.

The path which the King took to board his ship has been known ever since as King's Gap.

The lake is now no more and its disappearance is due almost entirely to the interfering hand of Man. In the early eighteenth century the River Dee beyond Shotwick was canalised in an attempt to form a navigable channel to Chester. It was not successful, but many acres of land were reclaimed and so altered the flow of the tide that the protective Hoyle Bank was constantly gnawed at until at last it was cut in two. The 'lake' slowly silted up and by the late nineteenth century its original half-mile width had been reduced to little more than a hundred yards and at low tide it was almost dry.

But by this time Hoylake, like Parkgate, had become a health resort. Sir John Stanley, the then Lord of the Manor, who had hitherto regarded the area as fit only for rabbit-shooting and wild-fowling, decided to take advantage of the vogue for the curative powers of sea-bathing and sea air. In 1792 he built the Royal Hotel in what is now Stanley Road. The building was demolished a few years ago and the housing development which now stands on the site is called 'The Royal'.

Some fifty years later on ground adjoining the hotel the Liverpool Hunt Club laid out a race-course with a grandstand and held annual race meetings there. The quality of the turf was such that when the rabbit holes and scratchings had been made good it was considered beyond compare. Eventually competition from more accessible race-courses brought about the abandonment of the meeting in 1868 and the course and the land adjoining was converted into the famous Royal Liverpool golf links we know today. Initially, the golf club had its headquarters in the hotel and the licensee was the same John Ball who became Leasowe Golf Club's first professional. He was a fine player, and subsequently won the Open Championship, but in 1907 he was involved in one of the most extraordinary rounds of golf ever played over these, or any other links. In dense fog! Ball accepted a wager to complete the 18 holes in under two and a half hours, in less than 90, and without losing the ball, which he was allowed to paint black. It will bring despair to the hearts of many golfers to learn that not only did he complete the course within the time, he did not lose the ball once and returned a score of 81.

It was on these same links, too, that in 1937 the late Frank T. Copnall, the portrait painter, arrived with what is believed to have been the world's first golf trolley. Made locally to his own specifications, it ran either on pram wheels or cycle wheels, no-one can quite remember which.

The town centre of Hoylake was originally called Hoose (the name is perpetuated as an electoral ward) and between what is now Market Street and the water's edge 150 years ago there was nothing but a sandy waste with a few scattered fishermen's cottages. Half a dozen families had it to themselves, and since they all inter-married and had many children the town is full of their grandchildren – great, great-great, and even greater – who, of course, are all cousins, first, second, and now probably third and fourth. Then, gradually, prosperous Liverpool and Birkenhead businessmen built houses there for their families' summer use and when the railways opened they moved in permanently, travelling daily to their offices.

Harold Edgar Young, writing just after the turn of the century, describes Hoylake as 'a place of residence for those who collect their incomes elsewhere' and goes on to lament that 'the old sand-blown road, with the links on one side and wide hungry-looking fields on the other that used to connect Hoylake with West Kirby is now called a "Drive" and large and pretty houses cluster along it all the way to West Kirby'.

The drive he alludes to is Meols Drive and although it is a fine, tree-lined highway and one of the district's best addresses it is interesting to know that originally it was nothing less than a piece of ribbon development!

Alas, as elsewhere in Wirral, the bell is tolling for many of these attractive homes. While domestic appliances have more or less filled the void left by the vanished race of domestic servants, the cost of maintaining the fabric is prohibitive. Inevitably, when any of them becomes vacant an application is often lodged for permission to demolish and build a block of flats on the site. There is always an outcry, but there is no real alternative and the flats get built. Yet, no matter how expensive and constrained they may be to tone in with the neighbourhood, blocks of flats aesthetically seldom match houses.

This area, and West Kirby and Caldy, were opened up by the establishment of the Seacombe, Hoylake and Deeside Railway and, a few years later, by the motorcar and the motor-bus.

Caldy, by general consent, is now considered to be Merseyside's most exclusive place in which to live, but Ormerod when he came to see it found it to be just 'a collection of miserable huts and hovels'. Then, in 1832, Richard W. Barton, a rich and philanthropic Manchester businessman, bought the manor and at his own expense had every cottage rebuilt or renovated. By the time the prosperous Merseyside businessmen arrived on the scene looking for good sites for their houses it was an attractive place.

For his own occupation Barton built Caldy Manor or, possibly, adapted and added to an already existing house. As Caldy Heart Hospital, which it eventually became, it is spoken of by people who were patients there with such deep affection that an attack of angina pectoris seemed a small price to pay for the privilege of being admitted. Its recent closure in the face of fierce opposition was greatly lamented.

Most of the very large houses on the leeside of Caldy Hill, enjoying shelter from the weather's excesses and breathtaking views right across the Dee estuary to Wales, were built in the early nineteen-hundreds and the years leading up to the First World War. As the years went by the size of the houses diminished somewhat so that those built in the 'twenties and 'thirties are not quite so grand, while those built in the last 35 years or so are smaller still. But by today's standards they are still large and very expensive. 'Cheshire is the Surrey of the North', said Sir Nikolaus Pevsner, 'but Surrey has nothing like this'.

Not least of the attractions in this part of the peninsula are the two promenades – one running from Dove Point, Meols (still so-called although the Point has long since vanished beneath the waves) to the King's Gap at Hoylake and the other from Riversdale Road to the sailing club at West Kirby. (You can walk from one to the other along the sand dunes, skirting the golf course.) The former brings you face to face with Liverpool Bay; the latter fringes the Dee estuary. Both can provide a delightful stroll when the weather is fine and balmy, or a bracing, blood-tingling walk when a keen breeze is blowing. When the breeze becomes a strong wind, they are best avoided.

From the West Kirby promenade there is a lot to see. A mile out in the estuary are the three islets of Hilbre ($11\frac{1}{2}$ acres), Middle Hilbre (3 acres) and Eye ($\frac{1}{2}$ acre) which not all that long ago were one. John Speed in his famous map of Cheshire published in 1611 shows 'Hilbrie' as a single, roughly square area. Since then the elements have worn away the soft sandstone but at half-tide the three parts can be seen to be linked. Beyond the islands is the grey-brown panorama of the Welsh hills and, if the time is right, the scene in summer is enlivened by scores of dinghies and sailing-boats tacking and manoeuvring, while many a day dies spectacularly in a brilliant Turneresque sunset.

Then there are the birds. Perhaps I should have mentioned them first. Birds in great variety, birds in enormous numbers, providing a great ornithological festival, the bird-world equivalent of the Gathering of the Clans or the International Eisteddfod at Llangollen. The average promenade stroller who might not be able to distinguish a gannet from a gull cannot fail to be impressed at the autumn and winter spectacle of great wheeling, whirring clouds of birds which fly over the water ahead of every incoming tide to feed on the mudflats and saltmarshes. It is estimated that some 150,000 waders of varying species congregate here from October to March after flying in from Greenland and Iceland, and even Canada. It is also a winter staging-post for many thousands of other migrant birds.

The attraction lies in the fact that the 6000 acres of saltmarsh are nothing less than a vast avian larder which is getting bigger every year. The gradual silting up of the Dee, which began in the middle ages and was caused by shifting sands, was accelerated just over 50 years ago when someone planted spartina grass on the Welsh shore. It did not flourish there but a few years later it was found to be growing vigorously at Parkgate. Conditions were so to its liking that it rapidly colonised the sands, trapping the silt which was brought in by every tide. This in turn provided a foothold for reed grasses and samphire so creating a huge marsh. All attempts to halt the spread have failed and it has insidiously crept forward like a vast green carpet. At West Kirby and Hoylake attempts are made to keep it at bay with an annual 'dig'.

The spartina and reeds provide seeds in abundance and the marsh plays host to myriads of worms and lower orders of invertebrate life, while the incoming tides teem with vast quantities of cockles, shrimps and minor molluscs.

Where there are birds in such quantity there are inevitably predators. Weasels, stoats and foxes make their forays among the flocks and birds of prey exact their toll, but the ducks and geese also have to contend with the guns of the wildfowlers. The Dee Wildfowl Club have shown their appreciation of the ornithological importance of the area and have voluntarily limited their guns to 350, though to me, as neither an ornithologist nor a wildfowler, that seems akin to conserving pedestrians by reducing the speed limit over zebra crossings to 50 mph.

Not surprisingly, bird-watchers, both amateur and professional, are attracted to the Dee and the Hilbre islands afford a close-quarters view of the wader birds. When high tides cover the marshes huge flocks settle on all three islands so densely packed together that late arrivals are sometimes forced to land on the backs of other birds, and not even those of their own kind.

An added attraction at certain times of the year is the sight of grey seals basking on the sandbanks at low tide. It is something of a mystery why they favour these waters, but over the last few years their numbers have steadily increased and over 200 have been counted in a season.

Hilbre Island has not only attracted birds: it has played a full part in the life of Man. It is thought, though it cannot be proved, that there was a small religious settlement there as early as the tenth century, and after the Norman Conquest it came into the possession of the Abbey of St

Werburgh in Chester and a small monastic cell was established there.
There was also a shrine to St Hildeburgh (though who she was or why
she was sanctified no-one knows) and in the thirteenth and fourteenth
centuries the island became a place of pilgrimage. The name 'Hilbre' is
a contraction of 'Hildeburgh's Ey' (or islet).

Hilbre is also a place of legends and if we can believe the words of a
sixteenth-century Chester monk named Henry Bradshawe, of a miracle,
too. He recounts how one day when Richard, Earl of Chester (1101–
1121) was on his way to Holywell to visit the shrine of St Winefride, his
party was set upon by a gang of Welshmen. The earl sent a message to his
Constable, the Baron of Halton, calling for help. The baron gathered
together a troop of men and made for Hilbre in the hope of reaching the
Earl by boat across the Dee. But there was no boat available, so he
sought the advice of a monk who was present. He was advised to go
down on his knees and seek the intercession and assistance of St
Werburgh. Which he promptly did, ending with the promise of a
substantial reward for her efforts when he got back home. And, lo! As
the Red Sea did for Moses, so the waters of the Dee parted and the Baron
and his men crossed into Wales without getting their feet wet.

In the sixteenth century Customs officers were stationed on Hilbre to
deal with vessels using the port of Chester and since old records refer to
several ships as being 'of Hilbree' it is presumed that their owners lived
on the island. It was also used as a place of embarkation for troops going
to Ireland and smugglers and wreckers used it as a hide-out. In the early
nineteenth century there was an inn used by sailors from the ships
moored off-shore, though it is reported that the landlord and his wife
were at that time the only residents.

A telegraph station was established in 1841 by Trinity House, but this
was eventually taken over by The Mersey Docks and Harbour Board
who bought all three islands and had keepers there. In 1945 they were
sold to the Hoylake Urban District Council for £2500 for the use of the
public. There is a resident warden – a modestly salaried post which,
whenever it has become vacant, has attracted hundreds of applications
from all over the country.

Over the last 50 or 60 years the district has changed surprisingly little.
New houses and blocks of flats have been built in odd corners, but only
two non-residential buildings of any note have arisen. At West Kirby,
near the railway station, the Concourse has given the area a much
longed-for swimming pool, a sports hall and a new library, while on the
promenade at Meols has been built a less glamorous but arguably more
necessary effluent disposal pumping station. For many years the sewage
from North Wirral was discharged into the Irish Sea through a 300 yard-

long pipe at Dove Point. All agreed it was unsatisfactory, but finding an alternative took years of argument and wrangling (especially with Wallasey). Not many political parties can claim to have risen to eminence on an effluent-disposal 'ticket', but the Hoylake Ratepayers did. Moreover, at one time they came within an ace of gaining control of the town's affairs. In essence, they were no more than incensed Tories and once the sewerage scheme was under way they retired from the scene.

The eventual outcome was the North Wirral Outfall. A yard in diameter and three miles long, it is the largest and the longest sewage outflow pipe in Britain. But the people of the district take no particular pride in the fact for never was anything built with more public misgiving. Those who know something about the strength of the winds and tides, and the fierce seas which can rage in Liverpool Bay, say 'It'll still come back'. They find little comfort in the knowledge that the effluent before discharge is 'mascerated'.

Soon after the pipe was brought into use a further uproar was caused when British Nuclear Fuels asked for, and won, permission to discharge radioactive waste through it from their plant at Capenhurst. Even though the experts say the amount is so small it is harmless an active opposition group named 'Save Our Shoreline' regularly voices its doubts.

Heswall is another place where the merchant princes of Merseyside built country retreats into which they moved their families for the summer. Nine miles from Birkenhead was a distance not too far for horse transport, and when omnibuses made their appearance there was sufficient demand to warrant a regular service between Heswall and Woodside during the summer months. Then, when the steam railways arrived and a station was opened on the coastal line beween Neston and West Kirby, followed a few years later by Heswall Hills station on the Neston to Seacombe line, they became permanent residents, travelling to their places of business each day.

They built imposing residences among the heather and the gorse on the rocky slopes of Heswall Hill (the peninsula's highest point), surrounded them with large gardens and substantial walls and today an abundance of sandstone masonry is one of the features of the area. Not only did they enjoy a superb view from this elevated position, but the air was considered bracing and pure; so much so that a sanatorium (now Cleaver Hospital) and The Royal Liverpool Children's Hospital were built there.

The houses were built where the owners chose, without the irritation of having to ask for planning permission, and one of the great charms of

Heswall's Lower Village (the original Heswall, that is) is the haphazard way in which it has grown. Between Telegraph Road running along the crest of the hill and the shore hardly a road runs straight and the entrance to many an elegant residence is along a by-way no wider than – and, in some cases, little better than – a cart track.

And if on arrival at a house in such a road, after driving a drunkard's course between rain-filled potholes and fearing for the car's suspension with every revolution of the wheels, you venture the suggestion that a layer of tarmac might not go amiss, the idea is dismissed as absurd. It seems that the lunar-like surfaces not only help to retain the rurality of the place, but are also a defence against all but essential motor traffic. For all that, such lanes have not altogether proved a deterrent to builders in recent years and even in this hallowed Lower Village every available pocket of land has been seized upon and small estates erected. Great ingenuity has been shown by architects in the way they have insinuated clusters of houses into what, to the layman, seem unpromising places. One result is that there are so many cul-de-sacs that the district must hold the record for the number of 'No Through Roads' in relation to its size. In the Heswall/Oldfield/Gayton area there close on a hundred – and many of them are called 'Something Way' which patently they are not.

It has not, however, been growth without growing pains and from time to time the all-important view has been the cause of neighbourly friction. Some newly-built houses have been located in positions which gave them a view, but in acquiring it they sometimes obscured it from older houses which had previously enjoyed it. In other cases, new arrivals striving for a view have cut down mature trees and uprooted shrubs.

Now that there is hardly any more land left for development, an area centred on the parish church of St Peter has been declared a conservation area. This includes Village Road where the church is, the pub is, and the shops are. But the road has already been widened and a small car-park provided; and the shop fronts modernised; and the old rectory pulled down and a modern one built. Gone is the picturesque village of 20 years ago and although it is not unattractive, the conservation order might reasonably have been better made a couple of decades earlier.

Despite its mention in Domesday Book (as Eswelle) there is little to see of any antiquity. There is a one-time smithy in Dawstone Road which dates from 1604, where it is said King William III had his horse shod when he spent the night at Gayton Hall, but it is now a crafts shop and lacks any resemblance to a blacksmith's.

The oldest structure by far is the tower of the beautiful parish church of St Peter. This is about 500 years old and the present church, erected in

1879, is the third which has been built on to it. This church was erected following the virtual destruction of the previous building in a violent thunderstorm on 19 September 1875 when (to quote Sulley) 'the electric fluid pierced the roof during the evening service, killed the organist and the boy who was blowing the bellows, and put out all the lights'.

Interesting features of the church are the Glegg family memorials, which have survived the various rebuildings and been placed at the foot of the tower. One of them, of yellowing white marble, commemorates Katherine, the wife of Edward Glegg, who died in 1666 at the age of 40. She was married to him for 16 years and in that time bore him 15 children. She is described as:

'. . . having bene to all wives a president of chastitie; to all matrons an example of gravitie; to all persons a paterne of piety; she was most loving to her husband, careful of her children, respectful to her relations and equalls, courteous to her inferiours, charitable to the poore, true hearted to her friends, kinde to her servants, and a cordial lover of all pious ministers and good persons'.

In the last 25 years the Heswall area has probably grown at a faster rate than anywhere else in Wirral: a look at the map shows how the once separate villages of Gayton, Heswall, Pensby and Thingwall are now joined by continuous housing. Shopping facilities and other amenities have come in their wake and Heswall's 'top village' has taken on the appearance of a small town.

Gayton, too, is patently such a place of the present that links with its past have to be searched for, and they are few. Gayton Hall where the Gleggs lived is still standing and occupied, and at the point where Cottage Lane slides into the mud of the Dee there is a link with Gayton's maritime days where a house called Gayton Cottage marks the site of a former ferry house – though by no means obviously so. On the main Chester High Road, adjoining the well-known Devon Doorway Restaurant (was ever a place more mis-named?) can be seen the remains of Gayton's windmill. The miller's cottage has been converted into an attractive-looking house, but the mill itself which ceased working in 1875 is slowly being engulfed by an unrestrained ivy.

For many years Gayton enjoyed its own self-governing parish meetings and towards the end of the eighteenth century, and just after, an annual Gayton Wake was held at the White Horse Inn. It attracted crowds from all over North Cheshire and large numbers of people came by boat from the villages on the Welsh shore of the Dee. It was a day-long bout of roisterous, rustic games and sports of the kind which later marked the opening of Birkenhead Park.

As a place for 'incomers' Gayton did not develop as rapidly as Heswall since it lacked the facility of a railway station but gradually, as motor transport became more common, some large houses were built there.

Between Heswall and the other component parts of the old Wirral Urban District there is still some countryside left, but although it forms part of Wirral's Green Belt I feel I should add 'at the time of going to press'. Green Belts are not supported by any firm legislation and by no means inviolate (as the recent incursion by the silicon chip factory at Neston has demonstrated); and since a local government official has recently declared that at the present rate of house-building available land in the Wirral will be exhausted by 1986, I fear the worst. No matter how much local councillors protest about the essential need to preserve open spaces between built-up areas, and despite the continuous protestations of amenity societies, determined developers always have their way in the end.

SEVEN

The Urbanized Villages

Upton, Greasby, Irby, Pensby, Thingwall, Willaston

UPTON

The story of Upton is one which opens with a mention in Domesday Book, and goes on to see it become Wirral's second most important village after Neston in the seventeenth and eighteenth centuries, a seat of the gentry in the eighteen-hundreds, a highly desirable residential district in the nineteen-twenties and thirties, to being the outer suburb of Birkenhead it is today. It is the story of a village fighting expansion and development, but, in the end, losing the battle against total urbanization.

Upton's early importance arose from its position at the junction of roads from five neighbouring villages – Woodchurch, Greasby, Saughall Massie, Moreton and Claughton – and it was the scene of a large weekly market and twice-yearly fairs. They were the largest fairs in all Wirral and were the big occasions of the year for both male and female farm workers who came from miles around.

For centuries its appearance hardly altered. It changed hands occasionally as one Lord of the Manor sold his rights to someone else, but it remained a country village until well after the development of Birkenhead. It then became a desirable residential district; not as far away as some of the other places on the Peninsula yet out of sight and too-easy reach of that rapidly rising metropolis.

The main mansion, and the one which still dominates the village centre is Upton Hall at the cross roads. Now Upton Hall Convent for Girls, the house was built in the eighteen-hundreds. In 1863 it was greatly enlarged by the then owner and squire, Thomas Webster. To quote Henry Aspinall again: 'Squire Webster was a thorough sportsman and a preserver of foxes. He had near his residence many fine covers and plantations with good lying for foxes. Upton Hall was a recognised meet; and breakfast was ready for anyone who chose to call'.

It seems that his son, Egerton, however, did not share his father's belief in the foxes' preservation: 'He was fond of shooting but never rode a horse. He was cross-grained in temper, and even worse. One day the hounds found a fox in the gorse near the end of the hall. The fox broke cover and headed for Bidston. Egerton suddenly sprang from under a hedge and shot the fox dead almost in view of the hounds! The whole field instantly galloped up with the intention of horse-whipping Egerton . . . ' At the last moment they recognised him, but the indignation felt all round was such that he had to leave the village.

It was an episode which says much for the life of the times.

Upton Hall was later bought by Thomas Inman, the Liverpool steamship owner who founded the Liverpool, New York and Phila-delphia Steam Ship Company (the first Atlantic line to use iron steamships) and made a fortune carrying emigrants to the New World. He stayed in the Hall only long enough to build Upton Manor a few hundred yards away down Moreton Road, a house which is now converted to retirement flats.

Inman is remembered in Upton as the sole donor of the present Parish Church of St Mary. (He also paid for the building of Moreton Parish Church.) The village in its time has had three churches, the first – at Overchurch – dating from Saxon times, and all have been on different sites. It has also had four burial grounds; one at each church and another, in use today, in Salacre Lane.

The present church has a small tower containing a ring of five bells and a clock, and the chime before the clock strikes the hour is unusual. The chime does not start on the 'doh' as with Westminster chimes, but on the 'me' finishing on the 'sol' instead of on the 'doh'. The clock is one of six in the country which John Smith and Son of Derby made with a similar chime.

In the middle-to-late nineteenth century more 'gentry' arrived and took up residence and, for a period, Upton was a country village with five large mansions and lesser, but still large, houses where many of the villagers found employment in one capacity or another. Then came the railways, including a link with the Mersey Railway from Liverpool, and by the turn of the last century the upper middle class was joined by the middle class and Upton began to expand. Then, as the motor omnibus arrived about the time of the First World War and gave the village a regular, if not very frequent, link with Birkenhead, the builders moved in and built houses for the lower middle class, but it still remained a delightfully rural retreat.

When the war ended Upton folk, like everyone else, set their minds towards the provision of a memorial to their dead. They decided that a mere inert monument was not enough:it would be more fitting to provide an amenity which would benefit the community as a whole and the rising generation in particular. And it so happened that right in the heart of the village, almost opposite the church, a large house and estate called The Elms was up for sale. A public subscription was opened and the property, consisting of the house, gardens, tennis court, and a large field beyond was purchased for £2000. A conventional war memorial was erected in the front garden of the house and, in 1920, it opened as a sports and social centre. They called it Victory Hall. It quickly became the hub of village life and still flourishes today with an impressive variety of indoor and outdoor recreational facilities (including a ladies' croquet club which has passed its fiftieth anniversary), but in splendid modern buildings built and opened in 1964. The money for the new Victory Hall came from the sale of the frontage of their property for shop development and the football field at the rear for houses. But, sadly, the development robbed the village of much (some say all that was left) of its character. The war memorial was moved beyond the village centre to the lawn of the library in Ford Road; a large and ancient spreading chestnut tree was chopped down, and the architecturally-nondescript shops which have been built in its place do nothing to enhance the scene.

As Upton began to expand more rapidly in the years between the two wars there were demands for its name to be changed to avoid confusion with the other 35 Uptons and 14 Uptons-with-hyphenated-suffixes, especially Upton-by-Chester. Things came to a head when a lorry dropped off a load of heavy granite slabs at the gate of the vicarage, obstructing the free passage of Church Road. They were intended for the vicarage at Upton-by-Chester. The suggestion was that the village should be called Overchurch and, in 1931 this was generally agreed and the local Post Office went so far as to have new franking stamps prepared. But at the last moment the change was frustrated by (and I quote from a newspaper cutting which did not explain further) 'a strong religious section in the village'. Since Overchurch was the original ecclesiastical name for the parish it is hard to imagine what those objections were.

It can only be said that the urbanisation of Upton really dates from that year. The population had risen to around 2000 and facing the fact that the Wirral was becoming more and more residential, Cheshire County Council agreed to transfer certain parishes to neighbouring urban authorities. In view of the way in which the last local government boundary changes were brought about it comes as a surprise bordering on total astonishment to learn that the residents were given a completely free choice as to whether Upton should throw in its lot with Birkenhead or Wallasey. And both authorities energetically canvassed the electorate as though Upton were the end of the rainbow. The campaign even wound up with a lively confrontation in the village hall between representatives of the two boroughs. Birkenhead emphasised 'the economical advantages of citizenship in Birkenhead . . . you already have our gas and electricity; you can have our water too'. Wallasey replied that *its* gas, *its* electricity *and* its domestic rate were cheaper, whereupon Birkenhead pointed out that Wallasey's water came from Liverpool and the rate would double within the next five years. Birkenhead possessed its own supply and (could they have been so naive in those days?) 'as consumption increases so costs will dwindle'. And what's more (the trump card!) 'we supply you with your only bus route'. From Wallasey came the prompt rejoinder: 'Have no fear about the buses. Birkenhead's will stay if only to keep Wallasey buses out!'

To all this cut and thrust, the chairman (from Upton) commented: 'Upton is up for sale and we must make the best deal we can'.

Polling date was 10 March 1931 but on the 9th the Wallasey Fire Brigade suddenly arrived in the village in all its panoply, not in answer to any emergency call but bearing a large placard declaring: WE CAN REACH ANY FIRE IN UPTON IN TEN MINUTES.

Hearing of this Birkenhead lost no time. It rushed its recently-acquired, bang-up-to-date appliance to the scene, also bearing a placard asking: WHY WAIT FOR TEN MINUTES TO HAVE YOUR FIRE PUT OUT WHEN WE CAN DO IT IN FOUR?

The voting was 661 for Birkenhead and 240 for Wallasey. Councillor Fletcher of Birkenhead said: 'The parish has made a wise choice. Upton residents need have no qualms as to the future'.

Alderman Parkinson, for Wallasey, replied: 'Wallasey has been vilified and misrepresented. The residents may come to realise the decision they have taken today is not as wise as they appear to think it is'.

In the years immediately following this change more and more houses were built, but in 1937 *The Liverpool Daily Post* was still able to describe it as 'one of the most delightful spots in Wirral'. But in the years since then, especially in the 'fifties and 'sixties, the story of Upton has been one of successive battles with authority as various developments were proposed. And it seemed that as fast as a proposal was made so was an organisation set up to fight it. They won some, they lost some, and when each battle was over the protesting forces stood down. In the last twenty-odd years there has been an Upton Residents Association, an Upton Preservation Society, and an Upton and District Ratepayers Society, and an Upton Road Residents Association. They have all faded away. They stood no chance in opposing the vast council housing estate at Woodchurch; they won the fight against the building of what would have been Europe's biggest supermarket with a car-park for 300 cars, and another against a large tyre factory. They lost the battle over Champion Sparking Plugs and the other light industry factories adjoining. They also lost a decisive battle over the extension to the Woodchurch estate with the building of three 14-storey blocks and against the Ford estate at the foot of Bidston Hill.

That protests were made against all these plans is understandable. Those they lost have transformed the place; if all had come to fruition it would have been totally unrecognisable.

But one protesting episode in Upton's more recent history now seems barely credible; it is even astonishing that public time and money was expended on it. In 1957 a resident of Manor Drive, at the corner of Meadway, gave the hospitality of his front garden to a piece of stonework called *Man*. It could hardly be termed sculpture since it consisted of seven large granite slabs salvaged from a Liverpool bombed site and fitted together so as to resemble, somewhat roughly, a human form. Most people found it ludicrous and it was quickly christened 'John Willie'. Some people, however, called it a monstrosity, and an outrage, and protested loudly. They protested to such effect that it became the subject of a public inquiry. The question posed in all seriousness was this: *Has this 'sculpture' transgressed the Town and Country Planning Act by being put up without planning permission?* And highly paid legal minds debated at length whether 'John Willie' was or was not a building within the meaning of the Act. In the end 'he' was adjudged not to be a building and not, therefore, subject to planning permission, so 'he' stayed put. But they got him in the end. Despite the indestructibility he was supposed to represent, 'John Willie' had paint poured over him one night and a few months later collapsed (or was he pushed?) and 'died'.

Today the boundaries of Upton are blurred but the village centre has managed to retain its identity and special character. There is a good selection of shops, a bigger-than-average number of them still owner-occupied and giving old-fashioned service, but until recently at peak hours and on Saturday mornings it was often choked with traffic. The need for a relief road was recognised by the planners and when an estate of council houses was built nearby a swathe of land was left between the houses to allow for the building of a new road to divert the stream of traffic heading for Greasby and West Kirby.

The by-pass has now been built and Upton village is a safer and quieter place. But the interval between planning and execution was over twenty years.

GREASBY

Leaving Upton Village the road ahead drops downhill and suddenly narrows where it passes Upton Cricket Club on the right. Until the building of the by-pass there was open farmland on the left. This undeveloped stretch acted as a green 'moat' between Upton and Greasby, an area which was stricken with malignant urbanisation in the nineteen-thirties.

Greasby was never a place of much importance historically or otherwise and past chroniclers have mentioned it only in passing or not at all and to tell the truth, there is not much to write about even now; it is really just a gigantic housing estate.

Recorded in Domesday Book as *Gravesberie* it was at one time in the possession of the monks of St Werburgh and subsequent owners have included the Gleggs of Irby and John Ralph Shaw of Arrowe Hall who was the last real squire during the latter part of the last century. In Shaw's day it was wholly an agricultural village and so rural and open to the elements that it was deemed a suitable place to establish a smallpox hospital. It was built in 1879 by the Wirral Rural District Council to accommodate just eight patients and after subsequently serving as a convalescent home and a dwelling house it was in use for many years as a most inadequate branch library.

As demolition is so often the precursor of development what other relics remain of days gone by are decidedly scant. There are a few Victorian houses and cottages and here and there old sandstone walls still standing – or not quite fallen – fleetingly suggest antiquity. However, Manor Farm, which served for many years as the District Bank and is now a restaurant, dates from around 1675. Greasby Old Hall is a little older and Rock House is a wattle and daub cottage encased in a later but still very old, brick lining.

There is also a cast-iron cross set in the grass verge in Mill Lane, the road which leads to Irby. This is more of a curiosity than a relic in that it is neither genuine nor in the place where it was first erected. This runic cross is but a replica of Greasby's ancient hiring cross where, as at Bromborough, farm labourers gathered on a day in April every year to offer themselves for hire for the following twelve months. When they were taken on by a farmer they were given a shilling and a pint of beer to seal the bargain. The replica was erected on the village green at the instigation of John Shaw in 1862 (his initials and date are still legible), but was removed in the early years of this century by the Hoylake UDC. Thanks to the efforts of Councillor Victor Pickerill it was re-erected on the present spot in 1969. After his death a year later a plaque was fixed to the base dedicating the cross to his memory in recognition of his work for Greasby during 27 years as a councillor.

When buses made the Wirral country areas less isolated after the First World War, some housing development took place in Greasby, raising the population to 750. Then the floodgates were opened. Land was sold for as little as 1½d. a square yard and building proceeded so fast that where there had been vast acres of potatoes and vegetables one season the next Harvest Thanksgiving saw houses with people living in them. Within 20 years the population reached nearly 5000 and, with a pause only during the years of the last war, development continued until 1958 when the drains and sewers could take no more.

The lull lasted until 1972 when the go-ahead was again given and the

UDC was so swamped with planning applications from builders that extra staff had to be recruited to deal with them. Today the population is about 8000 and still growing.

Mortimer, writing in the first half of the last century, said of Greasby: 'It is inconveniently situated, at some distance from the Ferries, in a remarkably poor and cold country. Greasby is by no means an eligible site for the agricultural occupations by which its inhabitants are supported. The land is generally inferior, the rocks in many parts rising to the surface'. If that were so then perhaps it might be argued that its present role as a dormitory area is the proper one. That at least seems to be the view of the powers that be. Only the other day permission was granted for the building of yet another 200 houses.

IRBY

Irby, and neighbouring Pensby and Thingwall, are like Greasby in that they, too, are comparatively modern single-class dormitory suburbs but Irby is saved from any archetypal label by its still-discernible village centre. It has been spoiled by the building of a characterless block of shops, but the presence of Irby Farm, Irby Hall, and the old Anchor Inn, together with the retention of many old typically Wirral sandstone walls round about, saves it from the commonplace.

For some reason, Irby Farm, dating from 1612, was not annihilated with the rest and remains incongruously and defiantly in the midst of the shopping area. Until recently its 50 acres were given over to rearing beef cattle. The powerful bucolic vapours which pervaded the village centre from time to time evoked a pungent reminder of Irby's rural past.

Irby Hall, of red sandstone with black and white timbering on the first floor, occupies a prominent position near the T-junction of the village and stands on the site of an eleventh-century manor house which belonged to the abbey at Chester. It was one of four such houses to which the abbot and his retinue repaired at regular intervals to exercise his right of 'infangthief, wayf, stray, goods of felons, and view of frankpledge' in respect of Irby, Greasby, Woodchurch and Noctorum. Which means that he had jurisdiction over thieves, should take possession of ownerless goods and stray animals, seize the property of felons, and establish suretyships to ensure the proper collection of tithes.

The present house dates from the early seventeenth century and was the home of the Irby branch of the Glegg family. When Sulley mentioned it about 90 years ago the then owner rejoiced in the name of Birkenhead

Glegg. But he seemed neglectful of his property. What had been a fine example of a typically Cheshire black and white house was described as 'rapidly falling into decay'. In 1888 it was reconstructed and the half-timbering was left only on the upper front face. In modern times it again fell into a state of near-dereliction and although it was listed as a Grade 2 building of historical and architectural importance, up to a few years ago it was an eye-sore. It was eventually put up for sale by auction in 1971 and to the delight of the residents who had fears that it would end up as something undesirable it was bought by a local builder, John Atkinson. Although open to the skies and seemingly beyond reasonable repair he restored it and made it into a beautiful home for himself and his family. With its sandstone scrubbed to its original pink and the black and white refurbished it adds greatly to the Irby scene.

The village stocks which stand on the lawn near the library are, like Greasby's iron cross, not the genuine article but a replica. About 30 years ago an observant resident spotted that a nearby wall included some irregularly-shaped stones and some time later when the wall had to come down to allow for road widening they were carefully removed and examined. Stood on end they were seen to be the pillars of the old stocks, each deeply grooved to take the wooden beams. Two other stones were identified as the sills on which they would have rested, while a piece of shaped ironwork found with them turned out to be one of a pair of struts which would have supported the upper beam while the miscreants were put in place. The stones were carefully measured and drawings were made, and then they were put into Council storage with the intention of re-erecting them when a suitable site became available. Unfortunately, when the chance came the stones could not be found and it is presumed that yet again they are doing service somewhere in another wall.

But the drawings were not lost and, determined not to let history slip through their fingers entirely, the Council built this replica.

On the other side of the rose garden, opposite the stocks, are Irby's public lavatories – and thereby hangs a tale which shows that Clochemerle was not alone. The building of these lovely loos in 1972 brought to end an argument which, incredibly, had raged in Irby for over 30 years. The advocates claimed that with the rapid growth of the area there was a crying need for a public convenience, while opponents vowed that the provision of such an amenity would attract undesirables. It was stalemate until local councillor, Mrs Doris Sissons, bravely seized the nettle and called a public meeting. The depth of feeling over the matter can be gauged from the fact that over 200 people turned up!

After a heated debate the project was approved and the lavatory was built. Since it was designed to blend in with the new library and the feared hordes did not materialise (was it the presence of the stocks?) the hullabaloo quickly died down.

PENSBY AND THINGWALL

If ever there was nothing to say about a place then that place is Pensby. For centuries it was no more than just a small farming community. No village, no church, no pub. Nothing. At the 1801 census the population was just 27. Like Greasby, the soil was described as poor and thin but over the last 50 years it has produced an abundant crop of bungaloid and semi-detached houses.

Adjoining Thingwall, on the other hand, merits special mention. It was a hamlet of sorts with, at one time, a windmill and an inn and it found a place in Domesday Book as *Tuigwelle*. But legend has it that in a high-lying field was located the 'thing' or annual Parliament of the Vikings who settled here about the year AD 900. There is no proof, but the name is certainly significant and it compares with 'Tynwald' in the Isle of Man, the authenticity of which no-one questions.

WILLASTON

The residents of Willaston may feel a little piqued at finding their village included in this particular chapter and I agree it is a borderline case. Willaston is by no means as built-up as the other places, it is still largely surrounded by countryside, and the 'villagers' go to some pains to maintain an atmosphere of rurality, making use of their spendid village green at every opportunity. Nevertheless, the amount of development which has taken place there over the last twenty years would even force an estate agent to admit it has been well nigh urbanized.

It was the beginning of this century when Willaston was first discovered by outsiders and the houses built then – in Hooton Road, Mill Lane, Heath Lane and Benty Heath Lane – were for the richer commuters. It was not on a scale large enough to endanger the rural way of life very much and less than 50 years ago there were still no less than 21 farms working not far from the village green. Now there is not one.

The last war brought big changes. A Royal Ordnance Factory was erected at nearby Hooton and an estate of houses for the key workers was rapidly built in Elm Road. Then, when the war was over, several other small estates were built and, following a development plan conceived by the County Council in 1967, the building rate has accelerated. Willaston today, therefore, is a mixture of the old, the not so old, and the new. But what is old is very, very old.

Willaston can boast a long history. It is thought that it is the place where the Saxons first settled when they arrived about the seventh century and that the name is derived from 'Wiglaf's Tun', with Wiglaf probably being a Saxon chief like Bebba, Brun and Scirard. Another theory is that the name comes from 'Wirheal (or Wirral) Stone' for at the spot where Hadlow Road meets the Chester High Road is a stone which popularly goes by this name. The Wirral Stone, some say, marks the meeting place of the 'Wilavestun Hundred' (as recorded in Domesday Book) and is the centre of Wirral. Others say the stone was put there by the Romans as a survey point. But local opinion is that it is nothing more than an ancient mounting-block (which is what it looks like), placed there as a matter of convenience for the relief of men on horseback returning home from Chester. The fact that an old tithe map actually shows it as 'P-stone' seems to bear this out.

The Hundred of Wilavestun (a 'hundred' being a division of an English county which contained a hundred families) included what we regard as Wirral today plus several places beyond, and since each township in that area had to send its reeve and four chief men to a periodic assembly it is clear that Willaston was a most important place. This system continued to the end of the Middle Ages, but the Hundred Court (or Wapentake, as it was known) which grew out of it persisted until the middle of the last century. It was one of the last in the country to survive and although in its latter days it did not meet in Willaston but at various other places this seems a good place to relate the nigh-incredible story of how a couple of smooth-operating lawyers found a crock of gold.

The Wapentakes (a word of Icelandic origin which means 'touch arms', it being the custom of vassals to touch the spear of their overlords in token of homage) died out in other parts of the country as the police system was gradually introduced and justices of the peace were appointed *but they were never abolished*. In 1820 the Wapentake of Wirral franchise was auctioned and sold for £230, but it remained dormant until it was quietly purchased in 1854 by a Liverpool solicitor, Samuel Holland Moreton, for the sum of £99 19s. Less than a month later the residents of Wirral were staggered to read an announcement in the local papers that the Wapentake Court had been revived and that it would henceforth sit for the recovery of small debts.

Moreton appointed as his deputy judge a fellow solicitor, Robert Grace, who is generally credited with having foreseen that there was much more to be gained than the trifling collection of overdue accounts. The Wapentake was no less than a private court, answerable to no-one, with power to fine and imprison, and the right to keep the fines. The main weapon at its disposal was the power to fine for contempt. The Court travelled from village to village throughout the Wirral, sitting in the bar parlour of pubs. Anyone near at hand could be summoned to sit as a juror and people were often stopped in the road and called upon to serve alongside the riff-raff that Moreton and Grace attracted. A refusal to serve was met with a fine for contempt. A refusal to pay the fine was dealt with by seizing and selling property belonging to the defaulter.

The Court had the air of a festive gathering rather than a seat of justice. Moreton (or Grace) would sit like Nero on an elevated chair at the head of a long table which was laden with food and drink. The jury sat at the table and the rest of the space was occupied by the public, with everyone generously supplied with free food and ale, all paid for out of the fines and costs which the Court exacted.

It was this power to demand 'costs' which was exploited to the full. Actions for damages were heard and although the claims could not exceed 40 shillings this restriction was legally side-stepped by the award of 'costs'. The Court had jurisdiction over waste lands and highways and on the slightest encroachment by a building or a wall or fence the perpetrator was summarily fined. An Ale Taster was appointed to ensure the quality and price of locally-brewed ale and he quickly learned that he was not welcome at Court if he could not produce an offender for punishment.

The travesties of justice meted out by Moreton and Grace became a scandal, but there was little that anyone could do about it. With their legal knowledge they found ways and means of using the Court to their own advantage. But on one occasion they did act in the public good. Whether there was some hidden motive is not known, but it was brought to their notice that a railway bridge in Birkenhead was in such a bad state of repair that in rainy weather water leaking from above collected underneath, making the roadway almost unpassable. Pleas and threats from other bodies to the railway company had been ignored, so Moreton summoned a jury of the Wapentake to inspect the bridge and order the railway company to repair it under penalty of a fine of £100 or seizure of the line in the event of default. The company ignored this threat, too, and Wapentake bailiffs were ordered to seize some railway wagons. The railway ordered its workers to resist the Court officials by force, but eventually the bridge was repaired.

But the most financially successful exploit of Moreton and Grace occurred in 1856 when they took advantage of an ancient right of the Lord of the Manor to take possession of the goods and chattels of a convicted felon. The miscreant was a Robert Wilson, cashier to a famous Liverpool shipping company, who for years had been embezzling the firm's money and using it to buy houses and land in both Liverpool and Wirral. He was caught and sentenced to 14 years transportation. Among the property bought with the stolen funds was a large house and 29 acres of land near Clatterbridge – within the jurisdiction of the Wapentake.

Moreton wasted no time and within hours of Wilson's conviction he evicted his wife and family into the road and moved in himself. The rest of Wilson's property was seized by a receiver appointed by the shipping company but Moreton immediately started proceedings in Chancery and, to the utter astonishment of most people, the Master of the Rolls pronounced in his favour.

Thus encouraged, Moreton changed the name of the house to 'Wirral Manor House' and had a proper courthouse erected at the rear. The lofty, red-brick structure, 75 feet long, is still there today in use as a barn and store.

Eye-witnesses have described how proceedings in the courthouse were usually presided over by Robert Grace who, more often drunk than sober, gave verdicts which incensed the public. As before, the proceedings were always followed by sumptuous dinners paid for out of the 'takings' and frequently absentees from the celebrations were even fined for contempt.

But all good things come to an end and the local papers began to campaign against the Wapentake and agitate for its abolition. In 1856, a Parliamentary Bill was promoted to bring about certain amendments in the procedure of the county courts and the opportunity was taken of inserting a clause abolishing the Hundred Court of Wirral. Moreton and Grace were each compensated, Moreton receiving £250 and Grace £300.

As it happened, the passing on of Willaston's own rights down the years eventually led to the setting up of a court in the village, but not one so outrageous. The rights passed through many hands by inheritance and marriage and eventually came into the possession of John Vere, Earl of Oxford, and a courtier to Henry VIII. In turn, they were inherited by his grandson and about the year 1560 he sold them piecemeal to 21 freeholders. This immediately raised the question of who was to be Lord of the Manor. It was settled in a commendably democratic way: a different one would be elected each year at a court specially set up for the purpose. This Court Leet and Baron, as it was known, was held annually during November and during the month of October the village rang to the 'Oyez! Oyez! Oyez!' of the court crier as he publicly proclaimed the date and time of its meeting.

The court sat in one of the village inns and was empowered to inflict penalties for such things as trespass, encroachment by cattle, and wilful destruction of hedges and ditches. It was also the occasion for the payment of dues and chief rents. There was a jury of twelve (who each received 1s. for their services) and two 'burlymen' whose job it was to assess the extent of any damage.

When the business of the court was completed the whole assembly was then entertained at the expense of the current Lord of the Manor who was expected to foot the bill out of his dues received. The 'quality' revelled in the upper rooms and the peasants and labourers below. Hot punch was always served and special 'court cakes' eaten. Anyone present for the first time was expected to buy a full round so that his health might be properly drunk. Any reluctance to comply with the custom was countered by a burlyman armed with a red-hot poker.

This was a tradition which lasted for hundreds of years and although it was not unique to Willaston it was one of the last survivors, the last Court Leet and Baron being held in the Nag's Head in 1907.

The villagers, however, were not denied an annual treat. The Willaston and District Shepherd's Club (a sick benefit society) held their 'Club Day' on the first Thursday of July each year and, following a procession through the village, this, too, ended up with a beano for the adults in one of the pubs while the younger people went to a funfair which always arrived for the occasion.

'Club Day' ended with the First World War, but such traditions have not been entirely lost. The attractive village green, with its magnificent copper beech (planted in 1935 to commemorate the Silver Jubilee of King George V) is often the scene of some festivity or other. It comes into full use on occasions of national merrymaking, like the Coronation and Silver Jubilee of the Queen, and European Heritage Year, and even on non-occasions the Residents Society promote festivals and fairs in the best Merrie England tradition. At Christmas-time the branches of the copper beech are festooned with lights and carols are sung round it with the carollers being fortified with hot dogs and soup.

One of the reminders of the last Silver Jubilee celebrations are the mapped-out Village Walks. Three routes round the village past items of interest have been sign-posted and a framed map of them is fixed to the front of the Memorial Hall.

And for the antiquarian Willaston has more to offer than most, with no fewer than 13 Grade 2 listed buildings – though the fact that some of them are still there today is due to the initiative of 'incomers'.

The old Red Lion Inn for example. Dating from 1631 (possibly earlier) it has been unlicensed since 1928 and up to 1972 had been empty and totally neglected for many years. It had been bought by a brewery company which wanted to demolish it and build a modern pub in its place, but the opposition of the residents and its Grade II listing thwarted their plans, so it was simply left to rot. Happily, when it had reached the point where little but the preservation order was holding it together, the brewery put it up for sale and it was bought by Nigel Worth, an architect, who happened to be looking for a home in the area at the time. It has now been restored (or, more accurately, virtually rebuilt because it almost had to be taken down and put up again), and although it may not look quite like the original it is as near as makes no difference and has done wonders for the village scene.

The green itself was once, most unusually, surrounded by farm-houses and a number of them still exist, although they may not immediately be recognisable as such. The building which houses the National Westminster bank was once known as Home Farm and bears the date 1661. The Midland Bank a few yards away is in part of the old Pear Tree Farm, which is eighteenth century, and the tall building next door to the Red Lion, which is part-house, part-hairdresser's, was Laburnum Farm of about the same age.

One Village Walk takes you along a path at the side of the Memorial Hall past Corner House Farm which is older still, with parts of it going back to the early years of the seventeeth century, and possibly earlier. Its name comes from the fact that it was once on the corner of the village green, but over the years the green has suffered several changes of shape.

In its early days the green was much larger and rectangular and it has been suggested that its unusual size was necessary to accommodate the assembly of the Hundred Court.

Willaston Old Hall, which bears a datestone 1558 over the front door, also faced on to the green at one time. The date, however, is thought to be a mistake. The datestone was put there about 160 years ago when some repair work was being done and it is now confidently thought that someone probably mis-read a poorly-written '6' for a '5' and that the likely date is 1658. This attractive red brick and stone house, with its three storeys and low ceilings, is typically Jacobean and although it fell into disrepair it was restored to its present fine condition by the late Dr and Mrs J.C. Lawrie.

Ashtree Farm, its near-neighbour in Hadlow Road, is even older; part of it was a cruck-framed cottage dating from the fifteenth century and was once obviously made of wattle and daub. This lay empty and almost derelict for many years, but remained listed as being of historical and architectural interest. In 1970, when all seemed lost, it was rescued and restored by Bill Hardman, an architect, who now lives there with his wife and family.

The longer Village Walk takes you past the side of the Parish Church (not old, but noticeable for its lack of a tower or steeple) and across the Elm Road estate. Beyond, on the other side of the recreation ground, can be seen the tower of Willaston's old windmill, in its day the biggest in Wirral. It was built in 1800 and is the last of several which have occupied the same site since the fourteenth century. With the building of the large flour mills in Birkenhead, the making of flour ceased, but with the machinery driven by a gas engine it was used for making cattle food. In 1930 it was damaged by a storm which blew down the sails and all milling ceased from then on. It soon became derelict, but in 1937 it was bought by the Wirral Society to save it from demolition. It served as a Home Guard post during the war and is now in use as a private home.

It is claimed that Mr Shuttleworth, one of the millers in the last century, cut and threshed corn in the early morning, ground it into flour, and made the flour into bread, and delivered the loaves in London the same night.

EIGHT

The Unexpected Villages

1. Bidston, Frankby, Thurstaston, Barnston, Brimstage

On a piece of land which is surrounded by water on three sides, and is smaller in area than the Isle of Man, and has been subjected to more than a century of ceaseless building, and has a population of about three-quarters of a million, it might seem inconceivable that anything claiming to be a 'village' could possibly survive. But villages there are and some of them are scarcely more than hamlets.

For the newcomer, it is one of the Wirral's unexpected delights to chance upon the little thatched village of Burton, or ancient hide-away Shotwick, or to see for the first time the carefully-architectured splendours of Port Sunlight or Thornton Hough. The latter were meticulous products of the drawing-board and models of their kind; let's look first at those villages which just happened because some ancient Wirralians took a fancy to a particular spot for some reason and built their clay and wattle huts there.

BIDSTON

Not many people go to Bidston these days just to look at it. It was a showpiece not many years ago, but now this little village of sixteenth and seventeenth-century sandstone and thatch is slowly dying and no-one seems to care very much. At any rate, there are no signs that anyone is doing anything about it. Sandstone is crumbling, thatch is thinning; holes in roofs have been covered with unsightly corrugated iron or asbestos or, worse, tarpaulins. The village shop has long been closed and its windows boarded up; the almshouses are empty, their leaded lights stoned; and the lychgate of the church and gates to cottages have been damaged and daubed with paint. Yet, Bidston is arguably the most interesting village of them all.

In 1971 Bidston Village was declared a Conservation area and later a by-pass was built which, after many years of pleas, rid the village of a constant stream of through traffic. But what has been done in the way of renovation has been the work of private individuals.

The most extraordinary piece of restoration took place in the late nineteen-sixties when a local architect, Harold ('Max') Faulkner, bought Bidston Hall, an ancient 20-roomed manor house which had been declared as hopelessly beyond repair thirty years previously. When Faulkner first saw the Hall during an evening stroll with his wife on Bidston Hill he found the floorboards had rotted away, ceilings had collapsed, doors had fallen off their hinges, wooden beams had dropped and staircases crumbled when a foot was placed on the first tread. Every window was broken, the roof was open to the sky, and in the Great Hall which spans the breadth of the building at the front there was a pool of water big and deep enough to sail model boats. And what damage had not been done by neglect and the passing of more than three centuries had been eagerly and thoroughly wrought by the vandals of today. It took seven months to get rid of all the dirt and grime and tons and tons of debris and rubbish.

The building was made safe; the rustic oak beams were restored and put back in position; the stonework was cleaned and repaired; the mullioned lead-lighted windows were renewed and central heating and all the other amenities of modern living were installed. In 1968 Faulkner and his family moved in and Bidston Hall, thus resuscitated, came to life again.

The Hall was originally a seat of the Earls of Derby and the exact date of its building is not known. Most writers in the past have ascribed its beginnings to Ferdinando, the 5th Earl (who built the tower which became Leasowe Castle) and its completion to his brother, William, who became the 6th Earl. In 1894, however, 'E.Q.' in a publication entitled *Bidston Hill Preserved*, issued in support of an appeal for the hill's acquisition for public use, asserts that: 'The fourth Earl, it is now evident, was the builder of Bidston Hall which has hitherto been attributed to his son. The date is about 1580, not from written records but from evidence curious but fully conclusive, viz. the masons' marks which show that the men employed were the same who built Stonyhurst for the Earl's friend, Sir Richard Sherborne, about 1590'.

The particular Earls of Derby who were associated with Bidston were altogether a remarkable bunch. Ferdinando, the 5th Earl, is said to have died at an early age 'probably poisoned by his political enemies', while his younger brother, William, spent years wandering round Europe and the Middle East, coming home via Moscow and Greenland from where he made the voyage on a whaling ship. He was, in fact, away so long without communicating that he was unaware that his father had died and that Ferdinando had also met his death and that he was himself now the 6th Earl. Not surprisingly he had long been given up for dead and the estate had been settled on various nephews and nieces with the result that in the end he only obtained a portion of his due.

He spent most of his remaining time at Bidston and in 1891 a theory
was suggested that this widely-travelled and cultured man was really the
author of the works attributed to Shakespeare. It was known that
William Shakespeare was among a company of strolling players which
had visited both Knowsley and Lathom and it was argued that some of
the facts and events in the earl's life are reflected in the plays. The theory
was sparked off by the finding in State papers of two letters, both in the
same vein, and dated 30 June 1599, from London to different parties in
Antwerp and Venice, to the effect that: 'Therle of Daby is busyed only in
penning comedies for the common players'.

James, the 7th earl, inherited his father's adventurous spirit and
became deeply involved in the Civil War. A staunch Royalist, in 1649
he was forced to flee to the Isle of Man (which he also owned and was
Lord of), but, foolishly, he was not content to stay and enjoy the security
the island offered and returned to the mainland. He was captured at the
Battle of Worcester and a few days later (despite assurances to the
contrary) he was taken to Bolton and beheaded.

His widow, Charlotte, with her heroic defence of the Derby seat of
Lathom House and her ultimate refusal to surrender the Isle of Man
after her husband's departure, had nothing to commend her to the
Parliamentarians. With both Lathom House and Knowsley Hall in
ruins she was faced with near-poverty and with her son, Charles, the 8th
Earl, was forced to sell Bidston, including the Hall and the village, in
1653.

The estate changed hands three times within a short period,
ultimately coming into the ownership of Sir Robert Vyner, banker and
goldsmith, who made the Coronation regalia which is still in use today.

As well as the Hall, much of the land has now been sold but the village
itself is still in the hands of the Vyner family. In the 300 years of their
tenure they have never regarded it as a permanent home. They had (and
still have) estates in Yorkshire and as time went on they more and more
became absentee-landlords, entrusting the affairs of the estate to agents.
This obtains to this day and although the village is now part of a family
trust it is many years since a member of the family has been seen there.

While Bidston Hall itself was in the Vyner's possession it saw many
different occupiers, mostly farmers. The most illustrious tenant of all,
however, was the famous F. E. Smith, the first Earl of Birkenhead, who
is said to have been in the habit of rehearsing his speeches out on the
terrace.

The village itself is ranged on either side of a 200-yard-long S-bend on
Hoylake Road and high above the traffic on a commanding outcrop is
the Parish Church of St Oswald. There has been a church on this site
since at least the twelfth century, but the present building dates only

from 1856 with the exception of the squat tower which remains from the previous mediaeval church.

Of the old houses, the most venerable is probably 'The Lilacs' immediately east of the church. With its weathered stonework and irregular roof-lines, a tall chimney-stack on one end, and a front door somewhat off-centre, it is a hotch-potch of a house which looks as though it were built piecemeal by some eccentric as the need arose. The result is delightful. It was once the vicarage and a favourite subject for artists – but did they notice that it had no gutters or downspouts? And how many of them realised that it lacked all modern facilities – no gas, electricity or hot water; no inside lavatory and no bathroom.

It is a sad sight today. It is still occupied, but the roof is sagging, the slates are shattered and the adjoining tithebarn (latterly used as the estate workshop) has caved in. The notice proclaiming 'This building is dangerous' was stating the obvious.

On the other side of the church at the corner of School Lane is Stone Farm, a Cottage which was once the village inn called 'The Ring O'Bells'. Situated in the shadow of the church tower, it was well-named, but in its latter days it was more familiarly known as the 'Ham and Eggs house' because that dish was its speciality and at holiday times attracted customers from all over the Wirral. Unfortunately, it also became equally well-known for inebriety, of which Simon Croft, the last landlord, was as culpable as any of his customers.

Simon died in 1864, but his name lives on as the subject of the song 'Simon the Cellarer'. He is buried in the churchyard just a few yards away from his old inn, but his last journey was not made without some difficulty. He was a big man and on the day of the funeral it was found that his coffin could not be manoeuvred out of his bedroom and down the inn's steep and narrow staircase. His last exit was finally achieved through the bedroom window after the frame had been removed.

The inn's notoriety did not die with him and the sight of drunks propping themselves up against the church wall or sleeping it off on the footpath to the distress of Sunday morning churchgoers prompted Lady Cust to demand of the Vyners that it be closed down. The inn finally shut its doors in 1868 and became a farmhouse.

Opposite Stone Farm at right angles to the main road is Church Farm. The largest house in the village, it is believed to have once been a small monastery and has no less than 13 different floor levels. As a result the mullioned windows are as randomly sited as currants in a cake.

Possibly the worst thing ever to happen to Bidston was the inclusion of the parish within the bounds of the old Borough of Birkenhead. They seemed not to appreciate what a priceless asset lay within their jurisdiction and, possibly because it was in private ownership, showed no interest in its preservation. Latterly, when deterioration had set in, a gesture was made by declaring it a Conservation Area.

Like most other big towns Birkenhead has never been without a housing problem and all undeveloped land within its bounds therefore was in constant jeopardy. So it came to pass that between the wars council housing was allowed to creep right up to the very fringe of Bidston Hill and to the edge of Bidston village, and about 15 years ago the vast Ford Estate was built on the lush pastures of the Bidston farmers. The village is thus sandwiched between these council estates and no man in Bidston can now call himself a farmer. Their acreage has been taken away from them successively until each in turn has had to seek a different livelihood. Their farms today are no more than names on gates.

From time to time individual voices have been raised in protest at the shameful neglect of Bidston and one man in particular who tried to arouse some feeling and bring about a last-ditch effort to save it was Harold Faulkner. His heart bled for the village and after proving so convincingly with his restoration of Bidston Hall that he knew what he was talking about he drew up a plan of what urgently needed doing and how it could be done. At his own expense he published a half-inch thick brochure entitled 'An Appeal for Survival' and outlined an 11-point plan for conserving the village as a whole. Copies went to all interested parties and organisations, including both Birkenhead and Cheshire County councils, the Society for the Protection of Ancient Buildings, the Civic Trust, and the Department of the Environment. He suggested then (1971) that no more than £40,000 was needed to effect essential repairs and that a public appeal should be made for the money if it were not forthcoming from elsewhere. Such a sum seems almost paltry, but his efforts were entirely in vain.

FRANKBY

To the motorist, Frankby is that little sandstone blur on the busy road between West Kirby and Greasby, between a with-care bend and a narrow straight, with a pocket-handerchief green, a few ancient houses, a farm or two, and the last resting-place of many of Wallasey's citizens.

When most people go to Frankby they do so with a purpose. To visit the cemetery or, on a fine summer evening or weekend, to walk in Royden Park where the Wirral Model Engineering Society has a splendid model railway which gives rides to children. Or they go to ride horses.

It has been claimed that there are more horses per head of population in the Wirral than anywhere else in Britain and if you go to Frankby on a

Saturday or Sunday you may well think this is where the majority are. If you don't meet them being ridden in the lanes you will hear them chomping and snuffling behind almost every wall and hedge. Many of Wirral's horse-owning residents find stabling and grazing for their mounts hereabouts and Birkenhead Riding Club has its headquarters nearby.

I first came to know Frankby as a small child. My family used to come here for a holiday when we lived on the northern side of Liverpool, and although that does not seem far to travel nowadays it took quite a long time then. A tram to the Pier Head, a boat across the Mersey and a bus for the other eight miles from Woodside. Frankby looked very much then as it does now. And it stands a chance like Bidston of staying that way for it is now a Conservation Area. For all that such designations and declarations these days are every bit as fragile as a politician's election promise there is reasonably good cause for confidence in this case. Frankby has not one stately hall but two. And though the squirearchy have long departed they are both in relatively safe hands; they belong to the people.

Frankby Hall, a dour, square, castellated and turreted building which looks as though it would not be out of place on some Welsh headland were it not made of sandstone, adjoins the village and was built in 1846/7 by Sir Thomas Royden, a shipowner and Member of Parliament. And well-known and successful though he was himself, his best-known achievement was probably being the father of the famous Dr Maude Royden, the writer, university lecturer, social worker, preacher, broadcaster and tireless worker for women's causes, not least women's suffrage, who died in 1956.

Sir Thomas's parliamentary and business affairs kept him away from the Hall for long periods and for much of the time the sole occupant was his unmarried sister. In 1933 he decided to sell up and offered the Hall and its 61-acre estate to the then Hoylake Urban District Council for . . . £8000 the lot! But they could not think what to do with it so they turned the offer down. In the end he sold it to Wallasey Corporation for £12,500 for use as a cemetery.

Wallasey was fast running out of land when they acquired the estate and there were some misgivings about establishing a cemetery in another authority's area 6 miles away. The *Liverpool Daily Post* did not think much of the idea and made the point that: 'Not only will it be difficult for relatives of the deceased to visit but *motor* hearses will be required'.

In my delvings into the Hall's history I came across a catalogue of the sale of its contents and the last two items seemed to spell out the end of an era as nothing else could:

Lot 650: 18 pots of well-grown aspidistras
Lot 651: Hudson Limousine car, 30 hp 6-cylinder, dark green, in
          good running order.

It took seven years to transform the estate into a cemetery. Many of
the trees had to be felled and the areas grassed over, while the main part
of the Hall itself was converted into two chapels – one Church of
England and Non-Conformist, the other Roman Catholic – complete
with tall Gothic windows. The cemetery officially opened in 1940,
giving space for 36,000 graves, and almost as though they were making
sure that no Wallaseyan could ever have cause for complaint at being
interred in Sir Thomas's front garden, the opening ceremonials and
consecrations of the different denominations were fully comprehensive
and took over three hours to perform. But as cemeteries go it is a
beautiful place.

The other stately home of Frankby is 'Hill Bark', one of the sights of
Wirral. This beautiful, black and white, half-timbered, pseudo-Elizabethan mansion enjoys what has often been described as an unrivalled
situation. Built on the top of Frankby Hill – albeit a *low* hill – with
Thurstaston Common rolling away beneath its windows, its particular
view of the Dee estuary and the Welsh hills is uninterrupted.

This was the home of Sir Thomas Royden's younger brother, Sir
Ernest, and it is built on the site of a former house of the same type which
belonged to Septimus Ledward, JP. Sir Ernest married Ledward's
daughter and went to live in a beautiful, black and white, half-timbered
pseudo-Elizabethan mansion called 'Bidston Court' in Noctorum,
Birkenhead. It had been built in 1891 for Robert Hudson, the soap
manufacturer, but the site did not do justice to the house. It was near to
and below the level of the road and although it enjoyed extensive views
when it was built they diminished as the outer fringes of Birkenhead
were developed. When Septimus Ledward died 'Hill Bark' came into
the possession of Lady Royden and Sir Ernest decided to move there –
but he decided to take 'Bidston Court' with him. 'Hill Bark' was
thereupon demolished and, in 1929, 'Bidston Court' was dismantled
and moved, lock, stock and barrel; stone, brick, and beam, to Frankby
Hill, where it was re-erected. Every stone, every brick, and every piece
of wood was carefully marked and, using local architects and local
builders, it was re-assembled ready for occupation by 1931, and given
the old name of 'Hill Bark'.

Sir Ernest died in 1960. This time Hoylake UDC did not drag its feet
and promptly acquired the property. Mind you, they took their time in
deciding exactly what to do with it, but in the end it was re-opened as
what must be one of the stateliest homes for the elderly anywhere.

On several occasions the house has been the setting for an open-air production of a Shakespeare play performed by the Hill Bark Players, a company of local amateurs brought together specially for the occasion.

Going to and from Hill Bark and/or Royden Park and (depending where you are coming from) Frankby Hall Cemetery, you will pass 'Catch Ums' – the name by which the locals always refer to their pub. A tiny pub, nicely in keeping with the size of the village, it is really 'The Farmers' Arms' and nobody seems to be quite sure how old it is. The landlord told me it must be at least 200 years old and took me outside to inspect the brickwork. 'Hard as iron', he said, 'we had an electrician here not long ago who wanted to bore a hole in the wall. He broke two masonry bits doing it'.

But why is it called 'Catch Ums'? 'It's because of its situation at the road junction. If we don't catch'um on the way out, we catch'um on the way back'.

THURSTASTON

Most people not liking the fact that a main road ran past their front door would solve the problem by moving away. But at Thurstaston can be seen an alternative solution. A former resident there simply moved the road.

In 1880, Sir Thomas Ismay, the immensely wealthy founder and chairman of the old White Star shipping line, bought a house called 'Dawpool' which nestled at the foot of Thurstaston Hill with nothing – apart from the road – but green fields and farmland between it and the shores of the Dee. Four years later, to mark his silver wedding, he had the house demolished and replaced by a magnificent mansion designed by the highly regarded Victorian architect, Richard Norman Shaw, who had also designed the White Star offices in Liverpool.

The main road between West Kirby and Heswall ran close to the house, so at Ismay's expense a 'by-pass' was cut through the rock higher up the hill. Not only did he thus achieve seclusion for his home, but the old road with a gate across it became his entrance drive. It can be seen today as one comes uphill from Caldy Cross Roads going off to the right just before the rock cutting.

A few years later Ismay's peace and quiet was threatened yet again by a plan to run a railway down the Wirral Peninsula parallel to the same road. So he took the obvious step – he had the railway re-routed as far away from his house as possible, running instead parallel with the shore. Since he owned all the land between his house and the shore and was also chairman of the railway company this was not difficult to arrange.

This second 'Dawpool' for all its magnificence had a comparatively short life and was demolished in 1927, just over fifty years after its erection to make way for a small estate of houses of more manageable proportions.

Both Ismay's actions proved to be blessings in disguise. First, the re-routing of the railway not only made Thurstaston and Heswall shores more accessible for day-trippers, but now that the railway has gone the old track has given us today the marvellous Wirral Country Park. Secondly, the diversion of the road has left the 'village green' area round the Parish Church and Thurstaston Hall completely unspoiled.

The scene provided by the elegant church and the ancient Hall, the old school with its lead-lighted windows, and the fortress-solid Dawpool Farm, looks as though it might have been specially built as a setting for a costume play. Many people driving down to the Country Park or the shore take in the scene at a glance, but it is worth stopping for a closer look.

Thurstaston Hall, slumbering at the end of a straight drive beyond iron gates fixed to lofty, fluted pillars, is the seat of the Lord of the Manor, Richard Turner. His grandmother was a Glegg and his ancestry can be traced back, albeit by a somewhat circuitous route, to Robert de Rodelent who was given the manor by Hugh Lupus in AD 1070. It is thought that he built a manor house on the site then and Richard Turner told me that a visiting architectural historian had recently identified one room, formerly used as a chapel, as being Norman. All ancient houses are inevitably an amalgam of the restorations, altera-tions and additions of succeeding generations and this is no exception. The entrance goes back to 1350, the west wing is mediaeval, and the central portion bears a datestone 1680. The east wing was built in 1836. In all its nine centuries Thurstaston Hall has never been sold. In the entrance hall in a niche on the staircase is an impressive life-size carved wooden figure of a man in armour. Patently a man of authority, it is certainly as old as the oldest part of the house and is thought to be a statue of Hugh Lupus himself.

Though there has been a church at Thurstaston for a very long time (the list of rectors goes back to 1303) the present building, dedicated to St Bartholomew, dates only from 1886. It supplanted a church built in 1824 and that, in turn, took the place of a small, rudimentary place of worship which stood within the grounds of the Hall.

To the puzzlement of many visitors, the tower of the 1824 church is still standing uselessly nearby. It seems that when the old building of the present church was sanctioned permission was given to use stone from the old church to build a wall enclosing the new churchyard. The stones were removed as required and when the wall was completed the tower remained over and so was simply left.

The present church was erected to the memory of Joseph Hegan by his two daughters. He was the owner of the first 'Dawpool' prior to Ismay. The organ, in turn, was built to the memory of Ismay by *his* two daughters. Though the church is smaller inside than one might expect from its outside appearance, it is a graceful building with some beautiful stained-glass windows and an interior richly ornamented with marble and alabaster.

The narrow road leading up from the church on the left is part of the original main road and, looking back, it can be seen how it would have linked up with the part which Ismay made his own.

BARNSTON

Between Heswall and the other component parts of the old Wirral Urban District there is still some semblance of countryside left and Barnston, though on a busy main road, is in the middle of it. It has so far escaped much development and is little more than a church, a pub, a tiny post office, a Women's Institute and a couple of farms, though modern housing does exist on the roads leading into and out of it.

The building of the church, with school and vicarage, incidentally, was paid for by Joseph Hegan of 'Dawpool', who owned land in Barnston.

The unexpected aspect of this part of the Wirral is not so much Barnston as Barnston Dale. Strangers driving along the road to or from Birkenhead are usually surprised to find about half-way between Thingwall and the Glegg Arms (or Devon Doorway) that the road drops suddenly for a couple of hundred yards and winds through an attractive rocky glade with a couple of old cottages nestling in the dip. In a book of rambles (*Across the Fields of Wirral* by Andrew Blair) which I read the other day and which was published in 1927, it is described as: 'One of the beauty spots of Wirral. It is deservedly popular, and during each year many thousands (*sic*) of pleasure-seekers travel thither by cycle, coach or train. Large numbers, too, go on foot. . . .'

I doubt whether anyone makes a special point of going there now and in a car one is in and out of it in half a minute. There was obviously much more of Barnston Dale available to the public in those days than there is now. The dale is actually the valley of a stream which runs into the Prenton Brook, which runs into the River Fender which, in turn, meanders northwards to join the River Birket which flows into Wallasey Pool. None of these watercourses is of much significance and both the Fender and the Birket, once they reach the neighbourhood of Birkenhead and Wallasey, suffer the indignity of being culverted.

BRIMSTAGE

Brimstage (variously known at times as Brunstall, Brunstath, Brumstache and Brumstagh) is another of those places which many a motorist passes through without a glance. It lies on what a niece of mine when small called 'a snakes-and-ladders road', so it is a case of looking where one is going anyway. And, truth to tell, there is not all that much to see. The road follows the line of a brook at the bottom of a mini-ravine; there is a row of estate houses along the top and in between them and the road there is a small village green and a village hall. But there is no village as such. No church, no pub, not even a shop. The interest lies on the other side of the road, behind the trees.

Here stands Brimstage Hall once the family seat of the Domvilles, one of the richest and most important families in Cheshire. Only the tower of the original hall now remains and it is known that this dates from at least 11 February 1398. A licence for the building of a private chapel was granted to the then owner, Sir Hugh Hulse, on that date, but whether it was for incorporation in an existing building or a new one is not known. The property had come to Sir Hugh through his wife, Margery, the sole heiress of the Domville family, and in due course it passed to their only son, Thomas, who obviously regarded the Domville name as the more illustrious and reverted to using the title and arms. But – as so often seems to have been the case in Wirral history – there was no male heir, only a daughter, Margaret, and since she was a minor when her father died she became a ward of Sir William Troutbeck. In 1432 she married his son, Sir John Troutbeck, and he not only became Lord of the manors of Brunstath, Oxton, Raby, Barnston and Little Neston, but was Lord of Dunham-on-the Hill, Chamberlain of Chester and, a most important post for which he had to thank his wife's forebears, Sergeant of the Bridge Gate, Chester. He was eventually killed fighting at the Battle of Blore Heath (near Market Drayton) in the Wars of the Roses in 1459, but his wife had died three years earlier.

Through marriage of a succeeding great-granddaughter, the vast estates eventually came into the ownership of the Earls of Shrewsbury.

A village inn called 'The Red Cat' (now in use for a modern pub in Greasby) once stood where stands the present village hall, erected at the expense of the first Viscount Leverhulme. But, I wonder, what prompted him to build it at all? No more than a couple of dozen people could ever have lived there even at its most populous.

2. Raby, Eastham, Ness, Burton, and Puddington, Shotwick

RABY

If you want some idea of how Wirral looked before the conquest – the builders' and developers' conquest, I mean – go to Raby. So far, it is largely untouched. There is a nibbling of new houses at one of the edges forming the sort of estate usually advertised as 'favoured by the young executive' but that is about all. If you approach from the Bromborough end, passing Bromborough Golf Club on the left, you will come upon a sight as attractive as it is unexpected. A lake, no less, tree-fringed and picturesque, and the only sheet of water above pond-size in the whole of the Wirral. This is Raby Mere. The Mere is a quarter of a mile long and was man-made over three hundred years ago to provide power to drive a mill for grinding corn.

Raby Mere has long been one of the Wirral's day-tripper spots. Even before the coming of the car it was a place to visit by bus-and-foot or bike. Before the last war, when Sundays meant Sunday School and Sunday Schools had treats, Raby Mere was a favourite venue. Apart from its natural attractions there was boating on the Mere and swings and tea in the Tea Gardens.

Back up the road from the Mere, near the entrance to the golf club, stands Raby Hall, an imposing Georgian-style, twelve-bedroomed house in four and a half acres which was built about 125 years ago. From being a private residence, it was for many years a nursing home. In 1975 it was put up for sale by auction and bought by a businessman for nearly £50,000 as a surprise for his wife. But the real surprise was his. His wife refused to move! So within 24 hours he was seeking a buyer and the house was acquired by the Wirral Society for Autistic Children to provide residential accommodation, with educational and training facilities for autistic adolescents.

Beyond the Mere, for a mile towards the tiny village of Raby, there are fields and trees and country lanes unmarred by anything built in the past 25 years. Even the motorway has not spoiled it, passing as it does in a cutting below field level. This area – from the Mere to the village – used to comprise the old Parish of Raby. This was an administrative delineation not an ecclesiastical one, for there is no church. Nor is there a school or a shop. The nearest church, school, and shop are at Thornton Hough one-and-a-half miles farther on. But there is a pub and it is as much one of Wirral's attractions as the Mere.

'The Wheatsheaf' is a free house just as it always has been since it served its first pint of ale in 1611. It is a single-storey, whitewashed, half-timbered and thatched building enlivened in the summer months with hanging baskets of geraniums. Inside, the tiny bar with its tiled floor, low beams and wooden settles, is the sort of place where you would not be surprised to find a serving-wench dispensing rough cider and mulled ale to besmocked and gaitered farmworkers. Instead, most of the customers now come in cars from a distance or from that estate on the other side of the Mere.

'People who live on that estate', said a man I met in the bar, 'say they live in Raby. They don't. Raby is round here. Twenty houses, four farms and cottages, a pub, a telephone-box and the school'.

The school is a sturdy, Gothic, sandstone building which has not heard the scratch of chalk for more than 75 years. One half is now a house and the other is a village hall which is now only used once a fortnight for a church whist drive and the occasional children's party. The building is unique in that it is the only piece of property in Raby which is not part of the Leverhulme estate. It belongs to the Parish Church at Thornton Hough.

The man whom the Troutbecks of Brimstage had to thank for the prestigious post of Sergeant of the Bridge Gate at Chester was Robert de Raby to whom it was given in 1350. His duties were 'to find bars, locks and keys for the bridge gate, the horse gate, and the ship gate, and men to watch the gates, and to open and shut them' – and since the bridge was the main point of entry for the Welsh the signal importance of his task will be appreciated.

He also had to furnish the Earl of Chester's household with coleworts (a kind of heartless cabbage) from Michaelmas until Lent, and with leeks during the 40 days of Lent, be responsible for the Castle gardens, and the fruits of a tree called 'The Restyngtre'. For all these responsibilities and duties he was given a house, the tolls from the gates, the profits from the fishery and ferriage, threepence a day, various rents, and all the apples remaining on the trees after the first taking'.

In those mediaeval days, too, Raby was where the Earl of Shrewsbury's Court Leet and Baron was held for all his manors – Raby, Oxton, Brimstage, Thingwall, Thornton Hough and Barnston – so it was obviously a place of some importance.

Now it is a place of no importance and it gives me great satisfaction to record the fact.

EASTHAM

It also gives me great satisfaction – nay, I rejoice – to report that Eastham, like Mafeking, has been relieved. It happened on Monday 17 July 1978 when, as was the case with Baden-Powell's little force during the Boer War, relief came when it seemed that all was lost. It marked the end of a siege which had lasted more than ten years.

To explain. That mid-summer day marked the opening of a £295,000 by-pass road which took away from the village an almost continuous stream of monstrous road tankers carrying all manner of highly dangerous petro-chemicals. At their peak 150 of them thundered through the twisting roads *every single day*. Only on Christmas Day was there a lull. The noise and the fumes, the dirt and the dangers had to be experienced to be believed. And this in a village which, a century before, Nathaniel Hawthorne had described as: 'The finest old English village I have seen, with many antique houses, and with altogether a rural and picturesque aspect'.

The cause of the trouble lay in the passing of the Manchester Ship Canal Act of 1949. This gave the Manchester Ship Canal Company powers to construct the Queen Elizabeth II oil dock at Eastham where the canal enters the Mersey and also – incredibly – the right to develop their adjoining land without having to obtain prior planning permission from the local authority. One wonders how such an astonishing privilege came to pass unchallenged. And what made it even more extraordinary was that permission to build houses in the village itself was denied because it was in the Wirral Green Belt.

The oil dock in itself gave little cause for complaint. It is largely hidden from view by earthworks and, after all, with a capacity for accommodating tankers up to 35,000 tons was it not the biggest and finest in the land? And did not the Canal Company give assurances that the oil would be pumped direct from the ships through pipelines to the refineries at Stanlow? Little did anyone guess that within a decade tankers would be built to a size which would make the dock look ridiculously small. Nowadays crude oil-carrying tankers are gargantuans of 200,000 tons and even bigger. So the smaller ships which use the Eastham dock bring in a variety of liquids, many of them highly volatile and some of them dangerous. There was no question of piping them anywhere. They had to be stored and on the green fields beside the canal the company quickly erected an enormous 'tank farm', an ugly, despoiling complex of Brobingnagian proportions. And to convey their contents to refineries and factories in all parts of the country needed the use of scores of road tankers.

But, miraculously, Eastham has survived and when I was there the other day you could almost hear the quiet. If Hawthorne could return for another look I am sure he would still recognise it. 'It was not merely one long wide street as in most New England villages (he wrote at the time) but there were several crooked ways, gathering the whole settlement into a pretty compass. In the midst stood a venerable church of the common red freestone, with a most reverend air, smaller than that of Bebington, but more beautiful and looking quite as old'.

That description still holds good, but some of the buildings he saw are now serving other purposes. A former mansion, Eastham House, which in more spacious days was the home of Mr John Tobin, a prominent Liverpool businessman (to whom the village cross is a memorial) and, later, Sir William Vernon (the flour miller), has been converted into 28 flats for the elderly.

The entrance lodge of Eastham House has been turned into two separate dwellings, though in its time it has also served as the village Post Office. This building, more than any other, felt the impact of the tanker onslaught. Literally. Situated right on the corner of Rivacre Road, a country lane which leads to Ellesmere Port, tankers taking the corner badly several times crashed into the house and had it been a modern 'semi' and not built of solid sandstone it would not be there now. I remember Mrs Sheila Kelly, the occupant, showing me how the wall had been gouged and scarred and the corner stones broken by the collisions. Right opposite was a sign denying access to vehicles over two tons unladen, but this was blatantly ignored. Proof-positive that the menace was now ended was indicated by the renewed stonework bearing not a scratch.

A farm which stands almost in the centre of the village just beyond the church has also been given a new lease of life. Eighteenth-century Hall Farm and its outbuildings have been imaginatively converted by the council into a number of attractive homes. The council has erected a plaque to its own cleverness, but it is well deserved.

Hawthorne might not now recognise St Mary's Church. Beautifully situated among the trees, its origins go back to the twelfth or thirteenth century, but what Pevsner calls 'a drastic restoration' was made in the eighteen-seventies. But the church spire would be familiar; that has not changed. In architectural terms it is a 'broach' spire, an octagonal cone rising out of a tower devoid of a parapet. The only other like it in Wirral is on St Andrew's, Bebington, and though most people find it as graceful as it is unusual Pevsner did not care for it very much. 'Ponderous, unhappily detailed' (he described it) and 'very odd'. The spire was originally built in 1320 and must have been well built at that, for it lasted over 400 years until it was restored without alteration to the design in 1732.

The rest of the church has undergone at least two rebuildings and in view of the last restoration (after Hawthorne's time) must now be classed as Victorian though earlier fragments remain. It is nevertheless a handsome building with some very fine stained glass windows and some interesting relics, including the tombs of the Stanleys and an ancient circular font, almost certainly Saxon and possibly a thousand years old.

But older still is the Eastham Yew. This venerable tree, which must have furnished who knows how many longbows in its time for the archers of this part of Wirral, stands in the churchyard near the church door, its trunk eroded and blackened as though it were on the point of death yet with leaves green and bountiful enough to give promise of many more years to come. It looked the same when Sulley gazed upon it a hundred years ago and, if it is dying, as some people suggest, it is taking an admirably long time about it.

A plaque attached to the protective railings records a visit made by The Royal Archaeological Society to see it in 1898 and their conclusion was that it was probably planted against the east end of the original wattle-and-daub mission chapel in Saxon times. And that could make it more than 1500 years old and Britain's oldest tree.

The Guinness Book of Records accords the distinction to the Fortingall Yew in Glen Llyon near Aberfeldy, Perthshire, '*part of which* (my italics) still grows'. Recently, in correspondence with Norris McWhirter, the editor, I challenged this assertion on behalf of Eastham's yew. Since the age of neither can be exactly determined I feel at the very least the honour should be shared.

The road from the village past the tank farm to the oil dock leads to the old Eastham Ferry, for so many years the point of embarkation for Liverpool. It declined with the increasing use of the ferries lower downstream after Brassey's New Chester Road was built, but it was not put out of business and a service of tall-funnelled paddle-steamers was introduced. They ran for more than 50 years and at week-ends and on Bank Holidays many thousands of Liverpudlians came for a day out in Eastham woods, an area so beautiful it was advertised as 'the Richmond of the Mersey'. Visitors from the bricks and mortar jungle were not only able to enjoy the beauties of nature but could also visit a zoological gardens and a variety of side-shows (including on one occasion a performance by the great Blondin on a high wire). But in the decade following the First World War the hawkers and the hucksters moved in and drunks and rowdies gave the place such an unsavoury reputation that decent people ceased to go there. In 1929 the steamer service ended and the old ferry boats were broken up. The little iron pier and landing stage were demolished in 1935.

But like the village, the ferry area lives again. There are no actual ferry-boats, and the old booking office has been turned into a public lavatory, but the woods have been tidied up (too much so, say the ornithologists) and turned into Eastham Country Park. There are picnic areas and nature trails and an old bear pit from the former zoological gardens has been excavated. A café has been opened and a car park has been imaginatively sited to give a view across the Mersey which is two miles wide at this point and looks like a vast lake. It provides a grandstand view of shipping making for the dock or the ship canal entrance and of aircraft flying into Liverpool Airport at Speke almost opposite.

The Eastham Ferry Hotel has also been renovated. Built in 1845 by Sir William Massey Stanley, it was a much-used hostelry in the ferry's hey-day and, latterly, was very popular with the tanker crews who gave it a cosmopolitan atmosphere. It is full of nautical knick-knackery and until lately was graced with an early Victorian glassed-in veranda. Its removal during the recent restoration and replacement with an open terrace brought an outcry from the residents of Eastham – but this was a skirmish they lost.

The final rout of the road tankers seems, not unnaturally, to have given Eastham new heart and on a fine, sunny day there recently I noticed how many houses and shops seemed to have been newly painted and pointed. I took particular interest in one house receiving careful attention. It was in the middle of a row of seven, but not obviously so. Not one of them had a front door. From the road, this terrace looks like the side of a school or a hall for all the entrances are at the rear – which, I suppose, makes the backs the front. The row was built by a wealthy Victorian preacher who could not abide the sight of women gossiping on their doorsteps. If they must chatter, he said, let them do it out of sight.

NESS

Nowadays the village of Ness is no more than an extended arm of Neston, but it remains noteworthy on two counts. Lady Hamilton and Ness Gardens.

Ness was no more than a small farming hamlet until the Stanleys opened up a colliery at adjoining Denhall in 1760 to extract coal from a seam which ran under the Dee towards Flintshire. It was mined for 180 years. Working conditions even towards the end were bad and in the early days they were appalling, not far removed from slave labour. Boys began work there as early as seven years of age and everything was done by hand – or feet. The seam was thin and Mortimer describes how the coal, of poor quality, was brought to the bottom of the shaft along two canals in small boats. Each boat carried four baskets, each holding four hundredweights. Four or five at a time were roped together and the motive power was supplied by a man lying on his back on the coals of the first boat and pushing with his feet on the canal roof.

This inhuman system was, in due time, replaced with ponies drawing tubs along rails. Latterly owned by the Wirral Colliery Company, the pit ceased working in 1928.

Legend has it that Emy Lyon, the blacksmith's daughter who became Lady Hamilton, was born in Swan Cottage. However, when Mortimer saw the village he described it as 'one of the most miserable in the Hundred, consisting of a mere mass of hovels inhabited by colliers'. Is it likely that a blacksmith of sixty years earlier would have been so much better off that he could afford to live in a house like Swan Cottage, even allowing for its being a more humble abode than it is today?

Nevertheless, Emy's birth in Ness and her baptism in Neston Church are well authenticated. According to the church register, she was born on 26 April 1765 and baptised on 12 May 1765 – just six weeks before her father died.

Her mother, Mary Lyon, was unable to support herself and the child in Ness and returned to her native Hawarden. Emy was brought up there until, in her early teens, she went to London to become a nursemaid in the family of a man who was the part-owner of the Drury Lane Theatre. With a situation in such a household where leading actors and actresses were constant visitors it is not surprising that she was soon dazzled by London life. A captivating beauty who was befriended and painted by the famous artists of the day – Romney (no less than 25 times), Gainsborough, and Reynolds – she changed her name for some reason to Emma Hart and by the time she was 17 she had become the mistress of the Hon. Sir Charles Greville. Two years later she transferred her affections to his widower uncle, Sir William Hamilton, the British envoy at Naples. They married in 1791 and within a very short time she had become a leading figure in Neapolitan society and an intimate friend of Queen Maria Carolina of Naples. There, too, she met Lord Nelson for the first time, but their intimate relationship did not develop until after his return from the Battle of the Nile in 1798. She became his mistress and two years later a daughter, Horatia, was born.

After the deaths of Hamilton (1803) and Nelson (1805) she enjoyed legacies from both but led such an extravagant life that she ran into debt and was imprisoned. She escaped and made her way to Calais where she died, a lonely alcoholic, in extreme poverty in 1815.

The twisting road out of Ness towards Burton leads to Ness Gardens – or, to be precise, The University of Liverpool Botanic Gardens. These beautiful gardens must number among Wirral's special delights. They attract about 80,000 visitors a year (and they are open every day of the year except Christmas Day) and though the number is steadily growing they are still not as widely known as they deserve to be. The gardens were created at the end of the last century by Arthur Kilpin Bulley, a wealthy Liverpool cotton broker and a keen horticulturist. He was also the first of the great twentieth-century patrons of plant collecting.

The 30-acre site on which Arthur Bulley chose to build his home is on high ground known as Mickwell Brow which slopes gradually down towards the Dee. On this south-facing site he laid out gardens and a small commercial nursery which grew and developed into the famous firm of Bees Seeds Limited. And if you have ever wondered where that firm got its name from, now you know. 'Bee' is for 'Bulley'. He was a man who liked to share his good fortune with others and he not only allowed the public free access to his grounds but provided a tennis court for the young people of Ness and furthered many a romance by placing a carefully-sited seat in the area known as The Pingo. Screened with bushes, access was through wicket-gates fitted with latches which made a loud click to give ample warning of intrusion.

Bulley believed that many colourful plants and flowers which were to be found in foreign countries would acclimatise themselves if planted in gardens here at home and spent a considerable fortune financing expeditions by a number of plant hunters, including famous names like George Forrest, Frank Kingdon-Ward and Reginald Farrer. From the Himalaya, Burma, China, and elsewhere they brought back thousands of specimens, the 'descendents' of which are so happily settled that a lot of people don't realise that what we think of now as a typically English garden is really half-Asiatic.

The first to go was George Forrest, an assistant in the Botanic Gardens in Edinburgh, who left for China in 1904. He spent most of the first year reconnoitring the area and learning to speak Chinese and training teams of native collectors. His method was to set up camp in a favourable area and send out small teams who brought back specimens of plants and seeds for his examination. It was a unique 'factory' method of plant-hunting and it worked well. The summer of 1905 found him staying at a French Catholic mission station in a vast mountainous area through which flowed four of the world's mightiest rivers – the Mekong, the Yangtze, the Salween and the Irrawaddy. By this time he had collected a large quantity of seeds and bulbs and nearly a thousand dried specimens when word came through that a band of marauding Tibetans had driven the Chinese troops out of a nearby town, murdered some French missionaries who were there and were now heading in their direction. It was decided to evacuate the mission and flee under cover of night. Including Forrest and his 17 collectors, a party of 80 people set out.

Out of that number only George Forrest was to survive. It took him nearly another month to reach safety after crossing a mountain range during the monsoon period and meeting glaciers and snow. He suffered a severely injured foot and kept himself from dying from starvation by eating parched barley which he picked up on the way. Despite those terrible experiences Forrest returned to the region six times in the next 25 years and, in all, he sent back home the astonishing total of over 31,000 specimens.

Some of the plants he introduced bear the name of his sponsor – like the *Primula bulleyana* and *Salvia bulleyana* – while others have been given his own name – like *Primula forrestii* and the *Iris forrestii*. But perhaps the most famous of all is the *Pieris formosa forrestii*. This shrub with its strikingly vivid scarlet bracts in May does well on the west coast and at Ness there is a superb specimen which I never fail to stop and marvel at. It was raised from the actual seed sent back by Forrest and it is an admirable memorial to this astonishing man.

Arthur Bulley died in 1942 and during the war years, with the staff much depleted, the garden became neglected. In fact, it was often down to just a couple of men, one of whom was the head gardener, Josiah Hope. He began work there in 1911 and lived into his nineties and never wholly retired. In 1948 Miss A.L. Bulley presented the house and the estate, together with an endowment of £75,000, to the University of Liverpool to be maintained as a practical and fitting tribute to the memory of her father. She stipulated, as her father would have wished, that a certain acreage should always be open to the public.

In the 30 years since the University took over – and especially in the 20 years since the present Director, Kenneth Hulme, arrived on the scene – the gardens have been extended and transformed. Now covering some 60 acres and superbly landscaped, they are not only beautiful, but as everything is carefully labelled they also provide a living horticultural encyclopaedia of great interest to anyone who has ever held a hoe or pulled a weed.

BURTON AND PUDDINGTON

Of all the 'natural' villages in the Wirral (as opposed to the purpose-built) Burton is probably the most visited by sight-seers and Puddington arguably the least. Burton is firmly established on the route of the day-out motorist as he passes through on the way to Ness Gardens and/or Parkgate for the ice-cream climax to the trip. Not so many bother to turn off and have a look at the little hamlet at the end of Puddington Lane. From the inside of a car there is not a lot to see, unlike Burton where the street of ancient and picturesque cottages can be taken in at a glance.

The way to see the village properly, of course, is to get out and walk about, but you may not find it easy to park your car. There is not much parking-space, but this is a deficiency which ensures that it does not become over-run and spoiled. That Burton today is still such an attractive place is no accident. It is no mere chance that the pink and white sandstone thatched cottages, some of them 400 and even 500 years old, are still standing and a delight to the eye. Three of them are actually cruck cottages and there are not many of those about.

The fact is that Burton, in the main, has been taken over by the professional classes (including half a dozen architects) who have spent a lot of money on the restoration of individual houses. And though some purists may mutter that it has lost its authenticity and that what is olde worlde on the outside should not be all mod. con. within, where would Burton be now if these people had not come?

For some reason Burton does not share Puddington's distinction of being included in Domesday Book, but in its early days the manor belonged to the church and was part of the see of Coventry and Lichfield. In the middle ages it became the biggest place in Wirral with a population of about 250, and in the thirteenth century a market was held here every Thursday with a three-day fair on the feast of St James.

In the fourteenth century when the waters of the Dee were nearer, Burton was also a port, but its maritime era was ended by the ever-advancing silt and the building of the New Quay at Neston. It gradually regressed into a small agricultural village and took on something of the appearance it still has. Approaching from the Ness end, the first cottage on the left in the single street is bigger than most of the others and probably the most photographed. This is not only because it is beautifully restored and attractively thatched, but it was here that Thomas Wilson, the famed Bishop of Sodor and Man, was born in 1663.

He was the fifth child in the family of a yeoman farmer and at the age of 23 he became a minister of the church. He also became tutor to the son of the then Earl of Derby, a post he held for six years, and he so impressed his Lordship that when the Isle of Man bishopric became vacant he gave him the job. At 29 he was a very young bishop and he served for a very long time. He held the post for 58 years, constantly refusing to leave the island and accept better sees offered to him at various times by King William and Queen Anne. When he died in March 1775 he was 93. He wrote a number of books and came to be described by Dean Farrer (of *Eric, or Little by Little* fame) as 'the last survivor of the Saints of the English church'. With his son, who became the Prebendary of Westminster, he established a school in Burton 'for the free education of the Burton boys and girls and four from Puddington whose parents should be unable to pay for their learning' – with the added proviso that 'scholars are not admitted till able to read'.

The school building is still there today on a rocky outcrop at the entrance to the village and was in use until the modern primary school was built in Puddington Lane. It is now a private residence.

From 1775 until his death in 1782 the manor of Burton was leased to the Reverend Richard Congreve, of Congreve, Staffordshire. In 1806 it was purchased from the church authorities by his son, also named Richard, and down the years since then Burton has basked in the reflected glory of this famous family.

An illustrious forebear was the Restoration playwright, William Congreve, who was famous for his bawdy comedies, and two later Congreves, father and son, were both awarded the Victoria Cross. Colonel Walter Congreve won his VC for attempting to save the guns at Colenso during the Boer War in 1899 while his son, Major William La Touche Congreve, won his VC for gallantry displayed at St Eloi in Flanders in 1916. Curiously, the elder Congreve won his Victoria Cross in part for saving the life of Lieutenant Roberts, son of Field-Marshal Roberts, VC. The Lieutenant survived also to win a VC, so that the Roberts and the Congreves are two out of only three families in history where both father and son have won the supreme decoration.

Richard Congreve built a mansion for himself at the end of the village where the view was best, right opposite Bishop Wilson's cottage. He called it Burton Hall and it stayed in his family until 1902 when it was sold to a member of another distinguished family, Henry Gladstone, third son of *the* Mr Gladstone.

Two years after buying it Henry Gladstone had the house completely remodelled and enlarged and it became Burton Manor. Today that is a name which hundreds, even thousands, of people throughout the north-west and even beyond hold in great esteem and not a little affection. As Burton Manor for Adult Education it is a venue for courses of learning lasting for a day, two days, a week-end or a week, ranging from acupuncture to zoology and every subject in between, from the commonplace to the esoteric. There are few who go there who do not come away singing its praises and many return time and time again.

Burton's church, dedicated to St Nicholas, stands on a sloping site protectively overlooking the village and set against the deep green backcloth of Burton Woods. It is located on a site where there has been a church since Saxon times, though the present building with its tall square tower and one-handed clock dates only from 1721. A double-naved building, it has a number of interesting possessions on show including a tiny book of prayers and meditations in Bishop Wilson's own handwriting and a first edition of John Foxe's *Book of Martyrs*. Bound in leather with brass corners it was printed in London in 1562–3.

In the path which runs through the woods behind the church are two sandstone flags carefully railed off to preserve them from the wear and tear of unknowing feet. As a plaque on the wall explains, these are the graves of a Quaker couple dating from 1663 who were presumably denied burial in the consecrated churchyard.

The 20 acres of woodland behind the church belong to the National Trust and were donated by Mr and Mrs Bulley in 1928. It was an act of generosity which may well have saved Burton from a fate akin to Upton or Irby's. Whilst the trees have long served as a screen sheltering the village from the chillier east winds, today they form a bulwark against the insidious developer. As it is they have come as close as they can and immediately the woods peter out there is an invasive line of modern houses and bungalows.

In Station Road, which leads from the village to the marshes and what was once Burton railway station, is another piece of woodland, no more than a small dell, which has also been preserved for posterity, this time as a memorial to a man whose name was revered in the village. Councillor Horace Green died in 1937 at the age of 87 having served as Burton's local government representative for 28 years. He was also an outstanding botanist on whom the University of Liverpool bestowed an honorary MA degree. This delightfully landscaped garden incorporates the old village well, or Hampston's Well as it became known, and which is thought to have existed as far back as the Iron Age. The earliest written reference to it found so far in 1602/3 shows that the Constable of Burton was charged with cleaning the well each year and that all able-bodied men of the village were required to help under pain of a fine of six pence – and nearly 400 years ago when pennies were of silver that was no token penalty.

Puddington may not be as pretty as Burton, but it is a pleasant place with a tiny triangular village green which, more than once, has proudly borne a sign proclaiming it to be 'CHESHIRE'S BEST KEPT VILLAGE'. And what it may lack in aesthetic appeal it makes up for in its history, mainly due to the activities of the Massey family who lived at Puddington Hall.

The old Massey house is now called Puddington *Old* Hall to distinguish it from a second Puddington Hall which was built about

1760 but which was all but destroyed by a great fire in 1867, only two wings escaping.

The Masseys generally were a feuding, fighting, fearless lot. As far back as the thirteenth century a Hamon de Massey fought on the French side at Poitiers against Edward, the Black Prince, and though captured was granted a pardon. His son, John, fought in the French wars and was knighted for his services, but met his death at the Battle of Shrewsbury in 1403. His son is not recorded as taking part in any wars but he carried on a most unneighbourly ten-year feud with the Hockenhull family of Shotwick despite being bound over several times to keep the peace. The last of the direct line was William Massey, a devout Roman Catholic and Jacobite, who took part in the Battle of Preston in 1715 against the Royalists. When the Jacobites were obviously on the point of defeat Massey mounted his horse and, successfully making his way through the enemy lines, rode as fast as his beast would carry him to the shores of the Mersey. Somewhere near Hale where the estuary was shallowest, and at low tide was even fordable, he crossed into Wirral and made his way to Puddington. Sadly, the long dash proved too much for his horse which, legend has it, delivered its master and dropped dead.

Unfortunately, it was not all over for Massey, either. Word got round that he was home and he was soon apprehended and imprisoned in Chester Castle where he died a few months later.

It is something to wonder at that in these days these two neighbouring villages remain so little spoiled. Those marshy wastes, for instance, have long been regarded as a challenge to generations of planners, who feel that leaving them to the birds is not good enough. Various schemes have been drawn up to reclaim vast acres and one at least was actually put in train. There were once lofty sandstone cliffs at Burton Point, but last century the stone was cut away to reclaim the stretch of marshland up to Shotwick. They misjudged the force of the tides and the embankment slowly crumbled and disappeared.

Later, there was a plan to build an embankment from Burton across to Connah's Quay and establish a Wirral and Connah's Quay Junction Railway to bring stone and slate across from Wales. And less than ten years ago came yet another plan to build a barrage with a six-lane motorway, together with huge reservoirs and facilities for boating, swimming, fishing, and sailing, and car parks for thousands of people. The plan is still extant but, happily, the scheme is so grandiose and costly that Burton residents are not losing sleep over it at the moment.

A few years ago, however, a more immediate threat to Burton was staved off at the very last moment. A Nottingham firm bought three vacant farms in the area with the intention of establishing a broiler factory which would rear no less than $7\frac{1}{2}$ million chickens a year. To the consternation of the villagers the old Neston UDC gave planning permission despite the fact that the firm wanted to erect enormous broiler houses which would not only be a blot on the pastoral scene but would bring a constant flow of lorries through the village.

The subsequent outcry from the residents, backed with impressive documentary evidence of what such a development had meant elsewhere, brought decisive action by the Cheshire County Council which revoked the planning order and bought up the three farms.

SHOTWICK

If ever you are seized with an uncontrollable urge to get away from the twentieth century, and yet know that you cannot afford to let such a feeling be anything other than transitory, then go to Shotwick. An hour there will do you the world of good. This little hamlet with a population of just 28, half a mile off the busy Two Mills–Queensferry road, is almost unbelievably out-of-time, as though some all-powerful hand had brought it to a halt 300 years ago. Only a public telephone kiosk and what looks like a modern bungalow but is actually an ancient cottage newly-renovated, serve to show that it is an illusion. In the unreal quietness of the place, as you look upon the ancient church and the venerable manor house and the old cottages, the feel of history will enter your bones.

The village has no shop, no Post Office, no school (at the time of writing only the vicar's son is of school age), no buses grind up and down its narrow lane and electricity only arrived in the mid-fifties.

There was once an inn called *The Greyhound*, but this was closed down for the same reason that Bidston lost its Ring O' Bells – an excess of drunkenness on the Sabbath.

It was not, however, the villagers who over-indulged but the Irish farm labourers from the farms on the other side of the Welsh border just three miles away. Denied a drink by the Welsh licensing laws which closed all pubs on Sundays, they tramped over the fields to the nearest English pub at Shotwick. There they imbibed as though wreaking vengeance on the puritanical Welsh and the inevitable drunken disturbances brought about the closure of the pub in 1915. It is now a private home.

For all its rustic air Shotwick was nevertheless once a place of some importance. A mile away stood Shotwick Castle, said to have been built by Hugh Lupus himself as the first of a line of fortresses intended to protect his Cheshire domain from the persistently marauding Welsh. Sulley suggests that this stronghold even replaced an earlier one built by the Saxons to defend themselves from the Danes and reproduces a ground plan drawn about 1680 showing a building roughly hexagonal in shape. Today only the earthworks on which it stood remain.

The village itself was established at a point where there was a Ford across the Dee to Flint and it is believed that this was the main trading route from England into North Wales long before the Normans came. It later became an important military highway and as Chester declined as a port Shotwick also took over that role. Thus, kings, barons, and knights met at the castle to assemble armies and plan campaigns against the Welsh and to subjugate the Irish. It was from here that Henry II set sail to bring Ireland under English rule. Henry III led a great army across the ford into Wales in 1245 and Edward I made the crossing in 1278 and again in 1284.

Shotwick's reign as a port lasted for about a hundred years before the water became too shallow and the shipping moved downstream to Burton. The ford, however, remained the recognised route from Cheshire into Wales and continued in use throughout the eighteenth century. That careful diarist, Nicholas Blundell, Squire of Ince Blundell, the little West Lancashire village on the main road between Crosby and Formby, records that on 26 June 1707: 'My wife, Mr Plumb, and I came from Holywell over Shotwigg Ford. It was very deep'. He went to Holywell again in 1721, crossing the ford on 8 July, returning on the 10 July: 'We came from Holywell to Flint, thence to Shotwick where I rode over without a Guide & came back again with one to fetch my wife over'.

That suggests the ford was not without its hazards and it speaks well of Squire Blundell that he was unwilling to risk his wife making the crossing without a guide.

The hamlet is dominated by St Michael's Church which stands guardian facing out across the Dee, except that the Dee is not there any more. When Shotwick was a port the waters of the estuary lapped the churchyard walls (and there is at least one iron securing ring left in the wall to prove it). Now the water cannot even be seen from ground level. Not only is the view obscured and disfigured by the unlovely sight of Shotton steelworks, but beyond the village there is now three miles of flat farmland.

When that attempt was made to restore Chester's maritime fortunes by canalising the river in 1735 (so ruining Hoylake in the process, you remember) one beneficial result was that thousands of acres of 'sea-land' were reclaimed between Chester and Shotwick. Which is how Sealand got its name and Shotwick became a farming area.

Nobody knows how long there has been a church at Shotwick. It certainly goes back to Domesday and possibly for another hundred years before that but the present building is, relatively speaking, fairly new. The massive, fortress-like tower is thought to date from the sixteenth century but the rest dates only from 1871 when a vast restoration took place. Happily, the restorers left intact that which was still in a reasonable state, including some fragments of fourteenth-century stained glass and the Norman doorway – all that remains of the first post-Conquest church.

The porch was added later and in its time is said to have served as a schoolroom (not many children even then, obviously) and, until the sixteenth century, as a place where marriages were solemnised (did the guests sit on the tombstones?).

In fact the porch seems to have played a prominent part in Shotwick life at all times. It was evidently the place where the menfolk gathered in their idler moments to gossip and discuss the things that mattered, just as in other places they gathered round the village pump or the cross. In the stonework are deep vertical furrows which were caused by the sharpening of arrows while the chit-chat flowed, for there was a time when all men were legally obliged to practice archery at the butts every Sunday after church. Some may also have been caused by one or other of the king's companies of archers while they waited at Shotwick for the right tide and fair weather conditions before embarkation.

Inside the church (and it is a proud boast of the villagers that it is always open) there are rare box pews and an even rarer three-decker pulpit, but I found that superabundance of dark woodwork tended to give it a solemn and sombre air. The pulpit (and possibly the box pews, too) came from a Chester church in 1812. The bottom deck of the pulpit was for the clerk who recited the responses to the prayers said by the parson in the middle deck, while the top deck was used by the clergyman preaching the sermon.

In the early years of the seventeenth century the incumbent was the celebrated Dr Samuel Clarke. He was appointed to Shotwick at the age of 25 and stayed for five memorable years during which the quality of his preaching was such that crowds came flocking from miles around to hear him. Holding strong Puritan views acquired whilst he was at Cambridge he was eventually compelled to leave the parish to answer charges in the Chancellor's Court that he had flagrantly omitted recognised church ceremonies. His persistent non-conformity made him many enemies among the more orthodox clergy and in 1662 he was forced to give up his ministry. Nevertheless, he continued to attend his own church as a member of the congregation and devoted the rest of his life to writing. He produced some 15 books and died a highly-respected figure at the age of 83 in 1682.

Shotwick Church today could not be sustained or even justified in a village of little more than two dozen inhabitants, but fortunately it not only attracts a congregation from beyond the village boundaries but holds a place in the affections of people even further afield. In 1971 when an appeal was launched to save the building from the ravages of wet and dry rot and to arrest the deterioration of the stonework the response was so good that there was enough left over to restore the organ as well.

It is heart-warming to report, too, that Shotwick Hall, the manor house, is in good hands and good heart. The hall was built by Joseph Hockenhull in 1662 to replace another building a few yards away and is a picturesque red-brick, gabled house typical of its period. Built in the shape of an E, it stands at the end of Shotwick's only other lane just before it peters out into the footpath to Puddington. The manor came into the Hockenhull family in the reign of Edward I when Cecily de Shotwicke married Richard de Hockenhull. It remained in Hockenhull hands until the mid-eighteenth century when, to repay debts, it was sold to Samuel Bennett of nearby Great Saughall. He, in turn, bequeathed it to his great-nephew, John Nevitt who promptly added the name of Bennett to his own. The Nevitt-Bennetts retained the whole estate until quite recently when, on the failure of the direct line, the village and some 600 acres passed to a nephew, Mr R.B. Gardner of Sevenoaks, Kent.

NINE

The Purpose-built Villages

Bromborough Pool, Port Sunlight, Thornton Hough

BROMBOROUGH POOL

It might well be argued that the little village of Bromborough Pool is more unexpected than any of those I have mentioned in the last chapter. It is not on any through route and, unless on business thereabouts, few ever come upon it unexpectedly. Like Shotwick it has to be sought out, only more so. And what's more it is located in a most unexpected place, right in the middle of an industrial cosmos, surrounded on all sides by factories and sheds, and great round storage tanks, and railway sidings, and concrete walls embroidered with barbed wire. Yet to come upon it for the first time is an eye-opener. Orderly streets of neat, well-kept houses, a football pitch and a bowling green, a neat little church in the Early English style and a round-roofed village hall.

To get there look for the sign-post off the New Chester Road, more or less opposite Port Sunlight.

In 1964 the village seemed doomed when it was announced that it had been zoned for future industrial expansion. Subsequently about a third of the houses were demolished as they became vacant. Happily, there has been a change of heart and the rest of the village is safe. Many people know it better as Price's Village for it was established in 1853 for the workers of the new northern factory of Price's Patent Candle Company of Battersea. That was 35 years before William Lever arrived to build Port Sunlight.

The men behind the village were not Londoners, however, but Scots. James and George Wilson were directors of the candle-making firm which their father, William Wilson, had founded. The Wilsons came from a well-known and once-prosperous family in Lanarkshire. In the late seventeen-hundreds iron-ore was discovered on some land they had recently purchased and three sons of the family, Robert, John and William, established an ironworks to produce pipes and rods and other cast-iron items, including cannon balls for use in the Napoleonic Wars. This had meant bringing labour out of the towns into the countryside so they had to provide accommodation. They also built a small school for the children, and though it was by no means a comprehensive village it became known as Wilsontown.

John Wilson had a son, also named William, who had emigrated to Russia and set himself up in business in St Petersburg but as the ironworks flourished he was persuaded to return home and help in its running.

But the need to modernise the works towards the end of the century proved too much of a financial burden and in 1808 the business collapsed. It was sold and the sum realised was not even sufficient to pay off the debts. William took himself off to London and making use of his knowledge of the Russian trade set up in business as a Russian broker and was successful. Then one day in 1830 he met a man who had devised a way of separating coconut oil into its solid and liquid parts and he bought the process from him. The solid proved to be a substitute for tallow in the making of candles and not only gave a much better light but a much-reduced smell.

In partnership with a Mr Lancaster, William Wilson set up a company to manufacture these 'patent' candles and, for some unknown reason, they chose to trade under the name of 'E. Price', borrowed from one of Lancaster's aunts. It has been suggested that neither of the partners wanted their names overtly connected with the tough world of industry (what about the ironworks?) but I feel it could just have been modesty on both their parts.

Lancaster eventually withdrew in favour of a venture in Ceylon and sold his interests to three sleeping partners, leaving the candle factory effectively in the control of William Wilson and his two sons, James and George, who had since joined him. It prospered and in 1847 it became a joint-stock company under the title of Price's Patent Candle Company.

From the outset, the Wilson brothers took more than an ordinary interest in the welfare of their workers. As devout Christians (and James was very devout) they believed that they had a moral obligation to guide their employees along the paths of righteousness and a general responsibility for improving their lot in any way they could.

The start of work every day was preceded by a ten-minute service, with five minutes 'donated' by the company from the working hours and five minutes 'given' by the workers out of their midday meal break. They also organised lessons in the three R's for a few of their youngest employees. The instructor was one of the foremen and the lessons took place in a room in the works – after hours. The boys were so enthusiastic that the original half dozen grew to around 30 and a special classroom was built for them. Later, this evening class was supplemented by a day class of boys who had been laid off from the works during slack periods.

In 1849 Price's bought out a night-light manfacturer who employed many boys and girls and soon separate boys' and girls' schools had been established.

The Battersea factory was not in the most salubrious area and in 1849 it was smitten with an epidemic of cholera. The Wilsons were told by a doctor that the best preventive measure for their workers was fresh air and exercise, so they closed down the schools temporarily and rented a field in the nearest countryside. On one part of it, James organised games of cricket on three evenings a week (ending with a few prayers on the pitch after stumps were drawn) and on the other part brother George, a keen horticulturalist (whose house at Wisley in Surrey eventually became the trial grounds of the Royal Horticultural Society), established allotment gardens. Further social benefits followed. There were factory outings (at the firm's expense) and a Mutual Improvement Society 'to promote the intellectual, moral and social advancement of its members by means of instruction and intellectual recreation'. In due course, a full-time works chaplain was appointed and he combined the functions of minister of religion (taking over the 5.45 am pre-work service), welfare officer, teacher and cricket coach.

By this time thoughts had turned towards expanding the business with a second factory, but not in the already-congested, run-down area of Battersea. Not even in London, but out in the countryside where the air was fresh and clean. Two factors had already suggested to the Wilsons that the new works should be somewhere in Merseyside. At the Great Exhibition of 1851 they had done a deal with a French firm whereby they acquired the French patent for making an improved textile lubricant (or 'cloth oil') in exchange for Price's particular method of distillation of fats and oils. As a result the supply of cloth oil to the northern textile mills became an increasingly important part of their business and it made sense that their factory should be within easy reach. The second factor was that Liverpool was the chief importing centre for West African palm oil, their main material.

After looking at various sites along the Wirral shore of the Mersey they found what they were seeking on the southern side of Bromborough Pool, just north of an already existing hamlet. This was known as Magazines Village, just a few houses which accommodated the families of men who worked on the powder magazines, three wooden hulks moored off-shore, in which gunpowder was stored for export. They were used for this purpose until shortly after the end of the World War II and the last remaining houses were demolished in 1971.

It was clear from the outset that if they were to build their factory in such an out-of-the-way spot they would have to provide accommodation for their employees as their father and his brothers had done in Wilsontown. But with all the experience gained at Battersea to guide them they were determined not just to build rudimentary houses but to establish a proper village community in which the residents could enjoy a good, uplifting, healthy and intellectually-satisfying life.

The land belonged to the Lord of the Manor of Bromborough who rejoiced in the name of Salusbury Kynaston Mainwaring. At first he would only agree to releasing the land long-term, but the Wilsons wanted freehold rights and deadlock seemed to have been reached when a timely article about the whole project appeared in the influential *Quarterly Review*. Mainwaring happened to read it and was so impressed he not only agreed to sell the land outright, but allowed them to purchase a further 19 acres which they found they needed. The price paid for the land was £12,267 10s. and construction work began immediately after signing the contract on 2 August 1853.

The village was built in stages as the finances of the company allowed. To begin with there was just one street, York Street, of 32 houses consisting of four blocks on each side of the road. Larger and more soundly constructed than the average artisan house of the day, they also had small gardens front and rear (George's influence) and – a real advance – water-borne sanitation.

The first residents were key-workers from Battersea who were needed to train locally-recruited workers and get the factory into operation.

In those early days, of course, there were no shops or school or any other amenities. The nearest places of any note were Bromborough and New Ferry, both two miles away in different directions, while Birkenhead was an hour or more's walk along the New Chester Road.

Elementary education for the children was undertaken by a Mrs Cowderay in the front room of her house at No. 5 York Street and for shopping the new 'villagers' had to rely on itinerant tradesmen. Later, a schoolroom was provided in the factory itself by hiving off one end of a building with a canvas wall and a shop was opened in a garden shed. This, in fact, was a village co-operative and, in due course, became the Industrial Provident Society which paid a dividend to its members.

As more houses were built and the population rose a start was made on providing social, educational and recreational facilities. Part of the land was laid out as allotment gardens for which the residents paid a rent of 6d. a year. They were so enthusiastic about growing-their-own that many a man would spend every evening on his plot and even put in a couple of hours before starting work in the morning at 6 am.

A feature of the village was – and still is – the large Green on which a cricket pitch and bowling green were laid and children's swings provided; and in 1858, by which time there were 76 houses and a population of 460, a proper school was opened.

One of the earliest societies formed was The Mutual Improvement Society (in imitation of the one at Battersea) the objects of which clearly reflected the interests of James, the more aesthetic of the two brothers. They were 'to promote generally the intellectual, moral and social advancement of the members' and its activities took several forms. Part of the factory Iron House was equipped as a reading room and classes for reading and writing were held there on four evenings a week, with two of the foremen as tutors. Later, the Society's syllabus expanded to include 'Penny Readings', lectures on a wide variety of topics, and, eventually, light orchestral concerts.

About five years after the foundation of the village, however, the company hit a bad patch and ran into financial difficulty. A committee of shareholders was formed to review company costs and were concerned to discover that the amount spent on building the village in the first year alone had come to £142,000. Nor were they pleased to learn that £40,700 had been spent on religious and educational instruction between the years 1852–1856. The brothers were rebuked: 'It is not the business of the company to promote Christianity'. The result of this admonition was that James and George immediately offered their resignations, but these were not accepted, the shareholders wisely recognising that the firm could not carry on without them, but it did bring all building work in the village to a halt.

There was, in fact, a space of 12 years between the construction of the first stage and the second. Building restarted in 1872 and went on for another six years until, once again, the firm ran into financial trouble. This time it was 20 years before they were in a position to continue and this third phase lasted until 1901. By this time the village had a purpose-built school (under the headmistresship of a Miss Humble who, when the need arose, would send for the Assistant Works Manager to administer corporal punishment), a church, a village hall, a hospital for infectious diseases, and a total of 142 houses. The population was 728. The houses built last were more spacious than the rest and may well have been influenced by the sight of those which were by now being built in nearby Port Sunlight.

The village enjoyed a particularly lively community life, bolstered no doubt by its comparative isolation and certainly by the encouragement given by its founders. The societies which were established ranged from the Mutual Improvement to the Fur and Feather Society, and particularly successful were the Horticultural Society, the Village Band, and the football and cricket clubs. The Horticultural Society promoted an annual flower and vegetable show from its inception and one is still held every summer in the village hall. It has long passed its centenary and is certainly the oldest annual show in the Wirral and must be one of the oldest in the land.

The Silver Band flourished for 82 years until 1938, when shift work made it impossible to get sufficient numbers together at any one time for rehearsals. In its time it had enlivened the village scene with concerts in the village hall in the winter and on The Green in the summer and always led the procession of the Rose Queen at the annual carnival.

The cricket club enjoyed enormous success against teams from all over Merseyside. Their superb pitch on The Green gave hundreds of spectators who turned up to watch the Sunday afternoon matches an uninterrupted panoramic view of the Mersey and the Liverpool shore from Garston to the Dingle and even beyond. It was an idyllic setting but, as happened with Birkenhead's little priory, the unfeeling demands of industry eventually blotted out the scene. In 1932 an immense embankment, 6500 yards long, was raised in connection with the Bromborough Dock scheme and as the waters of the Pool were pushed back the village found itself well inland. On the reclaimed land in between a storage tank depot was built to the north and to the east more factory buildings went up. The Green, although completely encircled now, is still fine and spacious, with the pleasant aspect of the church and village hall to the south and the view to the west graced by some fine Georgian-style houses which were built for some of the works managers.

For a time the football club played their matches on The Green, but they moved several times and now occupy a pitch at the entrance to the village adjoining the sports and social club. The football team were, if anything, even more successful than the cricket team and in the 1870's they even played a match against Everton. (In my delvings I've come across mention of this several times, but how and why it came about or who won and what the score was is never stated. I hope this reticence does not mean they were trounced!)

Both cricket and football teams still flourish, but few of the present members actually live in the village.

James Wilson died in 1890, living just long enough to see the church erected, and his brother, George, died in 1902. At that time the company was yet again experiencing some difficulties posed by the supplanting of the humble candle by the incandescent gas mantle and the arrival of electric light. The recession had its effect on the village and no more houses were built after that date.

A new and larger school had been erected in 1899 and a new Infectious Diseases Hospital in 1901. During the 1914–1918 war it had been used as a military hospital and in 1921 it was turned into a maternity unit. In 1941 it suffered severe blast damage from two bombs which landed nearby during an air raid and the patients were all transferred to Clatterbridge. That marked the end of its life as a hospital and later in the war it was converted into a sports and social club, a role it fills to this day.

The only additions to the village this century have been the war memorial, tennis courts and a pavilion, and a new bowling green.

With the virtual passing of candlepower, the manufacture of night lights and candles was concentrated at Battersea and the Bromborough Pool works went in for the production of oils and fatty acids. In 1937 the firm became part of the Unilever organisation and the name was changed to Price's (Bromborough) Limited. Lately the name has been changed again to Unichema Limited. It is not an easy name to pronounce at first sight and it will be a generation or two yet before the workers stop calling it 'Price's'.

All that remains now of the original factory is a small building with a clock tower. When the village finally disappears I hope they will have the sensibility to leave this standing as a reminder of a great Victorian social experiment and a memorial to the Wilsons.

PORT SUNLIGHT

For William Hesketh Lever, the first Viscount Leverhulme, making soap and making money was far from the be-all and end-all of his life, but from the money he made from soap he was able to indulge his real passions. Though he enjoyed big business and the excitement of planning and organising, there still remained an early boyhood desire to become an architect. Time and time again it manifested itself in some guise or other. Everything created or built in the Lever name, whether it was factories or workers' houses, or his own several stately homes and their gardens, bore his personal imprint. He was never happier than when poring over maps and plans and dreaming up new buildings, or alterations and extensions to old ones. During his lifetime he lived in a dozen different houses and every single one of them was altered to suit his taste and requirements. He built houses for crofters on the Hebridean Isle of Lewis and plantation villages for native workers on his Belgian Congo estates. But his greatest achievement was Port Sunlight – the factory itself and the deservedly world-famous model village adjoining with its unique and beautiful Lady Lever Art Gallery.

Lever came to this area of the Wirral after failing to find a suitable site for a factory in the immediate vicinity of Warrington where he was then located. He sought the help of a Warrington architect, William Owen, and after poring over Ordnance Survey Sheets they decided to look at the undeveloped land around Bromborough Pool just to the north of Price's.

It could not have been more unpromising. It was an area of near-marshland and muddy creeks, dank and desolate, and liable to flooding at high tides, with a slimy tributary of the Pool snaking through it. Nevertheless, Lever had the example of the Wilson's candle factory to show what could be done and his lively imagination could see the possibilities. It was flat and could be drained and he could foresee ships bringing his raw materials right up the Mersey to a wharf in the Pool, beyond Liverpool and the iniquitously heavy dock dues levied by the Mersey Docks and Harbour Board. Similarly, he would be able to load his finished products straight from the factory onto coastal vessels and be less dependent on the railways which tended to fix their transport rates in the knowledge that they had a monopoly.

Within a few months 56 acres of land had been purchased at a cost of £200 an acre from Thomas Green (great-grandfather of Roger Lancelyn Green). On 3 March 1888 a party of invited guests gathered on the Liverpool landing-stage and crossed over the Mersey by steamer to New Ferry where they transferred to a steam barge which took them up the tidal creek to the site. There 36-year-old Lever handed a silver spade to his wife and invited her to cut the first sod, saying: 'I have the greatest pleasure in presenting to her this implement of peace with which we, as Lancashire men, invade Cheshire.'

William Lever's excitement at the prospect before him can be imagined. The suppressed architect within him could be given free rein. And he knew exactly what he wanted. A model factory and a model village with

> 'houses in which our workpeople will be able to live and be comfortable; houses with gardens back and front, and in which they will be able to know more about the science of life than they can in a back slum, and in which they will learn that there is more enjoyment to life than in the mere going to and returning from work'.

The same sentiments, of course, which motivated the brothers Wilson.

The rough lay-out of both the factory and the village was Lever's own work; he was the master planner. William Owen and the other architects who were involved later designed the buildings and houses to accord with his wishes. Of the original 56 acres of land bought, 24 were allocated to the factory and 32 for housing. The building of Port Sunlight village began in December 1889 with 28 houses designed by William Owen in a road named Bolton Road after Lever's birthplace. By the turn of the century the number of houses had grown to over 400 and more and more land was acquired until the village reached its present size of 130 acres, forming a rectangle one mile long and a third of a mile wide. At the end of its second decade Port Sunlight village had nearly 800 houses and a population of about 4000 with facilities better than those of many a town. To the employees lucky enough to be living there within a few minutes walk of their place of work it must have seemed near-Utopian.

The houses, of high quality and carefully maintained by the firm, were in beautiful landscaped surroundings and of a density of only seven to the acre when building regulations allowed 45. There were no educational problems. Two large schools accommodated over 3000 pupils and a Technical Institute provided a three-year evening course for 500 students. There was also a library and a museum.

In times of sickness the villagers could call on the services of an air-conditioned cottage hospital with a resident doctor and four nurses. Their shopping needs were met by a large general store run by an employees' provident society, a post office, a butcher, a draper, a hairdresser and a newsagent.

There was a men's dining and recreation hall where 800 men could eat their dinners (no meals were provided, but the staff could cook or warm up the men's own food), and a large self-service canteen which catered for nearly 2000 women workers. Both these halls were also used for meetings, dances and concerts.

There was also a heated, open-air swimming pool, a gymnasium and a bandstand for al fresco concerts.

But no village is complete without a pub and one was provided in Port Sunlight – but from the customer's point of view it was a sham. The Bridge Inn, looking like an elegant old coaching house, was built round three sides of a forecourt and when it opened in 1900 it did so as a *temperance* hotel! Doubtless in the knowledge that their employer was a strict teetotaller, it was a couple of years before some of the residents plucked up enough courage to ask that it should be licensed. Privately, Lever did not like the idea but he arranged for a referendum of the residents to be held. The result was an eighty per cent vote in favour and their request was granted.

The general theme of the Port Sunlight houses is old English black and white with a wealth of half-timbering, but French, Flemish, and German influences can be seen in those houses built up to 1905. After that they become more English in character, albeit still with continental touches in many cases. The particular charm and attraction of Port Sunlight owes much to this and the fact that the houses were not all designed by the same hand nor built in facing rows a road at a time. William Owen was joined by his son, Segar Owen, in designing the second block, but over the years as the village grew a score or more architects were employed.

The scene is further enhanced by spacious lawns and trees, and well cared-for flower beds so that attractive vistas are revealed at almost every turn. Additionally, most of the houses are also fronted by unfenced grass plots which are always kept immaculately trimmed so that the generously-wide roads look even wider.

The village church was built at the personal expense of Lord Leverhulme himself and not of the company. It was designed by William and Segar Owen and was built in the years 1902–4. Leverhulme was himself a Congregationalist and the church was put into the trusteeship of the Congregational Union of England and Wales and there was a Congregational minister. Nevertheless, he stipulated that it should be interdenominational. Built of local red sandstone, it has a stone-slated roof and its finely appointed interior has a wealth of rich oak timber work and seats 800.

The church is Lord Leverhulme's last resting-place and he deserved somewhere rather special. He lived a comfortable life and was able to indulge his tastes, it is true, but he worked hard and thousands of people in different parts of the globe were better off for all he did. His tomb and that of his son, the second Viscount, and their wives is in the narthex at the north end. The church also contains bronze effigies of both Leverhulme and his wife, Lady Lever, sculpted by Sir William Goscombe John, RA.

Goscombe John was also the designer and sculptor of Port Sunlight's war memorial. Situated right at the heart of the village, the figures are of bronze set on a granite base and it is a most impressive work fit to be a national monument. Its theme is 'the defence of the home' and three soldiers, one of them wounded, are depicted protecting groups of women and children. Ringing the base are relief panels of more children and figures, male and female, representing various groups of the armed forces. Most war memorials are merely things of stone or metal accorded a dutiful but brief recognition once a year on Remembrance Sunday. This one is a work of art to be marvelled at the whole year round. Whenever I see it I seldom come away unmoved.

The first Lord Leverhulme rose to success and greatness through a combination of hard work, business acumen, courage, and – as he fully and publicly acknowledged – the unwavering love and devotion of his wife.

When he was six years old his father, a wholesale grocer in Bolton, sent him to the Misses Aspinwalls' private school across the road from their home in Wood Street and among the pupils was a draper's daughter, Elizabeth Hulme. She became William Lever's childhood sweetheart. When she was 12 her family moved to Southport, but the Levers and the Hulmes exchanged frequent visits so that they were never entirely parted. As they grew into their teens visits and outings were engineered, letters were surreptitiously exchanged, and gradually a courtship developed. William, however, was constantly nagged by a doubt that Elizabeth's parents might not consider him good enough for their daughter. But when he reached the age of 21 his father made him a partner in the business at the then princely salary of £800 a year and he felt sufficiently emboldened to propose marriage to Elizabeth and make a formal approach to her now widowed mother. Mrs Hulme had never at any time had any qualms about his suitability and in December 1872 the engagement was officially announced. They were married in April 1874 at the same Congregational church in Bolton where they were both baptised and by the same pastor.

Though she was never involved in any of his business affairs, Lever nearly always took his wife with him on business trips abroad of any length. These included a trip up the Nile, a six months round-the-world tour, and a three-months-long expedition up the Congo where she was the only lady in the party. It was notoriously unhealthy territory and not the sort of place for an excursion by a white woman of over 60, but she endured the rigours of it well and Lever was unashamedly proud of her – the more so when her exploit was marked by her being elected a Fellow of the Royal Geographical Society.

Sir William and Lady Lever (as they were by this time) arrived back home in March 1913 and on the 7 July they were guests of the Earl and Countess of Derby at dinner with King George V and Queen Mary who were staying at Knowsley whilst on a tour of Lancashire. A few days later Lever left to inspect some of his associated companies in Europe and for once left behind his wife who had some social engagements to fill. He was in Marseilles when he received a telegram saying she was gravely ill with pneumonia following a chill. He rushed back home and reached her bedside on 24 July just in time for her to recognise him before she drifted into unconsciousness. She died a few hours later.

It was the end of an idyllic partnership and in a public tribute later, Lever said: 'She was essentially a womanly woman and her knowledge of business was nil . . . but I am convinced that without her great influence there would have been neither a Port Sunlight nor a Lever Brothers as we know it today. It came because of the confidence she inspired in me!

'During the whole of our married life of forty years, however early business called me, I never breakfasted alone . . . and I always knew that whatever might happen in the course of the day the great event for her would be my homecoming in the evening. The greatest inspiration to me has been the wife I was fortunate enough to win.'

This brief background serves to explain why a man should raise such a remarkable memorial to his wife as The Lady Lever Art Gallery. The treasures it contains form one of the most extensive and important private collections in the world and it was typical of Lever that he felt that the works of art which he had been fortunate to acquire and enjoy during his lifetime should be shared with the public.

The building is in the classical renaissance style and was designed by the old firm of William and Segar Owen, though it is believed that it is actually the work of Segar. It stands imposingly alone at the end of a long, wide esplanade known (for some reason which escapes me) as The Diamond. It is planned in the form of a broad-stemmed cross with slightly projecting arms and contains some 30 rooms, including a main hall 130 feet long and 25 feet wide, two circular sculpture galleries top-lighted by glass domes, and two upper galleries. And collectors of items of useless information will be interested to learn that it has a ground area slightly larger than that occupied by Westminster Abbey.

Viscount Leverhulme was the only British collector of his age who came anywhere near rivalling the prodigality of the American million-aires. He was a collector with a catholic taste, though in his early days it was generally items representing the best of British craftsmanship which took his fancy. But it all began with two dainty eighteenth-century Derby bisque figures of a shepherd and a shepherdess. This was in 1877 when Lever was 26 and managing a branch of his father's wholesale grocery business in Wigan. The two figures were bought to adorn the mantelshelf in the parlour of the small house there in which he and his wife lived. This led to a life-long interest in porcelain, but as he moved into larger houses he began to collect furniture and pictures. Moving successively into even larger houses he added bronzes and tapestries and more furniture and so his collection grew. He was not ultra-possessive about his acquisitions, as some collectors have been, and he was happy to share them with others. Some of his pictures were even hung in the dining halls of his employees for their enjoyment and, on one occasion, when he snapped up a valuable oriental porcelain collection he promptly put it all on display in Port Sunlight.

Among the treasures to be seen in the gallery are one of the best collections of Georgian furniture in the country; paintings by some of Britain's most famous artists – Turner, Gainsborough, Reynolds, Romney and Constable, – as well as some remarkable enamels by Liverpool's George Stubbs. There is a marvellous collection of Chinese pottery, porcelain, jade, hardstones, and snuff bottles; and bronze sculptures, and tapestries; and one of the finest collections of Wedgwood ware to be found anywhere, all beautifully displayed in a specially-designed Wedgwood room.

The Gallery is now under the control of the Merseyside County Council and is open six days a week from 10am to 5pm and on Sundays from 2pm to 5pm. The *Sunday Times* has described it as 'one of the most beautiful small museums in the world' and if you have never been there, go now. You are unlikely to find it crowded. Wirralians generally don't seem to realise what a gem they have in their midst.

And if, from all I have written, you get the impression that I am somewhat awe-struck by Port Sunlight as a whole then so be it. I am.

THORNTON HOUGH

The handsome village of Thornton Hough is not so much purpose-built as purpose-rebuilt. It is the handiwork of two men – Joseph Hirst, a retired woollen manfacturer from Wilshaw near Huddersfield, and the indefatigable William Hesketh Lever who moved there from Warrington soon after work commenced on the building of Port Sunlight.

It was at the time purely an agricultural village consisting mainly of thatched and limewashed cottages strung out along an unmade road. Called *Torintone* in the Domesday Book, it was held in the reign of Edward II by Roger de Thornton whose only daughter became the wife of Richard de Hough. In the course of time, the conjoined names became the name of the village.

It seems not to have played any great part in the history of Wirral and when Mortimer saw it in the eighteen-forties he reported: 'The village is built on a slight elevation, the only street of which is cut through the solid sandstone, presenting a very unpleasant appearance, and though it possesses a few tolerably good houses, the greater portion are of a very inferior description.'

Lever found that while the cottages were not unpicturesque from a distance, inside they were dark, dank, and insanitary and quite unfit for human habitation. He was appalled to find living in one which boasted only a living-room and a single bedroom, a farm labourer and his wife and their twelve children.

It was Joseph Hirst, however, who arrived on the scene first and I find it curious that not only should a dyed-in-the-wool (so to speak) Yorkshireman leave his native county to retire, but that he should have chosen, let alone discover, this little hamlet in the heart of the Wirral. But Hirst was obviously not the archetypal, careful-with-his-brass Yorkshireman, for once he had built a house for himself he set about building a school for the village children and, in the following year, the

Parish Church of All Saints and vicarage. Two years after that he paid for the building of a village shop and a row of houses. Mind you, he did import his own architect and workmen from Huddersfield.

All Hirst's good works are nicely grouped together on the crest of the village. Thornton House where he lived is hidden in the trees on the left of the approach road from Clatterbridge, and just on the rise is his shop and the row of houses which he called Wilshaw Terrace after his home town. The shop on the corner is picked out by the short round tower with a conical roof and the attractive terrace of houses leads down from this to the church.

The church itself provides one of Wirral's curiosities by having a clock with five faces. There are two faces on the north side of the tower, one above the other. The higher one was added when Hirst discovered he could not see the time from his house.

The church almost adjoins the village pub (which was always there) and which is called 'The Seven Stars'. The name has given rise to an old village joke that Thornton Hough parish church has the highest steeple in the country – because it rises above The Seven Stars. It is not a common name and I wonder how it could have come about. Since the seven stars obviously denotes The Plough and this was – and still is – agricultural country, could that have been its origin?

Apart from a modern estate built on the fringe of the village at the Neston end, the rest of Thornton Hough is nearly all Lever's. Whilst he doubtless gained satisfaction and enjoyment from planning and building it, as with Port Sunlight he was fired by the best of motives. He was one of our greatest philanthropists and expended much time and money on improving the living conditions, not only of his employees but of others in more humble circumstances, in places as far apart as the Isle of Lewis in the Hebrides to the Belgian Congo and the south Pacific.

Lever came to Thornton Hough when he managed to rent Thornton Manor from Thomas Forwood, whose son became Sir William Forward, the Liverpool shipowner. Three years later he bought the property outright and – it almost goes without saying – he straightway set about altering and enlarging it. In fact he continued to add to it and change it throughout the rest of his life so that now there is very little left of the original. What was no more than a large Victorian country house when he moved in is now a beautiful neo-Elizabethan manor with extensive grounds and gardens which – needless to say – Lever largely designed himself.

All this work proceeded in tune with the re-shaping of the village which he bought piece by piece as opportunity offered. He found some initial resistance from some of the older villagers, but this was gradually overcome as they saw the style of house he was building. They were all in the Port Sunlight style (which meant, of course, they varied greatly) and each had three to five bedrooms.

When it comes to variety of style, take a look at the terrace of houses which go to make up Numbers 1 to 7 Neston Road, opposite The Green. Here Lever and his architects have really indulged themselves. Not only do the houses themselves differ, but the rich seam of architectural embellishment has been well tapped to produce decorative brickwork, sculpted stonework, ornamental plasterwork and carved woodwork. The doors are ornamented with ironwork and the window-frames are patterned, while the architects' imagination has been allowed full reign in the design of the chimney-stacks, some of which twist delightfully like candy sticks. That possibly makes it sound ostentatious, but it is not so in fact.

Lever went on to provide all the requirements of the stereotype English village centred on a village green of most generous proportions, large enough to contain football and cricket pitches, tennis courts and (though they have now gone) a bowling green and a quoiting ground. And a pavilion with, of course, a thatched roof. At the end of Neston Road terrace he built a blacksmith's shop and he planted what has now become a beautifully spreading chestnut tree alongside.

The small Church of England school which Joseph Hirst built became inadequate and Lever, a non-conformist, provided The Lever Un-denominational Day School which is still doing duty today as Thornton Hough County Primary School. He also turned one of the larger houses into an orphanage for girls and built a Liberal Club which locals may have found a curious addition to their village. But Lever was a staunch Liberal and from 1906–1910 was actually the member of Parliament for Wirral. He later decided, however, that a club restricted to one political party in a place like Thornton Hough was inappropriate and it became The Village Club open to all.

His masterpiece is St George's Church, originally Congregational but now The United Reformed Church, which sits comfortably and benignly in a superb situation at the focal point of the village. To me, it is one of the most aesthetically satisfying churches in the Wirral. Lever's architect on this occasion was J. Lomax-Simpson but, as always, he knew what he wanted. He decided that it should be Norman in style and he and his architect went to France looking at other Norman buildings to ensure that all the detail was correct. The result is a building of local red sandstone with an interior which is warm and inviting and unpretentious. The intricate carving of the arches, the supporting columns and the window surrounds left me marvelling at the craftmen's expertise.

For someone intent on building a model English village it seems
something of a contradiction that William Lever should have had a
passion for untypically English wide, straight roads. From Thornton
Hough he built a total of five miles of what he thought of then as arterial
highway. The longest, known as Lever Causeway, runs for three-and-
a-half miles through the villages of Brimstage and Storeton to join
Storeton Road, Prenton, – though only the stretch from Prenton to
Storeton village is open to public traffic today. The road was built on a
principle which would hardly find favour with modern highway
engineers, with three carriageways, the centre being intended for fast
traffic and the two outer lanes reserved for slow vehicles. The centre was
macadamised while the 'slow' lanes were left ready for macadamising
should the need arise. The three lanes were divided one from the other
by four lanes of trees, consisting of elms, poplars and sycamores. He also
built another road running for just over a mile as straight as an arrow
from his Thornton Manor gate towards the chimney of his Port Sunlight
works. It is said that he fixed the route simply by opening the map and
ruling a straight line across the land, all of which he owned. It must
surely rank as the quickest road plan ever devised. Using this road to
drive part of the way to his office by Stanhope and pair (a light, open,
single-seater conveyance) he arrived in half the time he would have
taken using the twisting country lanes. In the course of a year that added
up to many hours saved and the industrious Lever would have found
that a cause of great satisfaction. Today this particular road is not used,
but Lever Causeway is a most attractive feature of this part of Wirral.
But only the centre carriageway is used. The trees have matured to make
an impressive boulevard, but the 'slow' lanes which have not been used
for many years (if they were ever used at all) have become grassed over.

Not long after William Lever settled in Thornton Manor his brother
James (who joined him to form the firm of Lever Brothers) came with his
wife to live in Hirst's former home, Thornton House. It was a large house
by most standards, but in 1895 James had it pulled down and replaced
by a very grand Elizabethan-style stone and half-timbered building.
Ten years afterwards it was made even bigger. After Lever's mother
died he persuaded his father and his three unmarried sisters to move to
Thornton Hough from the Bolton area and a house was built for them
which they called Hesketh Grange (Hesketh being Mrs Lever's maiden
name). After the father's death the three sisters continued to live there
and in St. George's Church there is a colourful stained glass window to
their memory. There was Emily (1847–1939), Alice (1849–1944) and
Harriette (1855–1946) – and if you work it out you will see that Emily
lived to be 92, Alice 95, and Harriette 91.

While Hesketh Grange was being built father and the three ladies
lived in the house known as 'Thicket Ford' near the church. When they

moved out another sister, Mrs Bromley, moved in and it was she, in fact, who gave the house its name, bringing it with her from her previous home in Lancashire. Yet a fifth sister, a Mrs Ferguson and her husband, came and bought a house called Thornton Lodge so that Thornton Hough became a Lever enclave with (including William) seven of the nine Lever 'children' living there. And all in a style as befitted relatives of a multi-millionaire.

The metamorphosis of Thornton Hough wrought by Lever and Hirst was complete and there is no relic of the original village left. When they first set eyes upon it there was a village pump, a cobbler's shop, a woodman's hut and a toll-bar, some of which one might think would have been preserved, especially by a man like Lever who became one of Britain's greatest antiquarians. But I suppose they were hardly picturesque or in such a sorry state that the hard-headed (but soft-hearted) businessman would not throw good money after bad. In any case he was thinking only in terms of making a modern model village and had he thought a village pump or a cobbler's shop necessary he would have provided new ones.

On the corner of The Green facing St George's Church is a little raised garden with seats and a wooden signboard. This proudly proclaims that in 1964, 1968 and 1973 Thornton Hough was Cheshire's Best Kept Village, while in 1959, 1963 and 1972 it was the best-kept village in its class. It is a fine record but, alas, as the village is now in the Metropolitan County of Merseyside they can no longer enter the contest. A circumstance which has probably given some other places fresh heart.

TEN

Open every day including Sunday

Bidston Hill, Arrowe Park, Thurstaston Common, Caldy Hill and
Grange Hill, Wirral Country Park

Apart from some of Wirral's villages, among the Peninsula's unexpected delights are some of its open spaces. Not the man-made public
parks, nor the magnificent Ness Gardens, but the areas which were
fashioned by nature and are still largely in their natural state. Bidston
Hill, Thurstaston Common, Eastham Woods, Caldy Hill, and Grange
Hill at West Kirby, The Dales and The Beacons at Heswall, the woods
at Burton . . . to name but some of a commendably lengthy list.

In almost every case we owe their preservation to men of vision who
realised that if action were not taken in their lifetime succeeding
generations would have nothing but bricks and mortar to look at and
paving stones and tarmac to walk on. And, fortunately, these men of
foresight were also men of substance able to translate their ideas into
reality.

BIDSTON HILL

Bidston Hill is a perfect example of what can be achieved by tapping
the veins of public spirit. Strictly speaking, it is not a real hill, just the
end of a 200 foot-high ridge which runs down the Wirral Peninsula from
Spital through Storeton and Oxton, but not for nothing do I hold it in
high esteem. I came to know it first as a 17-year-old when my family
moved over the water from Liverpool and, later, it became my courting
country; so I know it in all seasons. Once, when I was preparing a radio
programme for BBC Radio Merseyside, I took a tape recorder down into
the woods about three o'clock one fine May morning, and sat on a log
while the machine captured a dawn chorus that made up twenty of some
of the most enchanting minutes of my life.

In summer and autumn the hill has its different delights, but I know it,
too, when the snow lies thick upon it and the wind is razor-keen, turning
a morning's walk into a slithering, scrabbling, gorse-grabbing, heather-
holding expedition. But often on these mornings the view makes the

effort worthwhile. The snow not only enhances all things natural but also acts as a cosmetic on the face of Man's ugly works, while the clear air extends the view right across Wales, beyond Moel Fammau to Snowdonia. And, with a half-turn right, to Blackpool Tower and the distant hills of Lakeland. Many claim to have seen (and I *think* I did once) Snaefell in the Isle of Man.

The most surprising thing of all about Bidston Hill, however, is that it is still there and not obliterated by houses. The last Corporation of Birkenhead seemed to bear malicious intent towards this end of the borough and built council housing estates right up to its edge and, given half a chance, I feel sure they would have gleefully encroached onto its slopes. Fortunately, a body of public-spirited men nearly 90 years ago had more feeling and foresight.

In 1894 a committee of distinguished men of Merseyside was set up to raise funds so that Bidston Hill could be bought and preserved forever as a public place. On it were such worthies as Joseph Heap and Daniel Wilson, the millers; Laird, Grayson and Clover, the shipbuilders; Ismay, Royden and two of the Holts, all shipowners; Lever and Hudson, the soap kings; Robb, the store owner; and Willmer of the *Birkenhead Advertiser*. Altogether a committee of 60 of Merseyside's upper crust, plus the Lord Mayor of Liverpool and the Mayor of Birkenhead.

They were initially after the 47 acres owned by the Vyner family, although for many years the public had been allowed free access to it. But they feared for its future. 'It has long been seen', they said 'that only a short time could elapse before it would be surrounded or covered by houses and its unique value gone forever'.

The money was raised within a year and the secretary of the appeal wrote: 'Whoever has walked over the heathery surface of Bidston Hill is aware that in extent, variety, and beauty, the views from it are rarely equalled. Many, however, do not know what a scientific botanist tells us; that it is the last sub-alpine spot remaining open within many miles, and that the air upon it is as pure as on Monte Rosa.'

More than being just a beauty spot, Bidston Hill is steeped in history. The famous windmill – the last of many on the same site – was built in the early days of the last century and went on grinding corn until 1875 when it fell into disuse and became a ruin. It was restored to its full-sail glory in 1894 by Mr R.S. Hudson.

The first lighthouse was erected on the hill in 1771 and lasted for almost a hundred years. It was rebuilt when the Observatory was established in 1867 but its light was extinguished during the First World War and has never shone forth since.

Long before the building of the first lighthouse the hill was a signal station and Liverpool shipowners and merchants had flag-poles erected in a line right across the topmost ridge. When a ship hove into sight the appropriate flag was raised and this could be seen through a spy-glass from Liverpool. A popular vantage-point where merchants gathered to 'read' the flags was St Nicholas Churchyard, but on clear days they could also be seen from Everton Brow and St James' Walk (on which the Liverpool Anglican Cathedral now stands), near which many of the merchants lived. Since in those days a further week could elapse before the vessel actually reached port the system gave timely notice of arrival. At the station's height there were over a hundred flag-poles in use, stretching from the signal station building near the lighthouse to beyond the windmill and if old etchings are anything to go by, it was a truly remarkable sight. The station fell into disuse about 150 years ago and time, weather, and the public's tread have obliterated most of the holes, though if you look hard enough you can still see traces of one or two.

The famous Observatory was erected by the Mersey Docks and Harbour Board for astronomical and meteorological observations to assist shipping. Over the years since its role has gradually changed. In 1929 its work was merged with that of Liverpool University's Tidal Institute and it became – as it still is – the world's leading tidal authority computing tide-tables for 160 of the world's major sea-ports. On one occasion it was even called upon to say what the state of the tide was in the region of The Wash on that day in October in the year 1216 when King John lost his jewels. This was for the benefit of an expedition which hoped to recover them. The Observatory staff also worked out the vital data for the D-Day landings in Normandy during the last war.

It is now known as the Proudman Oceanographic Laboratory. A large new extension, in no way architecturally related to the original but a very pleasing and strangely unobtrusive building for its size, houses a staff of a hundred and research into tidal questions is now conducted with all the benefits of modern electronic wizardry.

On the western slopes of the hill is the stately Bidston Hall, to which I referred when writing about Bidston village, and right on the edge of the hill, half-way along Boundary Road, is the incongruously-named Tam O' Shanter Cottage. Corn-coloured and quaint, it sits in an attractive leafy setting, with ducks and geese and hens waddling about and pecking away just as others of their kind did *circa* 1670 when the cottage was thought to have been first built. But like the antique hammer which has had two new heads and three replacement handles, *circa* must be construed in the broadest sense. Its origins certainly go back to the seventeenth century and even beyond – a stone found on the site actually bore the date 1511 – and it is the last of several cottages built by squatters who moved onto the land while two manorial lords spent three years squabbling over who owned what. By the time they had settled their differences the squatters had earned squatters' rights and were allowed to stay on payment of rent.

The cottage got its name in 1837 when the tenant was a stone-carver who embellished the gable-end with a carving of Tam O' Shanter (from Robert Burns' poem). It shows Tam fleeing on horseback across a bridge from pursuing witches whom he had caught unawares dancing in their 'cutty sarks' (or short shifts).

In the course of three and-a-half centuries the cottage several times fell into disrepair and was rescued and, in 1950, it was listed as a building of special interest. But it also proved to be of irresistibly special interest to the local vandals and in 1974 they triumphed with a fire which completely gutted it. Birkenhead is not over-endowed with things historical and it was appropriate that the initiative for clinging on to this particular relic should come from the Birkenhead History Society. They proposed an imaginative plan to rebuild the cottage (it was far beyond restoration) to its original appearance, using the old stones, and turn it into a Field Study Centre which would help bring about a greater appreciation of Bidston Hill by the public and particularly by schoolchildren.

Through the Job Creation Programme this was brought about and with the voluntary help of a group of Friends of Tam O' Shanter and a resident warden it is proving a great success. Schoolchildren visit it in parties during school terms, and after viewing an exhibition of photographs and drawings which tell the history of the cottage, the Observatory, Bidston Hall and Bidston village; and looking at an exhibition depicting the flora and fauna to be found on the hill, they set off on a nature trail which has been mapped out. The cottage is also open to the public and at week-ends voluntary helpers have revived an old Tam O' Shanter tradition by selling refreshments.

All these historic monuments are by way of being a bonus on what Nature has provided and make Bidston Hill the unique place it is.

Further purchases of land over the years have brought the total area open to the public to 90 acres. When the money for the first portion had been raised the appeal secretary declared:

'In buying these forty-seven acres, the Committee feels it has acquired a spot formed by nature, which in the combination of purity of air, varied and extensive views, and beautiful sky effects, stands perhaps alone in the kingdom, and such as no other large town possesses.'

What more is there to say?

ARROWE PARK

I know there are bigger public parks in Britain (though Roundhay Park, Leeds, is the only one I can think of off-hand), but Arrowe Park always seems particularly vast to me. I suppose because it contains a full-size 18-hole golf course, good enough to have been used for a qualifying round of the British Open Championship, about 40 football and/or cricket pitches and rolling acres of lush meadowland and trees like you get on big ducal estates, while room has been found in a spare corner to build a massive new hospital.

It is bigger than Hyde Park and it accommodated with ease that famous Boy Scout Jamboree of 1929 when 50,000 Scouts from all over the world spent a very damp ten days having the efficacy of their motto tested to the full. The park covers 425 acres and it is a sobering thought that it was once just one man's private garden. John Ralph Shaw (whom we met at Greasby) bought the land from the Trustees of Warrington Grammar School. His uncle, twice Mayor of Liverpool, had also bought land in the area and the two estates eventually became one.

Such a setting demanded a house to suit and between 1835 and 1844 John Shaw built an Elizabethan-style mansion which he called Arrowe Hall. Twenty years later it was extended and in 1876 it was enlarged yet again by the addition of a billiards room and a conservatory.

By this time the property had descended to Captain Otho Shaw, whose chief interest was travelling the globe shooting animals and birds. So great was his total 'bag' that he had to increase the size of the hall yet again so he could display them. His collection included no less than nine tigers (including one which was alleged to have killed and eaten men, women and children, and no less than 600 head of cattle which the gallant captain stalked for nine days and nights), black bears, elks, leopards, panthers, moose, yaks, bison and sundry other four-legged creatures, together with eagles, vultures and lesser birds of prey.

The captain was also an antiquary and the Hall was virtually a private museum with, among other things, a very fine collection of glass and some pottery more than 2000 years old which came from the tombs of Cyprus, much silver plate and many water colours and paintings. One bedroom contained a magnificent carved oak bedroom suite made in York in 1684. Two old carved oak chairs from Arrowe Hall are, at the moment, in store at Leasowe Castle and when I was being shown round I was invited to try one for comfort. I suspected something was afoot, but was not prepared for what actually happened. As the seat took my weight there was a great bang-clatter and a pair of nasty-looking wrought iron hooks shot out of the arms and imprisoned my legs above the knee in a near-tourniquet grip. It was obviously a chair to restrain anyone being a nuisance.

The Arrowe estate eventually came into the ownership of Lord Leverhulme and from him the Corporation of Birkenhead bought these 425 acres in 1927.

In 1929 it was the turn of Czechoslovakia to play host to the Boy Scout movements's world jamboree, but as it happened to be the twenty-first anniversary they generously suggested that it ought to be held in Britain where the movement originated. Birkenhead Corporation immediately offered the use of Arrowe Park to mark the fact that it was in the old YMCA in Grange Road, Birkenhead, on 24 January 1908 that Lieutenant-General Sir Robert Baden-Powell (as he was then) first mooted the idea. In 1910 Baden-Powell returned to the YMCA to unveil a plaque to commemorate the auspicious occasion. It is now on the wall of the theatre of the present YMCA building in Whetstone Lane.

50,000 Scouts of all shapes, sizes, races, colours and creeds packed their kit-bags and trekked to Birkenhead. They came from 31 different lands within the British Empire and 41 lands without. It was the greatest international conglomerate of youth the world had hitherto seen. They gathered in a vast tented town on an area which ever since has been called the Rally Ground. The Jamboree was opened on Wednesday 31 July 1929 with a speech by HRH the Duke of Connaught and the Chief Scout himself blowing on a Kudu (an African antelope) Horn, the one with which he sounded reveille at the first-ever scout camp on Brownsea Island. There was an enormous programme of events, but before anything could be got underway a deluge swept the camp ('various opinions obtained as to what it really was – a cloudburst, a waterspout, or something unlabelled by meteorologists') and tents were blown away like discarded newspapers. The whole Rally Ground was soon under water and though it drained fairly quickly it left behind a sea of mud. And Wirral mud is clinging mud.

But the Scouts were equal to it. 'Any ass can be a good scout on a fine day' quoth the Chief and the boys responded with such a will that by the time the public was admitted everything was spick and span.

For the opening ceremonies they pretended it was dry and 50,000 sat on the saturated turf uncomplainingly as they listened to the speeches until, at a given signal, they rose as one to take part in what was euphemistically termed 'The Urge Forward'. It was no less than a great mass stampede with all 50,000 yelling their heads off. It must have been a somewhat unnerving sight for the dignitaries on the platform but, say the newspaper reports of the day, they pulled up smartly and 'it was the sight of a lifetime and deeply stirring'.

It continued to rain on and off for the whole ten days but the programme went on uninterrupted. The Prince of Wales spent two nights under canvas, disdaining anything more luxurious than an ordinary Scout tent, and flying from London to Hooton Park Aerodrome in a Westland Wapiti aeroplane in order to foster this new-fangled mode of travel. He also played the last nine holes of the Royal Liverpool golf course, achieving a 5 at the long 16th and 4's at the 17th and 18th ('which is fine golf').

It was a notable week, too, for 'B-P' himself. A very popular national hero, he journeyed to Birkenhead by train as *Sir Robert* Baden-Powell and returned home in a brand new Rolls-Royce drawing a luxury caravan as *Lord* Baden-Powell of Gilwell. The Rolls and the caravan were a present to him from the Scouts of the world and his elevation to the peerage was announced half-way through the first week.

This historic gathering of youth was seen by over 300,000 members of the public and has been commemorated with a fine life-size statue in slate of a Boy Scout, sculpted by that superb Liverpool sculptor who did so much work in the Anglican Cathedral, the late E. Carter Preston. It stands in the grounds of Arrowe Park Hospital.

During the last war the Rally Ground was used as a military training ground and now, after many years of controversy, a 910-bed hospital has been built on 15 acres of it.

Arrowe Hall itself, after serving for many years as a very happy convalescent home is now a care centre for the physically and mentally handicapped.

THURSTASTON COMMON

If, one hundred years ago, three landowners of Thurstaston and Irby – namely, Birkenhead Glegg, the Lord of the Manor, the Reverend F.E. Thurland, the Rector, and Thomas Ismay, the shipowner, of Dawpool House – had not joined together and announced their intention of fencing in the land they owned on what was then generally known as Irby Heath then we might not be enjoying the delights of Thurstaston Hill and Common today.

Thurstaston Hill is arguably the most-visited beauty spot in Wirral, and rightly so. Like Bidston Hill, it is really the end of a long ridge rather than a free-standing hillock. A bracken and heather-covered escarpment rises sharply from Telegraph Road to a summit tonsured by the tread of millions of feet over the years to expose the orange-red sandstone pate. The Common slides away gently towards Irby, with the heather and gorse giving way to a belt of slender trees, mostly silver birch, with some beech and pine and stunted oaks, linking up on the northern edge with Royden Park at Frankby. It commands expansive views in all directions – to Wales, out to sea across the waters of Liverpool Bay, and right over the sprawling mass of Liverpool to the uplands of Lancashire. It is a good place to check on the way our generation is changing the face of Wirral. Like architectural models on a relief map, the impact of new development can be seen vividly.

The area had long been used as common, and although the owners were legally entitled to seek enclosure their intention was not at all well received in the council chamber of Birkenhead Town Hall, despite the fact that the land lay seven miles beyond their jurisdiction. Undeterred, the Council resolved on 29 December 1879 that: 'Having regard to the health, comfort and convenience of the inhabitants of the Borough of Birkenhead, and the benefits of the neighbourhood, about 60 or 70 acres of the highest and most most attractive part of the common should remain unenclosed as a place of recreation, with proper roads, ways, and footpaths to and over it in convenient directions'. Council representatives were despatched to the Inclosure Commissioners in London and instead of being told to stay in their own backyard and mind their own business they were allowed to argue their case and to such good effect that the Commissioners granted them 45 of the 60/70 acres they demanded. And what's more, they included the highest and most attractive parts.

It took another two-and-a-half years to complete formalities and on Wednesday, 26 July 1882, the Mayor of Birkenhead (who was William Laird, Junior) and the Corporation walked the boundaries and formally took possession.

The occasion was brought to a conclusion with an address by the distinguished Liverpool historian, Sir James Picton, from atop Thor's Stone. Thor's Stone, that mysterious flat-topped rock formation standing dramatically isolated in an amphitheatre-like depression on the Common is certainly the place from which to deliver an address – nay, make an oration – and Sir James would surely have made the most of it for he had a fanciful notion about the stone's origin.

'Standing thus isolated (he wrote) it forms a very remarkable object. How far its original shape has been modified it is impossible to say, but human labour has been largely expended upon it. The sandstone in this locality is nowhere else to be found in a similar form and position.

There is a legend connected with it. What can we infer as to the origin and purpose of a monument of this kind? The name of the parish may somewhat assist us – Thor-stane-ton, the town of Thor's Stone, seems to point very significantly to the association connected with it. Wirral was exposed from the eighth century onward to the incursions of the Danes who ultimately effected a settlement. Thor was a divinity common to the Anglo-Saxon and Danes. The feast of Yule, at the winter solstice, was celebrated in honour of Thor, or the Sun, in order to obtain a propitious year. The fete consisted of sacrifices, feastings, dances and nocturnal assemblies. Fat oxen and horses were sacrificed to Thor. Human victims were also offered; the practice not being abolished amongst the Northern nations until about the ninth century. The victims were laid on a great stone altar, and either strangled or knocked on the head. The bodies were opened and afterwards burned.'

Philip Sulley, writing half a dozen years later, took up the tale and even embellished it: 'The worship of Thor and Odin, of Frigga and Feia, for a time overshadowed that of Christ, and the great stone of Thor was reddened with the blood of priests and captives'. The Stone is certainly a sight to fire the imagination and Mrs Hilda Gamlin, in her turn, suggested it was raised (she did not venture to say *how*) to commemorate the Battle of Brunanburh.

But, sadly, just as the Americans have made nonsense of all the legends surrounding the Moon and Mars, so modern geologists have spoiled the stories about Thor's Stone. The hill has been extensively quarried over the years, they say, and the massive monolith is nothing more than stone which proved unsuitable for some reason, possibly because it was too soft. Stone has been removed from all round it so leaving the 'amphitheatre' in which it stands.

Since those days the weather and the feet of generations of scrabbling children and youths who cannot resist reaching its flat top have sculpted it into an abstract form. Its edges have been rounded and rainwater has gouged gullies and channels smooth and tactile enough to please Henry Moore, while countless initials and names carved into its amenable surface are, in the mass, not undecorative. Who knows, in the course of time they may well be regarded in the same light as the graffiti on the walls of Pompeii.

In the years immediately after the last war my wife and I found our way around the less frequented parts of the Wirral with the aid of one of Andrew Blair's little books of rambles of the sort I mentioned briefly when writing about Barnston Dale. This one was called *Wirral Fieldpaths and Byways* and cost half-a-crown and never was more value for money received. Andrew Blair, Fellow of the Royal Geographical Association, was one of Britain's best-known ramblers. He was the founder of the Liverpool and District Federation of the Ramblers' Association in 1922 and author of several books for walkers. There was not a footpath or public way on Merseyside or in North Wales that he did not know. He loved the Wirral and, in particular, he loved Thurstaston Hill. In his late sixties he was stricken with an illness which confined him to his bed, but what he achieved in his lifetime for walkers, hikers, and ramblers was so much appreciated that in 1942 it was decided to erect a monument in his honour on the topmost point.

For the unveiling he was taken to Thurstaston by ambulance and carried to the top of the hill on a stretcher, and stuck inside my copy of his guide is a yellowed clipping from the next day's *Sunday Express* describing the scene. It ends: 'Ramblers who climb the height of

Thurstaston Hill in future summers will find there a pedestal built from Thurstaston stone by Thurstaston craftsmen, and on its top you will see a brass compass engraved with the names of landmarks which the eye can see on a clear day'.

So next time you are there spare a thought for Andrew Blair for we owe him a lot, but at the same time remember those Birkenhead councillors of 1879. They really deserve a monument, too.

CALDY HILL AND GRANGE HILL

The sandstone ridge which starts around Shotwick did not always end at Thurstaston. It is thought to have continued all the way to West Kirby until some aeons ago it cracked and crumbled at this northern end, leaving stranded what we know today as Caldy Hill and Grange Hill. Like Thurstaston both today are in the care of the National Trust and they are as beautiful as any spot in the Wirral. Covered with bracken, gorse, and heather and ornamented with silver birch and pine tree, they probably provide the best views, too.

On Caldy Hill especially it is possible to manoeuvre oneself into a position where houses and humanity cannot be seen to obtain a panoramic view of the mouth of the Dee, with bright yellow gorse in the foreground, the Hilbre Islands as the focal point, and the Point of Air and the shadow of the two Ormes in the distance. And since that is looking westward, if you wait till sunset you can see it all gloriously overlaid with tints and tones of orange and red.

In one such spot is a seat 'To the memory of Mr and Mrs J.E. Hawkins who lived nearby and loved this view'. I know how they felt.

The sandstone column with the large ball on top standing on the summit of Grange Hill was erected in 1841 by the Trustees of Liverpool Docks 'as a beacon for mariners frequenting the River Mersey and its vicinity'.

WIRRAL COUNTRY PARK

The idea of tramping for 12 miles along a disused railway track will not immediately commend itself to everyone as a pleasant way of spending a fine summer's day. Unless, that is, your walk takes you along that particular stretch of disused railway which once ran from West Kirby alongside the sands o' Dee to Hooton. For these dozen miles of track have been transformed. The old single-track railway has become The Wirral Way, the basis of The Wirral Country Park, developed jointly by the Cheshire County Council and The Countryside Commission, and opened to the public on 2 October 1973.

Now, where the old tank engines ran for 80 years, there is a series of delightful walks with splendid views, a 'ride' for horses, picnicking areas with appropriately rustic seats and tables, specially stocked ponds for fishing, ponds reserved for studying pond life, fully-documented nature trails, particular areas of interest for students of archaeology and railways, and plenty of scope for ornithologists and botanists, artists and photographers, loafers and lovers.

At Thurstaston there is a camping site and a splendid purpose-built Visitors' Centre offering refreshment facilities, an enquiry desk with nature trail leaflets and other relevant literature, an exhibit showing how the area has developed almost from the beginning of time, and a small lecture theatre where a colour slide show can be seen accompanied by a commentary on the park's attractions. It is a most imaginative enterprise where the planners seem not to have missed a trick. The routes and the off-shoot footpaths are well signposted; the horse-ride is safely separated from the walk, and where a stile is necessary they have even remembered to make provision for prams. The park is superintended by full- and part-time Rangers dressed distinctively in a Lincoln-green rig.

The railway was established in 1846 when the Parkgate, Chester and Birkenhead Junction Railway Company was formed to establish a link between Parkgate and the Chester-Birkenhead line at Hooton. Exactly 40 years later, to cater for the increasing commuter population, this was extended to Heswall and West Kirby.

The single-track line had passing places at Willaston, Parkgate, Heswall and Thurstaston and to ensure there were no misunderstandings about who had the right of way, the drivers, like runners in a relay race, had to be in possession of a 'staff' before proceeding along a particular section. With such a system there could be no such thing as a through express and the constant stopping and exchanging of 'staffs' might suggest that journeys were tediously slow. But I suggest the businessman travelling in those less frenetic days would not have had it otherwise. Their train was a pleasant 'club' which they visited twice-daily. Indeed, the First-Class coach of the 8 am out of Heswall before the First World War was equipped with armchair seats and bridge tables, as befitting the company chairmen and directors who used it.

From West Kirby all the way to Hooton was a pleasantly scenic route by any standards, but its attraction was enhanced by the great rivalry between signalmen in maintaining their platform gardens. To get a brief glance of what it was like, go to Willaston where the old station (named Hadlow Road to distinguish it from the other Willaston near Crewe) has been restored to look like it did when it was in operation. There are milk churns and a four-wheeled trolley on the platform, time-tables and period advertisements in the waiting-room, while the booking office viewed through the glass looks as though the booking clerk had just slipped out for a moment.

The ingenious idea of turning an old railway-line into a linear park was first put forward in 1965 by Graham Walker of Thingwall, the then assistant secretary of the Wirral Green Belt Council, but its realisation was due in very large measure to a remarkable man, the late Laurence Beswick. By profession, Laurence Beswick was an architect, a town and country planner, a land reclamation expert, and a surveyor. In the First World War he won the DSM at Gallipoli (where, as a marine, he claimed to have been the first man ashore). But it was in the last 20 years of his life that his name became well-known in East Cheshire and Wirral where he was looked upon by many as an unofficial ombudsman. Wherever a developer dared to tread Laurence Beswick was hot on his heels asking why, and how, and by whose authority. In his capacity as secretary of the erstwhile Cheshire County Federation of Ratepayers and Kindred Associations he stormed the county in the wake of planning applications. He assisted and advised groups of residents worried about their environment, he addressed public meetings and gave evidence at countless planning enquiries, always with vigour and often with hackle-raising bluntness. Later, he became the secretary of The Wirral Green Belt Council, a body composed of representatives of some 40 organisations all with a positive interest in preserving as much of Wirral's countryside as possible. It was in this capacity that he drew up a detailed plan for making the old railway track into a linear park to be called The Wirral Way.

It was no armchair exercise. He spent three years making a detailed survey of the entire 12 miles of track and the land adjoining, calling on all the landowners and local authorities involved, obtaining their opinions, listening to their objections and arguing his case. Throughout this formidable task he was accompanied by a well-known Wallasey personality and one-time councillor for Seacombe, Miss Eliza Bestwick who acted as chauffeuse/factotum. More than that, he looked even further ahead and saw that The Wirral Way could be connected via footpaths at Mollington to a linear *water* park based on the Shropshire Union Canal between Ellesmere Port and Chester. Needless to say, he – and the faithful Miss Bestwick – surveyed that, too.

In 1970 his work was rewarded when The Wirral Way project was given a 'Countryside in 1970' award which Laurence Beswick personally received from the Duke of Edinburgh at the Guildhall in London.

He died of cancer in July 1971, aged 74, but lived long enough to see his plan adopted by the Cheshire County Council. A memorial, with a bronze plaque bearing his likeness, is sited on the cliff top at Thurstaston near the Visitor Centre. There were many occasions in his life when he fought a cause and lost. The Wirral Way was an exception and it was fitting that in a short ceremony after the unveiling of the plaque his ashes were scattered on the spot where one of his dreams came true.

ELEVEN

Over, Under, and Out

The River Mersey

The trouble with living on a peninsula, like living on an island, is one of communicating with those 'over the water'. Ancient Wirralians probably neither knew nor cared very much who or what lay on the opposite shores. All they knew was that every so often a strange aggressive race of men would appear out of the mists and take over the place. Not until the time of the Normans and after was there much doing in the way of intercommunication. After all, what is now Liverpool was just a bleak inhospitable area of muddy nothing and few wanted to go there, while the Welsh on the other side of the Dee were not known for their friendliness.

It was not until after King John made Liverpool a port in 1207 that any real need for a ferry arose. Before then anyone wanting to cross the estuary simply paid the nearest willing fisherman to row him across. However, someone (probably Henry de Lancaster) did officially hold ferry rights since the king, as part of his package-deal to attract settlers (or 'burgesses') to the area, offered 'all the liberties and free customs which any free borough upon the sea has within our land' and this included freedom from the ferry toll.

As the town grew there was doubtless a need for people to visit the important city of Chester to do business and several occasional ferries became established at divers points up and down the estuary where horse-coaches could be caught, but the main route was naturally between Liverpool and Birkenhead. And, as we have seen, the traffic grew to such an extent in the middle ages that the Prior of Birkenhead had to appeal to Edward II for leave to construct accommodation for travellers waiting to cross.

At that time the involvement of the monks themselves in ferrying was restricted to people who thumbed a lift in their boats plying between Birchen Head and their store in what is now Water Street, Liverpool. They would not be able to charge a fare, but I have no doubt they accepted contributions towards the upkeep of the Priory.

If the monks' boat was not running, however, the traveller had to rely on the casual boatmen who worked only when they wanted to and charged exorbitantly for the crossing. This became such a scandal that the Prior eventually sought royal sanction to run the ferry exclusively and to charge tolls. This was granted by Edward III on 13 April 1330 and a regular service has been running throughout the 650 years since.

In 1545, following the dissolution of the monasteries, Henry VIII bestowed the priory, its rights and its considerable possessions, including the ferry, to one of his courtiers named Ralph Worsley, of Worsley near Manchester. Among the multifarious offices he held was crown-bearer, keeper of the lions, lionesses and leopards in the Tower of London, grand train bearer, controller of the Counties of Chester and Flint, clerk to the duchy of Lancaster, and excheator (that is, one who looks after *escheats* or property which falls to the overlord for want of an heir) of the County Palatine of Lancaster. Some eight years before this the Molyneux family had come into the tenure of the Lordship of Liverpool and this included the rights of ferryage (that is, the right to levy tolls) from that shore to the Wirral. They, in turn, leased the ferry rights to various burgesses but it was still generally referred to as 'the king's ferry' and from time to time they had to resort to litigation against various 'pirate' ferryboats.

The Molyneux reign over Liverpool lasted for exactly 240 years, until the year 1777 when the Town Council bought all their rights, including control of the ferry, for the sum of £2250. Either in triumph or relief, the Corporation immediately threw the ferry rights open to the public, allowing unrestricted access to the quays so that anyone with a boat could ply for hire, charge what he could get and pocket the lot. It was an odd thing to do and they clearly could not have foreseen the day when thousands of people would need to cross the Mersey twice a day. It may well have been, however, that by this time the Priory-owned ferry, being more reliable, had already garnered most of the traffic to and from Birkenhead, athough there were also established ferry routes between Liverpool and Ince, Carlett (that is, Eastham), Rock Ferry, and Seacombe.

As we have seen in the chapter on Birkenhead, Worsley's windfall eventually came into the possession of the Price family who similarly leased the Woodside ferry rights to others eager to have them. It was a virtual monopoly but, in 1837, a man named Curell set up a rival ferry service from a point on the shore about 400 yards to the south. This, he claimed, was the spot from where the Priory monks actually operated and he called his enterprise 'Monks Ferry'.

The lessees of the Woodside Ferry immediately took legal action in defence of what they claimed was a breach of their royal rights. There cannot be many cases in legal annals where the court has been asked to consider a position which obtained 500 years earlier. But in their defence the Monks Ferry promoters claimed that the Priory's rights were rendered void from the beginning by the pre-existence of the 'king's ferry' from Liverpool. They lost their case, however, and were forced to close down in 1840.

The ferry service from Wallasey could be as old as that from Birkenhead, but there is no known record of one before 1515. There was certainly one operating in 1552 for in that year Ralph Worsley went to law, alleging infringement of his rights by a certain John Minshull, Lord of the Manor of Tranmere, who was operating a ferry to Liverpool from Wallasey Pool. Worsley claimed that his jurisdiction extended to Wallasey Pool, but Minshull's answer was that he was operating from 'Secum' on the west side of the Pool beyond the limits of Worsley's domain.

There was also a ferry from Tranmere at that time, probably operated by Minshull as well, for old records show there was some connection between the two.

By the mid-seventeenth century, as well as the established ferries, it is recorded that 'there were a number of bye-boats plying on the river that don't belong to the Ferries' and it is probable that they had no regular routes but simply picked up passengers at various points on the shore and landing them on the other side at places like Otterspool, Toxteth, Sandhills and Bootle.

In the eighteenth century the Rock Ferry and New Ferry services were also in existence and before long Egremont and New Brighton followed. The river was thus criss-crossed like lacings in a shoe and since the boats were all propelled by oar and sail the River Mersey, with all the ocean-going vessels sailing into and out of Liverpool as well, was as crowded and hazardous as it was picturesque.

The auspicious introduction of the steam-paddle *Etna* was to change the scene completely in the course of the next few years. As a ferryboat she was a vast improvement on anything which had gone before, but she was by no means in the luxury class. In fact, she was devised rather than built, being constructed from the hulls of two Mersey barges (or flats) placed side by side with a single paddle-wheel between them. Her engine is believed to have been on one hull and the boiler on the other and her decks were capacious enough for horses and cattle and carts and carriages. She was as open to the elements as a rowing-boat.

A contemporary advertisement for the *Etna* service proclaimed that:

'This vessel remaining at each side only Ten Minutes, the certainty with which Passengers may calculate upon crossing, at all times of the day, will be an advantage that never yet has been afforded to those whose business or pleasure lead them to cross the River'.

And so it was. She made her first trip at 8 o'clock on the morning of Thursday, 17 April 1817 and proved such a success that the other ferries had to follow suit. Within 20 years all the cross-river boats were steam-driven and the rush into Wirral was on.

One of the attractions of John Askew's new residential district of Egremont was that it had its own ferry, so obviating a walk along the shore to the boat at Seacombe, but it was not apparently in the original scheme of things. According to the Liverpool artist and historian, William Herdman, the Egremont ferry was actually established as the result of a quarrel between Sir John Tobin (who had a fishing lodge on the shore near Askew's property) and Thomas Parry, who owned both the Seacombe Hotel and the Seacombe Ferry. As a result Tobin and the ever-eager entrepreneur, Askew, set up 'The Egremont Ferry Company'.

A ferry was also an indispensable part of James Atherton's scheme at New Brighton and his prospectus mentioned 'that several gentlemen propose to erect there a handsome Hotel and a convenient Dock or Ferry to be called "The Royal Lighthouse Hotel and Ferry" and to establish a communication by Steam Packets between that place and Liverpool'. It went on to say that 'the Steam Boats will be frequently in requisition for the towing of Vessels or affording assistance to Ships in distress' and in the early days of the steam ferries this side-line often proved a great inconvenience to travellers. There were still sail boats in the river and in bad weather or, I suppose, moments of great calm, there must have been more money to be made acting as tugs. Would-be passengers were often left waiting for hours on both sides of the river without explanation. It did not seem to happen to the Woodside boats, however, and sometimes intending passengers from Seacombe gave up hope and walked all the way round the head of Wallasey Pool via the Poulton Bridge to Woodside.

The monopoly which the Woodside ferry enjoyed for the Birkenhead area, apart from the challenge from the Monks Ferry, was also broken by another enterprise established on the other side of the headland but against which they had no grounds for complaint, legally anyway, since it was founded with the consent of the Lord of the Manor, Francis Price. As part of a land deal in which he agreed amongst other things to build St Mary's Church, a waterside hotel and landing-place was built and called Birkenhead Hotel and Ferry. For a time it was very popular – not least because the Woodside ferry service was then being most inefficiently run – and was the terminus for four-horse coaches which ran regularly to Chester, North Wales and the Midlands.

The mismanagement of Woodside eventually led to the setting up of 'The Woodside, North Birkenhead and Liverpool Steam Ferry Company', but this did not improve matters and, in its turn, was taken over by the Birkenhead and Chester Railway Company. They also purchased and re-opened the old Monks Ferry to which they drove a tunnel to extend the railway beyond their station in Grange Road and using the ferry for the exclusive use of rail travellers. This was still illegal but it went unchallenged this time because the directors of the railway company were largely the directors of the new Woodside company. It so happened that most of them were also Birkenhead Improvement Commissioners – the forerunners of the Town Council – and when the Woodside Ferry continued to show little sign of improvement arrangements were made without too much difficulty for it to be transferred to the town.

From that point on the dealings between the Commissioners, the railway company, Mr Price and the Corporation of Liverpool who had acquired the Birkenhead Ferry are somewhat tangled, but the final outcome was that Monks Ferry and Birkenhead Ferry both ceased operating and Woodside, with the rail terminus at Woodside Station alongside, became the sole ferry from Birkenhead to Liverpool.

The running of the Egremont and New Brighton ferries, each in different hands, also left a lot to be desired and between the years 1861–3 Wallasey Local Board (which became Wallasey Town Council) bought them all out.

Under municipal control all the remaining ferries became reliable and as more and more people moved into the Wirral they were soon out of the red and into the black.

For all that, the previous unreliability and the fact that even the steam-paddle boats could be held up in bad weather turned the thoughts of some men to an alternative, reliable all-weather link between the two shores. Not necessarily over the water (although a bridge was considered) but under.

As early as 1825 when Birkenhead Docks were being built, Sir Marc Isambard Brunel (the father of Isambard Kingdom Brunel), prompted by the success of his Thames tunnel the year before, had seriously studied the possibility of tunnelling under the Mersey. This was before the coming of the railways and he was thinking of a road tunnel.

Twenty-five years later Sir John Hawkshaw brought out a most adventurous scheme known as the 'North Wales Railway' which would have its starting point in Liverpool, pass under the Mersey through a tunnel, follow the length of the Wirral Peninsula and then cross the Dee to Flint by means of a viaduct. The plan had the support of William Gladstone (who happened to have coal-bearing estates in Flintshire) but it came to nothing.

Next from the drawing board, in 1866, came the Mersey Pneumatic Railway, an idea sparked off by the opening the year before of the Post Office Tube Railway between Euston Station and Holborn Post Office whereby mail was propelled to its destination by compressed air. There seemed no reason why people should not be similarly encapsulated and despatched. The brain behind the scheme was the eminent engineer, Sir Charles Fox, and although it had the support of influential Liverpool and Lancashire businessmen and Parliamentary sanction was obtained, sufficient capital was never forthcoming.

In 1871, however, Parliamentary authority was obtained to proceed with the construction of an orthodox double-track railway, but it was another nine years before adequate funds were available to make a start. Within a year the contractor employed got into financial difficulties and Major Samuel Isaac was called in. He was an extraordinary character who made one fortune during the Crimean War as a contractor to the army and another during the American Civil War as a daring blockade runner into Confederate-held ports. But his engineering experience was nil. Nevertheless, Isaac had such confidence in his own abilities that he not only agreed to undertake the work but offered, in return for a large stake in the company, to meet all the costs - legal, Parliamentary, construction and other incidentals - until the Board of Trade gave their certificate of worthiness and the line came into use.

The pilot-heading was driven through the rock with a boring-machine invented by a Colonel Beaumont of the Royal Engineers. It was a gigantic pneumatically-operated drill and it was a great success, producing an almost perfectly smooth bore. But in one way it was too good. The machine produced a fine, dry, suffocating dust and within a few years every one of its seven-man crew was dead from silicosis.

The main tunnel was excavated with explosives and pick and shovel, with every labourer wondering if the next bang or blow from his pick would bring the River Mersey pouring in on top of them.

The line, which ran from James Street in Liverpool through Hamilton Square to Green Lane in Birkenhead was opened by the Prince of Wales (later Edward VII) in 1886. Two years later a branch line was built out to Birkenhead Park and in 1891 the line to Green Lane was extended to Rock Ferry. A year after that, the Liverpool section was extended to an underground station that was situated below Central Station.

Major Isaac lived to see the railway opened but died a few months later.

Initially, the line was an enormous success and it hit the ferries hard, but whilst the number of passengers carried in 1890 reached the 10 million mark after that there was a decline. The simple reason for this was that to haul the trains up and down the steep inclines particularly powerful locomotives had to be used and they belched smoke and sulphurous fumes to such an extent that the ventilation system could not cope. The stations and the carriages were never free from a dense, foul-smelling fog and whilst the journey was quick it was something of an ordeal. Moreover, by this time George Train's horse-powered street railway had been replaced by electric trams which had their terminus at Woodside and their time-table was designed to link with the ferry sailings. And a healthy, if somewhat slower trip, completed with a pollution-free ride on a fast tram was preferred by many.

To overcome the problem of the dreadful 'fug' it was decided that the railway line should be electrified and in 1903 the Mersey Railway became the first steam railway in the world to change over entirely to electric traction. And it is worth noting that the conversion work was carried out without any interruption to the normal service. From then on the railways once again became a threat to the ferries but crossing *over* the river was still the only way to transport goods and vehicles. The large, open-decked luggage-boats sailing from the floating roadways sufficed in the days of the horse-drawn vehicles but as the motor-vehicle age grew apace they were ultimately unable to cope. Long queues of lorries and cars waiting for the boat became a regular sight on each side of the river and naturally gave rise to thoughts of an alternative.

A bridge or a tunnel? That was the question which was argued at length, but nothing positive was done about it until Sir Archibald Salvidge, the then leader of the Liverpool City Council, instigated the formation of a committee to consider the possibilities. They appointed consulting engineers who reported that whilst a bridge might be aesthetically pleasing it would be costly to build, would require constant maintenance, could cause silting on both banks of the river, and in time of war (the Great War was still very much in mind, of course) if it were wrecked it would close the Port of Liverpool. They recommended a road tunnel. Its cost would be a little over half that of a bridge, it would require less upkeep and, if made completely circular and double-decked, four lanes of traffic could be accommodated on the upper deck while the lower deck could accommodate a two-lane tramway to provide a rapid-transit alternative to the passenger ferries.

There was opposition to the plan. Some people thought the problem could be solved more easily and more cheaply with a fleet of bigger and faster luggage-boats, whilst the Mersey Docks and Harbour Board saw the proposed branch tunnel to Seacombe as being a threat to their plans for the Birkenhead dock estate. It was also pointed out that a tram service, no matter how fast and frequent, could only carry a small proportion of the passengers carried by ferry boats and the fares would be prohibitive.

But, due mainly to the determination and zeal of Sir Archibald Salvidge who also advocated adoption of the scheme to combat the growing unemployment, the tunnel was built. Wallasey and Bootle were included on the original committee but in the end Liverpool and Birkenhead decided to go it alone.

Work on the pilot tunnel began in the week before Christmas 1925 at the Liverpool end and at Birkenhead the following March. The work which had been done by the pioneers of the rail tunnel helped in planning the precise route and on 3 April 1928 Salvidge and Miss Margaret Beavan, the Lord Mayor of Liverpool, went below ground where Sir Archibald took a pick and broke through the last thin wall of rock. There on the other side, with outstretched hand, was Alderman Naylor, the Mayor of Birkenhead. It must have been a dramatic moment. The engineers measured up and announced that the divergence of line, level and length was, at the most, no more than one inch.

The tunnel was opened to the public by King George V on 18 July 1934 (though pedestrians had already twice had the privilege of walking through it at a charge of sixpence each in aid of charity) and in honour of Queen Mary who was also present it was named Queensway.

Long before this the Mersey ferry services had undergone many changes. Tranmere Ferry had closed down in 1897, Birkenhead Corporation had taken over Rock Ferry and New Ferry two years earlier while Seacombe, Egremont and New Brighton ferries had been bought by Wallasey Corporation in 1862–3.

The extension of the railways throughout Wirral and their subsequent electrification and links with the Mersey Railway took its toll of the ferry traffic though it was less marked in Wallasey where the train only serves the outer areas.

The New Ferry service was closed down in 1922 and Rock Ferry in 1939. The Egremont service lasted until 1941 when the pier suffered irreparable damage from a colliding Dutch ship in the war-time blackout and in that year, too, the luggage service to Woodside was discontinued.

The Seacombe luggage-boats stayed in service throughout the war and after, but the competition from the road tunnel proved too much in the end and they went out of use in 1947.

The passenger boats at that time, however, were still holding their own. The post-war motorcar boom and defection from public transport was not yet in full swing and, in 1947, the still-confident Wallasey Corporation installed the world's first shore-based radar control by which the boats could continue to operate in the most dense fog, the skippers being 'talked' across by controllers watching the comings-and-goings of other river traffic on a screen. The service was subsequently extended to cover the Woodside boats.

The New Brighton service had by this time become a summer-only ferry catering for holiday traffic, but as the resort declined so did the ferry trade (though some would argue it was the other way about) and it was closed down in 1972.

In the immediate post-war years the *Royal Daffodil II* broke away from the Wallasey ferry fleet in the summer evenings, lifted up the hem of her skirts and went dancing. It was a diversion which began with two 'dance-cruises' laid on to celebrate VE-Day and VJ-Day, both of which were a great success and from which live radio broadcasts were made. It was fitting that the *Royal Daffodil* should have been chosen for she had something to celebrate. On 8 May 1941 she received a direct hit in an air raid whilst moored at Seacombe stage and sank. She lay on the bottom for 13 months before being raised. After repair and re-fitting she rejoined the ferry fleet in June 1943.

The dance-cruises (and the radio broadcasts from them) became a regular feature and led to the building of the biggest and most palatial ferry boat yet, the diesel-powered *Royal Iris*. What would the men who launched the *Etna* think if they could see her? Coming into service in 1951, she was purpose-built for cruising and entertainment: 'complete with ballroom, orchestra, cocktail and lounge bars, buffets, etc. she is an attraction no other resort can offer. Passengers are furnished with a commentary by the ship's Captain on passing ships and points of interest ashore and, should the weather be unkind there is ample air-conditioned covered accommodation throughout'. She was also used on the normal ferry run when not cruising and the regular commuters were aghast when they first set eyes on her. With *three* decks she seemed top heavy and in her gaudy pea-green and bright yellow livery she looked out of place on the Mersey.

But she has been a great success and during her service of nearly 40 years has carried millions of passengers on cruises and on the ferry run and thousands of children on educational cruises, while at lunch-times she ties up at the Liverpool landing-stage to serve as a floating restaurant (and very good it is, too).

New Brighton's decline, as we know, was accelerated by the boom in motorcar-owning which took Merseysiders further afield, and the great increase in traffic generally was also reflected in the Mersey Tunnel.

This was increased by developments in Wirral and every year, excepting for the war years, the traffic figures rose until in 1968 it approached the 19 million mark, with as many as 60,000 vehicles passing through in one day. At peak hours traffic in the Liverpool city centre and in Borough Road and Conway Street in Birkenhead was brought to a standstill. 'I've been stuck in the Tunnel queue!' took its place alongside that other immortal phrase 'The bridge is up!' as motorists became more and more angry and frustrated. Clearly something had to be done.

The warnings, in fact, had been heeded as early as 1958 when consultants were asked to study the problem and report. The upshot was a decision to build a second tunnel linking Liverpool with Wallasey. At first it was to be a single tube with just two lanes, as being all that was immediately necessary or could be afforded, but in 1968 the decision was taken to duplicate it, so that the Wallasey Tunnel has two lanes in each direction entirely segregated.

In the case of this new tunnel, instead of excavating with controlled explosives and pneumatic tools, it was decided to use a boring machine with the blood-curdling name of 'The Mangla Mole'. In essence, it was a boring machine like the Beaumont drill which was used in the rail tunnel but on a monster scale and complete with a chain of mechanical buckets which removed the spoil as it fell. Weighing 350 tons, with a 35-foot diameter 'bit', it was the biggest machine of its kind in the world and had already bored out five tunnels in Pakistan but none of them more than 1500 feet long. Whether it would work as efficiently in the wet conditions beneath the Mersey was very much open to question, but though they met with tremendous problems and set-backs the engineers in charge solved them all.

From different points of view, each one of the sub-Mersey tunnels constitutes a remarkable feat of engineering. This Wallasey Tunnel was opened by the Queen on 24 June 1971 and called Kingsway.

But, of course, building a tunnel is one thing; somewhere it has to come out. On the Liverpool side it was fairly clear where it would lead, but in Wirral the mouth of the tunnel would appear in Seacombe and, patently, there had to be a new road to take the traffic away down the peninsula. Hence the Mid-Wirral motorway, the M53. It took a long time in the planning and as with all motorways there were arguments and protests and petitions about its route.

It is 12 miles long and cost a million pounds a mile to build and when it was finished its opening was delayed by the national scare about the safety of steel box girder bridges after several disasters abroad. Its opening day was repeatedly announced and then delayed, and rumoured and denied, until, finally, on the cold freezing morning of 1 February 1972 a small party of dignitaries and workmen watched Lord Leverhume end the saga by quickly snipping a tape and making a one-sentence speech wishing godspeed to all who drove on her.

But it was still only partly open. The Tunnel link was closed and when the flyover bridges were eventually declared safe that was opened by a solitary anonymous police car.

To begin with, the M53 ended at Hooton where traffic once again had to join the congested A41 but the building of an extension to Ellesmere Port was authorised and this opened in December 1975. As motorways go the M53 is pleasant enough and provides the motorist with views he never had before. I know it has ruined farms, gobbled up lands and houses, and trespassed on people's solitude but it is there now. Whether it was wholly justified is a matter of opinion.

And, of course, it knocked another nail into the coffin of the ferries. The paradox is that as the Wirral has become more populated the demand for the ferries has got less. Commuters moving into new housing estates further afield and needing to cross the Mersey simply climb into their cars and instead of crossing over, they drive under – and out.

When the Mersey Passenger Transport Executive was set up in 1969 to take control of and co-ordinate all public transport in the area they were charged with running it – or attempting to do so – at no loss to the ratepayer. After a cold, clinical appraisal with the aid of a computer study it was announced that the loss-making ferries must go. But because it is a *royal* ferry it cannot be abandoned without the sanction of Parliament and so far their efforts to promote a Parliamentary Bill to achieve this end have been unsuccessful.

The MPTE's decision prompted a great cry of outrage and the launching of a 'Save Our Ferries' campaign which was enthusiastically supported by many who never use the boats but travel by train. What will we do, they asked, when the trains break down (as they sometimes do) or there is a rail strike (as has happened)?

That pertinent question apart, a River Mersey without ferries is unthinkable. As *The Guardian* remarked of that computer survey:

'Nobody had told the computer what it was like to stand on the deck of a ferryboat when the spray is flying on a blustery day and the crests whipped off the waves give a snow-flecked appearance to the greys and greens of the river. Nor could a computer turn into binary arithmetic the view of Liverpool waterfront from the middle of the river'.

If we were to rid our life of everything which did not show a profit or cost us money for upkeep we would close down the Williamson and Lady Lever Art Galleries, sell off Birkenhead and Arrowe Parks for factories, and raze Bidston Windmill to the ground.

The mighty Mersey bereft of ships is bad enough. Bereft of ferryboats would be like Blackpool without its tower, or Cowes without its yachts – or even Venice without its gondolas.

Index

Index